THE EVERLASTING
HATRED

THE EVERLASTING
HATRED

HAL LINDSEY

WND Books

THE EVERLASTING HATRED

Published by WND Books
Washington, D.C.

Copyright © 2011
by Hal Lindsey

COVER DESIGN BY MARK KARIS
INTERIOR DESIGN BY NEUWIRTH & ASSOCIATES, INC.

WND Books are distributed to the trade by:
Midpoint Trade Books
27 West 20th Street, Suite 1102
New York, NY 10011

WND Books are available at special discounts for bulk purchases. WND
Books, Inc. also publishes books in electronic formats. For more
information call (541-474-1776) or visit www.wndbooks.com.

ISBN 13 Digit: 978-1-936488-30-8

Library of Congress information available

Printed in the United States of America

10 9 8 7 6 5 4 3 2

CONTENTS

ONE

WE'RE AT WAR

"Over the rest of this decade, the divide between radical Islam and the industrial democracies will become the most destabilizing factor in world affairs."

—JOSEPH DE COURCY[1]

"The governments of the world should know that Islam cannot be defeated. Islam will be victorious in all the countries of the world, and Islam and the teachings of the Koran will prevail all over the world."

—AYATOLLAH RUHOLLAH KHOMEINI OF IRAN

THE VIDEO SHOWS the tortured face of American Daniel Pearl, a news reporter with the *Wall Street Journal*. He was captured after being lured to meet with a London-educated Muslim he had met before. The American is forced to confess on camera, "My father is a Jew, my mother is a Jew, and I am a Jew." Then suddenly a hand with a knife appears on the video screen and slashes his throat. Then his head is sawed off with a dull knife and held aloft by a hand in front of the camera. The video cuts to hooded murderers who repeatedly stab the lifeless corpse. The final scene cuts to Pearl's severed head lying on a pile of newspapers as a message scrolls across the screen: "If our demands are not met, there will be more like this."

The Muslim terrorist who actually cut off Pearl's head was later captured and, under interrogation, confessed that he committed this horrible murder. His name is Khalid Sheikh Mohammad, and he is the principal planner of al Qaeda's attacks on 9/11. This linkage demonstrates that hatred toward Jews is a shared hatred against Americans.

Islamic terrorists chose Daniel Pearl to slaughter for one reason—he was a Jew. The gory details of his videotaped murder are further evidence of the maniacal hatred that animates the movement to which the terrorists belong—Islamic Fundamentalism. But this particular butchery is but one of thousands of brutalities committed by Muslim zealots throughout history—and all for the same cause: They hate Jews with a visceral, bone-deep hatred that is almost impossible for the Western civilization to comprehend. In fact, this hatred goes back to the dawn of recorded history.

IMPERATIVE QUESTIONS

On September 11, 2001, Americans were suddenly thrust into the middle of this hatred, which is part of an ancient family feud. In actuality, we were involved in this conflict long before we realized its magnitude and the great danger it poses to our nation. But since September 11, Americans have been frantically groping to understand what is at stake. Many questions continue to be asked following the initial shock of those horrible first days and their aftermath.

In light of recent events, not just Americans but also the whole of Western Judeo-Christian-based civilization is now asking questions such as:

- Why do Muslims hate Jews?
- Did this hatred begin, as Muslims today claim, with the Zionist movement and the creation of the state of Israel, or is there evidence of this animus in history past?

- Why do Muslim fundamentalists hate the United States and call it "the great Satan"?
- Why do Muslim terrorists willingly sacrifice their lives to kill Americans?
- Do Muslims hate America only because of our support of Israel, or is there evidence that supports other possible motivations?
- Will Islamic terrorists gain access to weapons of mass destruction? If so, will they use them on the United States?
- Could terrorist organizations imperil the very survival of the United States?

This book intends to answer questions such as these on the basis of relevant Biblical and Islamic texts, as well as by examining the history of Jewish-Muslim relations. But in addition to this first set of queries, there are even more foundational questions about Islam itself that this book will seek to answer, such as:

- Are there calls for violence and conquest in the Koran and in the equally authoritative traditions recorded in the Hadith?
- What does the Koran teach about Judaism and Christianity?
- Are Islamic fundamentalists an aberration of the Muslim religion, or are they—as they claim—the true followers of Mohammad?
- Does the example of Mohammad's life teach us the true meaning of the Koran?
- What can we learn from the history of Muslim conquests?
- Were these conquests due to misinterpretations of the Koran or were they actually commanded by it?
- Can we get insights into Mohammad from his forefathers Ishmael and Kedar?
- The Muslim religion is tightly interwoven with the culture of the seventh-century Arabian Peninsula. Are there

aspects of that distant culture that shed light on current Muslim beliefs and behavior?

New Peril We Face

More than at any time since the Crusades, Islam poses a serious threat to the whole of Western Judeo-Christian civilization. Nations of the European Union (EU) and NATO are now being seriously threatened from within by a rapidly expanding and demanding Muslim population that is bent upon forcing Islamic Sharia law upon their host nations. Similarly, the United States and Israel now face in Islam the greatest threat to their survival.

As the chapter title declares, "We're at War." I warned repeatedly in 1991 that, with the fall of the Soviet Union, the greatest danger facing the world was no longer communism, but the revival of Islamic Fundamentalism. But I must confess that I wasn't fully aware of just how great a threat this would pose to the Western world.

How Nice the Old Enemy Looks Now

During the Cold War, we faced an enemy that was somewhat conventional. The Soviets were at work through operatives spreading the gospel of communism around the world. We fought their surrogates in Korea, Vietnam, and South America. They possessed nuclear weapons and had several means of delivering them accurately on target. They also had biological and chemical weapons of mass destruction (WMD) that could kill most of the world's population.

But during the fifty-year Cold War era, there were certain rational constants that helped prevent nuclear annihilation. If the United States were to be struck by any WMD possessed by the Soviet Union or one of its surrogates, we knew where and how to retaliate. They knew that to attack us meant an instant end of their civilization as well.

In short, as terrible as the prospects of nuclear war were, tenuous world stability was maintained by the doctrine of MAD-Mutually Assured Destruction.

MEET THE NEW ENEMY

With the new threat, however, we are confronted by entirely new dimensions of antagonism with enormously greater dangers. We no longer face a political force but a religion that has an estimated 1.4 billion followers worldwide. This religion produces an alarming number of passionate followers who believe it is their duty to Allah to die as martyrs in the pursuit of conquest against those who would restrain Islam from subjecting the world to their religion.

Today Islam is the fastest-growing religion in the world. And the increasingly radical fundamentalist Muslim represents not only the greatest threat to world peace and stability, but also the greatest challenge to the Western world, much of it now secularized but with roots in Judeo-Christian theism.

To appreciate the growing power and influence of Islam, you must look beyond the population figures. Muslims now control, to some extent, about fifty of the world's most important countries—from Indonesia in the East, through the oil rich states of the Middle East, to Senegal on the Atlantic. These countries control vast wealth and unappreciated commercial resources.

At least seventy of the world's 184 countries are considered part of the Dar-al Islam—the "House of Islam," land over which Islam rules. It is a religion practiced in the jungles of Africa, the sands of the Sahara, the oil fields of the Middle East, the mountains of Asia, and the islands of the Pacific. Islam is increasingly making its impact felt in traditionally Christian parts of the world.

Mosques Replacing Churches in the West

In "Bonny Old England" today there are more Muslims than Methodists. There are even more Muslims than there are evangelical Christians, and more active mosques than churches.

"Funded by the vast resources of Arab oil money, the Muslims are buying abandoned Anglican Churches and turning them into mosques at such a rate that some Muslims claim that England will soon be the first Muslim European country," writes author Robert Morey.

Islam is especially rapidly growing in Australia, Canada, Germany, Denmark, Norway, Holland, France, Spain, and the United States. There are an estimated six to eight million Muslims in the United States.

The latest demonstration of Islam's growing power is the Muslim demand to build a mosque a few blocks from "Ground Zero," in the precincts of the destroyed World Trade Center. Islamists have issued such threats of violent retaliation for perceived insults to the Koran and Mohammad that America is virtually intimidated into allowing Muslims religious liberties beyond those granted followers of other religions. Muslims are successfully bullying their way into extracting all kinds of religious concessions from our government.

Fundamentalisms the Real Threat

At least 10 percent of the 1.4 billion Muslims are fundamentalists and therefore are potential terrorist threats. And intelligence information indicates the percentage of fundamentalists is growing. History shows that the devout Muslim fundamentalists are one of the most lethal threats the world has ever known.

In contrast to the old enemy of the Cold War era, the new one is irresistibly motivated in the cause of Allah to become a "martyr," or a homicide/suicide bomber. Young men are promised the highest place in paradise with seventy-two beautiful virgins willing to fulfill every fantasy as soon as the Jihadis die as martyrs for Islam. This is a heady wine that attracts unlimited numbers of volunteers to hurl themselves against the "unbelievers"—especially the United States. Not even the Japanese Kamikaze pilots of World War II can compare with the danger these Islamic zealots pose. And the chilling news is that the fundamentalists are on the brink of possessing the most destructive weapons the world has ever known, thanks to certain terrorist-sponsoring Muslim countries like Iran.

Pakistan has many who have aided al Qaeda terrorists, assistance that includes sheltering them from U.S. troops fighting them in Afghanistan. And the father of Pakistan's nuclear weapons, Dr. Abdul Khader Khan, has been exposed for providing nuclear technology and aid to Iran and Libya. According to former Mossad chief Shabtai Shavit, Khan offered his nuclear knowledge to Algeria, Egypt, Syria, and Saudi Arabia. They all turned him down, but he continued to smuggle nuclear technology and equipment to Iran and Libya, and perhaps, the evidence suggests, to North Korea as well.

Contrary to the old Cold War, we can be hit by a major terrorist attack and not know exactly where to retaliate. This enemy hides in the shadows and mingles with citizens within our own nation. He has Muslim sympathizers who give him aid and shelter. He is also effectively protected by America's doctrine of "political correctness," which hamstrings our intelligence agencies and renders the enemy virtually "uncatchable."

As the Islamic world developed untold wealth through oil, its military might has been increasingly strengthened. The only thing standing in the way of the Muslim nations achieving some degree of parity with the West is their tendency to fight among themselves. But as you will see, there is one cause that can rally them together—hatred of the Jewish state and Western civilization. And Islamic Fundamentalism is the driving force that is rallying all Muslims to "Jihad" for obliterating Israel and replacing the Western world order.

United States in Serious Danger?

Since September 11, many Americans are wondering just how vulnerable we are. Is our nation truly in grave danger?

Here is just a sampling of warnings given by responsible U.S. leaders:

> "The prospect of another attack against the United States is just as real . . . as it was on September 12. It's not a matter of *if*, but of *when*." (emphasis added)
>
> —VICE PRESIDENT DICK CHENEY,
> MAY 19, 2002[3]

> "There will be another terrorist attack. We will not be able to stop it . . . I think we will see [walk-in suicide bombers] in the future. I think it's inevitable."
>
> —FBI DIRECTOR ROBERT MUELLER,
> MAY 20, 2002[4]

> "Terrorist networks have relations with terrorist states that have weapons of mass destruction . . . and they will get their hands on them."
>
> —SECRETARY OF DEFENSE DONALD RUMSFELD,
> MAY 21, 2002[5]

In addition, the United States has placed a high alert status on the following potential targets of terror:

- Major bridges, such as the Golden Gate or Oakland Bay bridges
- Tunnels entering major cities like New York

- Subways and railways
- Large shopping malls
- Aircraft and major buildings
- Statue of Liberty
- Computers that control our nuclear facilities and our entire electrical infrastructure
- Banks and financial institutions (cyber attack) such as stock exchanges

Are Counter Measures Possible?

These warnings came despite the creation of the new Department of Homeland Security, the complete re-organization of the FBI, placing the CIA on maximum alert, and directing U.S. troops in Afghanistan to destroy the operational headquarters of al Qaeda, the latest star in the Islamic pantheon of terror.

Our country has mobilized for a global war on terrorism, and already we are faltering. Our efforts in Iraq and Afghanistan have stalled because we have failed to understand Muslim beliefs and practices. We have set as our goal to turn these Islamic countries into democracies, even though a Western-style democracy is totally contrary to the kind of government taught in the Koran. In Islam, religion and government are woven together, and both are inextricably patterned after the tribal culture of the seventh-century Arabian Peninsula. This is why Islamic nations have such a hard time fitting into the modern world.

Take just two examples of this. The Shah of Iran used all of his power to separate religious structures from government organizations and to create a modern nation that could compete in the industrial West. Iran became a flourishing nation, but Shiite fundamentalists rebelled against the Shah's move toward modern culture. As soon as the Ayatollah Khomeini returned to lead a revolution, he drug Iran back to the seventh-century culture of the Koran. Personal freedoms were wiped out overnight, and hundreds of thousands of Iranians were imprisoned or executed. A country that had been our friend became our avowed enemy and labeled us "the Great Satan." If the United States and the West had stood by the Shah, the fundamentalist fanatics would never have been able to overthrow his government.

In 1923, Mustafa Kemal Ataturk, the heretofore-revered father of modern Turkey, brought Turkey out of its backward, non-productive society and began its transformation into a modern industrial state. He eliminated the Sultanate and Caliphate, which were the joint political and religious arms of the fallen Ottoman Empire. He declared Turkey a secular state and separated religious and state affairs. He gave women full political and social rights and eliminated polygamy and harems.

Turkey has flourished and grown under the application of Ataturk's plan. But for decades, Islamic fundamentalists have sought to overthrow it. In 2003, the fundamentalists finally came into power with the election of the Justice and Development Party, headed by Recep Erdogan. Since then, Turkey has begun to leave the Western world and re-enter the Islamic world of Iran and Syria. The Turks have pulled away from NATO, of which they have been a part since 1952. The United States and Israel have been snubbed. Both Israel and the United States gave much valuable military technology and training to Turkey during their previous times of friendship, and now both may face those weapons in future conflicts. I expected this turn of events to occur because Turkey is part of the Gog and Magog invasion predicted by the prophet Ezekiel.

These two examples show the pull of the Islamic view of government upon those who take literally the teachings of the Koran. This Koranic pull is why, in my view, the efforts of the United States to democratize Iraq and Afghanistan are misconceived and futile. Instead, we need to destroy their war making capability and leave. And then warn them that we will destroy them if they are complicit in further terrorist attacks against us. This is the only language that Islamic fundamentalists understand.

Probably more important than anything else is that the West, especially the leaders of the United States, understands Muslim beliefs and practices.

Who Is the Terrorist "Du Jour"?

Because of a lack of true knowledge about what Islam's sacred books teach, Western leaders are proceeding unknowingly down an impossible path. The mantra constantly repeated by our "politically correct" government leaders today is that "Islam is a religion of peace and love." I am sorry—that is just not what the Koran, the Hadith, and the history of Muslim conquests clearly teach. It is true that the majority of Muslims are not fundamentalists, thank God. But when any one of them gets serious about his faith and becomes zealous about what his holy books teach, he is a candidate for becoming what we know as a terrorist.

Under the Obama Administration, things have gotten even worse. Our government will not allow terrorist acts to be labeled Muslim acts of terrorism. The liberal media have bowed to this folly as well. Acts of terrorism clearly motivated by Islam are called instead the acts of mentally unbalanced individuals.

I believe the only reason the United States has not suffered more horrific terrorist attacks is because of the grace and mercy of God. There have been a number of attacks that would have killed hundreds of people if only the bombs had functioned properly.

On Christmas Day 2009, Umar Abdulmutallab, a twenty-three-year-old Nigerian man, attempted to blow Northwest Flight 253 out of the sky. Had his underwear bomb functioned correctly, 289 people would have been blown out of the sky. Al Qaeda took credit for the attempted terrorist attack. It was later found that he was trained and supplied by al Qaeda, which is the most dangerous Muslim terrorist organization facing the West.

In addition, consider the following challenges we still face:

- Our borders are as porous as Swiss cheese. In 2009, more than 56,000 non-Latin people were caught illegally crossing into the United States via the undefended Arizona-Mexican border. Most of these illegals were from the Middle East. We don't know how many successfully got into the United States. And we certainly don't know how many may have been trained as terrorists.

- Airport security remains a joke primarily because of the fear of being "politically incorrect." There is no way to correct this apart from using profiling techniques and firing many people that are not suited for this kind of work. The world's best airport security is Israel's. They use aggressive racial profiling and hire their brightest and best to man security. Machines will not take the place of these measures. Minimum wage, poorly educated people cannot "psych out" a trained terrorist.

- Our nuclear plants are vulnerable to terrorist attacks because they are not properly prepared to defend against coordinated Islamic suicide assaults by highly trained terrorists. According to military intelligence, a suicide plane could hit them. Terrorists using scuba gear could infiltrate them from adjacent waterways and launch an attack.

- Our drinking water and food-supply chain are vulnerable to biological/chemical attacks.

WE ARE IN DEEP POOH-POOH!

I continue to report on my TV show, *The Hal Lindsey Report*, on the imminent threats facing the world. The following are just a few of them:

- A holocaust will occur in the Middle East if Iran is allowed to get nuclear weapons.
- Iran has formed a binding pact with Syria, Hezbollah in Lebanon, and Hamas in Gaza to launch a coordinated attack against Israel as soon as they have nuclear weapons.
- Iran has slipped an estimated 100,000 rockets and missiles into Syria, Lebanon, and Gaza to be used against Israel if it attacks their nuclear facilities. This makes it possible for every population center in Israel to be bombarded with lethal missiles.
- Israel has long had a carefully prepared contingency plan known as the "Samson Option." This plan provides that in the event Israel is hit by biological, chemical, or nuclear weapons, Israel will launch a massive nuclear strike against the cities of every enemy state attacking her.
- To make matters worse, Iran's president, Mahmoud Ahmadinejad, is a devout believer in an Islamic prophecy that says the Muslim messiah known as the "Mahdi," is ready to return and only awaits the beginning of an Armageddon-type war to break out that will cause him to return and lead Islam to world victory. Ahmadinejad believes that Allah has chosen him to start that global conflict. I believe this is why he is so determined to get nuclear weapons. As he has warned, he will blow Israel off the map as soon as he can—and this, Ahmadinejad believes, will start the war that will cause the Mahdi, also known as the "Twelfth Imam," to return and lead the Muslims to world domination.

At this moment in history, Islam represents the single greatest threat in the world to the survival of Western civilization.

RELEVANCE OF AN ANCIENT FAMILY FEUD

I believe all of these clear and present dangers can be understood only by learning how this conflict began between the descendants of the Biblical patriarch Abraham four thousands years ago. There is a perfect word that describes the Arab's virulent feelings toward Israel. It is the word *enmity*. The dictionary defines enmity as "the extreme ill will or hatred that exists toward an enemy." It infers a state of hatred that has been nurtured over a long period of time.

At the beginning of the twenty-first century, it is hard to imagine how a four-thousand-year-old family feud could cause the whole world to become involved. Yet this is exactly what the Bible predicted would happen in the last days. These prophecies spell out an exact scenario of events that will come together shortly before the end of history as we know it.

Central to this scenario is the re-igniting of the ancient conflict between the Israelites and Arabs. The conflict has risen and subsided at various times since the destruction and dispersion of Israel in A.D. 70.

It is as a consequence of the rebirth of the state of Israel, the Bible prophets predict, that the whole world will become involved. The Bible specifically predicts what will be the final flashpoint that ignites the war of Armageddon. It will be an unsolvable dispute over Jerusalem between the sons of Isaac and Jacob and the sons of Ishmael and Esau. We know these people today as the Israelis and the Arabs.

Who Would Have Dreamed?

Who would have believed as the twentieth century dawned that a small, backward, neglected land that had become as desolate as the moon would become the center of a controversy so great that all the major world powers would be dragged into it? For centuries, world attention focused on the Gentile civilizations of Europe, the Americas, Russia, and the Far East. Until the middle of the twentieth century, many people couldn't even find Palestine on a map. But today, the headlines aren't about Western or Asian civilizations; they are about the peoples of the Middle East. For the first time in modern history, ancient Biblical names are making global headlines.

One of the main predicted signs that the world is entering the "last days and the end of history as we know it" is that the strategic center of the world would shift back to the region where history began. Today, the world's focus has returned to a place that had been bypassed by the modern developments of science and technology.

Prepare to Be Shocked

This book will reveal many vital facts about the Middle East conflict that are little known. It will take you into history and reveal the real causes of the growing world crisis that will seriously affect your life. Writing this book has been a great sobering adventure. So press on through the history and facts. I promise it will be rewarding. And I believe you will find a vital basis for hope in the coming perilous times.

TWO

FOUNDATIONAL IRREVOCABLE COVENANT

"Emperor Napoleon Bonaparte, while on his Palestinian campaign, asked one of his generals, 'Can you give me a proof that the Bible is the Word of God?' He replied, 'Your Majesty, the Jew. Against all historical precedence, he has survived centuries of dispersion and yet has remained a distinct people—a nation in exile—though scattered over the entire world and terribly persecuted, just as the Hebrew prophets predicted he would be, patiently waiting for his promised return to the land of his fathers.'"

—Napoleon Bonaparte, A.D. 1798

ISRAEL CHOSEN? WHY?

Most of us have heard at some point in our life the saying that "the Jews are God's chosen people." But in view of their catastrophic history over at least the last two thousand years, one wonders, "If they are God's chosen people, for what purpose were they chosen?"

From the founding of Islam onward, Muslim Arabs have disputed the Jewish claims of being the chosen people. Ishmael, Abraham's first-born son and the father of the Arabs, was angry over the foundations of the Jewish claim from the very beginning. This smoldering enmity toward the Israelites was passed along to his descendants from generation to generation. Mohammad enshrined this enmity toward the Jews in the Kuran and teachings of the Muslim religion.

So the origins of the Arab-Israeli conflict really took root more than four thousand years ago. A man was called for a special mission that would forever change the course of human history and the destiny of mankind. It is impossible to understand the hatred behind the present Middle East crisis without knowledge of what exactly happened then and why.

This all began at a time when all nations were determined to push the knowledge of the one true God out of their culture and memory. The Bible records that because of this, God chose a man for the purpose of creating a special nation. God's purpose for this nation was to preserve a true revelation about Himself, to reach out to the world through it, and ultimately to provide salvation for all mankind. God's great love for all mankind is what motivated Him to create this special people and nation.

The Bible records how God chose a man named Abram, whom He later renamed Abraham, from an advanced civilization known as Ur of the Chaldeans. God made a special irrevocable covenant with him and his descendents to facilitate this purpose.

In this covenant made with Abraham, God's plan for all mankind is laid out in broad outline. In terms of its effect upon the history and destiny of mankind, nothing else can be compared. It is truly amazing, but the rest of the Bible is a commentary on the full meaning of this covenant. To put its importance into perspective, the main focus of the Bible message from Genesis 12 to Acts 2 are the recipients of its promises—Abraham and his descendents.

IRREVOCABLE COVENANT

The covenant is formed around God's declaration of four direct and three understood "I wills." This is the God of the Bible's consistent formula for expressing an unconditional promise.

When God makes a promise and says, "I will," it is the end of all uncertainty as to its fulfillment. The one condition on Abraham's part was to, by faith, leave his country, his home, and his relatives to travel to a land that God would show him.

In response to that faith, God promised Abraham the following:

Now the Lord had said to Abram:
"Get out of your country,
From your family and from your father's house,
To a land that I will show you.
I will make you a great nation;
I will bless you
And [*I will*] make your name great;
And you shall be a blessing.
I will bless those who bless you,
And *I will* curse him who curses you;
And in you all the families of the earth shall be blessed."

—Genesis 12:1–3, (emphasis added)

So much is contained in these few words that they must be carefully analyzed. Let's consider the passage above point by point.

★ *The Promise of a Nation:* "*I will* make you a great nation."
This statement implicitly contains the promise of a son through whom this nation would be created. It also implicitly promised the land to which Abraham was ordered to go, since you can't have a nation without a land.

However, there was one major problem—Abraham and his wife were childless. Yet everything God promised Abraham depended upon him having a son. Now since he was seventy-five years old and his wife was sixty-five years old, Abraham understood that it would take some kind of divine intervention for him to have a son. But Abraham had a lapse of faith when God delayed fulfilling this promise. He kept checking his biological clock, thinking the promise was becoming more impossible by the day.

* *The Promises of Special Personal Blessings:* "*I will* bless you and [I will] make your name great; and you shall be a blessing." God promised to bless Abraham in three ways: First, God blessed him with special protection, great wealth, with vibrant health even into old age, and made him successful in all his dealings. Second, God promised to make Abraham's name great—and his name has been reverenced all over the world for more than four thousand years. He is recognized as a spiritual father by three of the world's major religions—Judaism, Christianity, and Islam. And third, God promised to make Abraham a blessing. Untold millions of people have recognized him as the father of their faith. The example of Abraham's faith, permanently recorded in the eternal Word of God, has been a blessing to countless millions throughout history.

PROMISES THAT ANTICIPATED ANTI-SEMITISM

* *The Promises of Divine Protection:* "*I will* bless those who bless you, and *I will* curse him who curses you." These "I wills" anticipated that Abraham and his descendents would be the objects of special attack. In view of their special mission of redemption to the world, it is only logical that they would be singled out as prime targets by the devil. Anti-Semitism has been a relentless fact of history.

Abraham and his divinely chosen line of descendents through Isaac and Jacob have been consistently persecuted and attacked. There is a mystical quality behind the intensity of hatred toward the Israelites. This is especially true of the descendents of the

Southern Kingdom, which is composed of the tribes of Judah, Benjamin, and Levi. The Israelites were first called "Jews" while in Babylonian captivity, the word *Jew* being derived from the name of their geographical origin, *Judea*. The Jews have been singled out for special hatred since they were driven into global exile after the destruction of Israel in A.D. 70. The name *Jew* has come to be indiscriminately applied to survivors of all twelve tribes of Israelites in recent centuries.

Only a person who understands the one the Bible calls "the god of this age" (2 Cor. 4:4) can begin to understand this mystery. Any objective study of the irrational outbreaks of hatred all over the world toward the Israelites—the mindless slaughter of them in every century—will reveal that there is a malevolent spiritual force behind it all.

★ *The Promise of Blessing upon All Who Bless Israel:* "*I will* bless those who bless you." Individuals, groups, and nations that have sought to help Abraham and his descendents in their times of need have all been blessed by God. The United States has received, helped, and protected the dispersed Israelites. The United States has stood for Israel's survival as a nation from its rebirth in 1948. I believe this is one of the main reasons God has so blessed America in the past. But as we will see, our attitude toward Israel is changing—to our peril.

★ *The Promise of Judgment upon All Who Curse [Harm] Israel:* "*I will* curse him who curses you." Since God chose to create the nation of Israel for the special mission of redeeming the rest of mankind, beware of mistreating or harming the Jewish people. God's promise of protection to Abraham and his seed serves as a warning to the nations or Gentiles—"*I will* curse him who curses you." All attacks upon Israelites will ultimately bring retribution from God. When Gentiles attack them, they are attacking God's chosen instruments of their own redemption.

This promise of God's protection was confirmed by Isaac when he passed on the divine blessing to his son Jacob, "Cursed be those who curse you, and blessed be those who bless you." (Gen. 27:29)

Almost four hundred years later, God made even the apostate prophet Balaam pronounce this solemn warning to King Balak, who had hired Balaam to curse the nation of Israel. "How shall I curse, whom God has not cursed? And how can I denounce, whom the LORD has not denounced? . . . *Blessed is everyone* who blesses you, and *cursed is everyone* who curses you." (Num. 23:8 and 24:9, emphasis added)

This account is extremely important. These verses prove that the promise of God's protection included all the descendents of Abraham, Isaac, and Jacob.

To illustrate how seriously God takes this promise, note that the Hebrew prophet Zechariah, sixteen hundred years after Abraham, warns that the Messiah's first action when He comes to set up God's kingdom on earth will be:

For thus says the Lord of hosts, "After glory He has sent me against the nations which plunder you, *for he who touches you, touches the apple of his eye.* "For behold, I will wave My hand over them, so that they will be plunder for their slaves. Then you will know that the Lord of hosts has sent Me. "Sing for joy and be glad, O daughter of Zion; for behold I am coming and I will dwell in your midst," declares the Lord. "And many nations will join themselves to the Lord in that day and will become My people. Then I will dwell in your midst, and you will know that the Lord of hosts has sent Me to you. And the Lord will possess Judah as His portion in the holy land, and will again choose Jerusalem."[6] (emphasis added)

We know this event as the Second Coming of Jesus the Messiah. It is certain that this refers to the time of the second coming because the Messiah sets up His throne in Jerusalem and dwells among His people. According to this prophecy, the first thing He will do is judge all of the Gentiles who have mistreated His people, Israel.

Much more will be said about this important subject later.

PROMISE OF MANKIND'S SALVATION

The final line of this prophesy in Genesis 12:1–3 is the most important: "And in you all the families of the earth shall be blessed." Abraham and his descendents will be the vessels through which all the peoples of the earth will be blessed. The literal translation is, "And in you *I will* bless all the families of the earth."

This promise reveals the main purpose for which Abraham and his descendents were chosen. They were to be the vessels through which God would reach out to the world with His plan of salvation.

In embryonic form, this promise predicts the provision of salvation for the whole world through one of Abraham's seed. It reveals that the ultimate purpose of God through Abraham and his seed is redemptive.

As the Bible unfolds this promise of blessing, four reasons for why God chose and created Israel are discernable. These are the purposes for which He chose them:

- First, they are to receive, write, and preserve the Word of God. As the Apostle Paul testified, "They were entrusted with the oracles of God."[7]

- Second, the way God deals with Israel in response to their faith or lack of faith is a living historical lesson about God's character. The way God dealt with Israel as a nation teaches principles of how He deals with the individual who believes in Him.[8]
- Third, the Jews are to be the physical race through which the Messiah the Savior of the world would be born. Isaiah predicted the mission of this Messiah, "It is too small a thing that You should be My Servant to raise up the tribes of Jacob, and to restore the preserved ones of Israel; I will also make You a light to the Gentiles so that My salvation may reach to the end of the earth."[9]
- Fourth, Israel is called to spread the message of the true God and His salvation to the world.[10]

THE ONLY LAND-DEED GOD EVER GAVE

God expanded upon the original covenant with another essential covenant. It concerns the land on which He would establish the nation given to Abraham and his descendents. There are several promises regarding this land that together carefully spell out: (1) to whom it is given (2) its borders (3) the conditions of ownership, and (4) the duration of its ownership. God foreknew the great troubles that Israel would encounter concerning the rights to their land throughout history—especially during the "Last Days." So He stated the terms of their "Title Deed" to the land in a comprehensive covenant, backed by His own oath.

As mentioned above, the one condition Abraham had to fulfill was to leave his country and relatives and go to the land that God would show him. Apart from that requirement, which Abraham met, all of the promises that followed were unconditional.

This is what God promised Abraham shortly after He gave him the first covenant:

And the Lord appeared to Abram and said, "To your descendants *I will* give this land." God also promised: "For all the land which you see, *I will give it to you and to your descendants forever.* And I will make your descendants as the dust of the earth; so that if anyone can number the dust of the earth, then your descendants can also be numbered. Arise, walk about the land through its length and breadth; for I will give it to you."[11] (emphasis added)

It is very important to note the features of this covenant God made with Abraham. They have a direct bearing on the controversy raging in the Middle East today. Note first that it is given not only to Abraham but also to his descendents. Second, it is an unconditional covenant. God swore, "*I will*" do this—without attaching any conditions upon the recipients. Third, this covenant is "*forever*," thus the behavior of Abraham or his descendents cannot prevent its ultimate everlasting fulfillment.

BOUNDARIES OF THE DEEDED LAND

The border of the land to be possessed ultimately by Abraham's descendants is spelled out very specifically in the next expansion of the land covenant. Something else is added that is unique in God's dealing with mankind.

Despite his advanced age, Abraham believed the Lord concerning a promised son who would come from Abraham's own body, and offspring as numerous as the stars of heaven. But Abraham still wanted more assurance regarding possessing of the promised land. So he asked, "O Sovereign LORD, how can I know that I will gain possession of it [i.e., the land]?"[12]

God's response is one of the greatest demonstrations of how patient and gracious He is with mankind. God chose to accommodate Abraham's continuing need for strong reassurance. He did this by performing a covenant-making ritual that was the most solemn and binding known to man in the culture of that time. Here is the account of how God reconfirmed to Abraham the title deed to the land and its boundaries. It is so important that I am quoting the ceremony in its entirety:

So the LORD said to him, "Bring me a heifer, a goat and a ram, each three years old, along with a dove and a young pigeon."

Abram brought all these to him, cut them in two and arranged the halves opposite each other; the birds, however, he did not cut in half. Then birds of prey came down on the carcasses, but Abram drove them away.

As the sun was setting, Abram fell into a deep sleep, and a thick and dreadful darkness came over him. Then the LORD said to him, "Know for certain that your descendants will be strangers in a country not their own, and they will be enslaved and mistreated four hundred years. But I will punish the nation they serve as slaves, and afterward they will come out with great possessions. You, however, will go to your fathers in peace and be buried at a good old age. In the fourth generation your descendants will come back here, for the sin of the Amorites has not yet reached its full measure."

When the sun had set and darkness had fallen, a smoking firepot with a blazing torch appeared and passed between the pieces. On that day the LORD made a covenant with Abram and said, "To your descendants I give this land, from the river of Egypt to the great river, the Euphrates—the land of the Kenites, Kenizzites, Kadmonites, Hittites, Perizzites, Rephaites, Amorites, Canaanites, Girgashites, and Jebusites."[13]

This passage gives important details concerning the irrevocable nature of the covenant. This strange ritual gets at the heart of the meaning of the Hebrew word for covenant. It comes from the verb *barath*, which means "to cut." In Hebrew, the expression for making a covenant is "to cut a covenant." The Hebrew scholar Franz Delitzsch writes concerning this ritual:

> The proceeding corresponded rather to the custom, prevalent in many ancient nations, of slaughtering animals when concluding a covenant, and after dividing them into pieces, of laying the pieces opposite to one another, that the persons making the covenant might pass between them. . . . God condescended to follow the custom of the Chaldeans, that He might in the most solemn manner confirm His oath to Abram the Chaldeans.[14]

This reveals much about the character of God. Certainly it shows that He is gracious and considerate of our human limitations. It demonstrates that He takes into account our degree of maturity and knowledge of Him in His treatment of us.

AN OATH THAT CAN NEVER BE BROKEN

As the custom dictated, Abram laid the sacrifice halves opposite each other, making a path in the middle for those making the covenant to walk. The parties would then hold hands and walk together between the sacrifices, taking an oath on the terms of the covenant. They would then swear an oath that the one that breaks the covenant is to be hewn in pieces as the sacrifices had been. We are talking serious covenant making here.

But in this case, a most unusual thing happened. Abraham was put into a deep sleep and shown a vision of God alone walking between the sacrifices and swearing an oath by Himself that He would give the land with its specific borders to Abraham and his descendents as an everlasting possession.

For God to give His Word in a promise is enough to make it unbreakable. But God swore an oath by Himself that He would fulfill this promise concerning the land. Thus by two immutable things, His Word and His oath, it is made certain beyond all things. *So let all who contest Israel's right to that land today beware.*

WHY THE CANAANITES WOULD BE DESTROYED

A prophecy was also given to Abraham as to when his descendents would first take possession of the land. It would be after they spent four hundred years in the land of Egypt. The reason for the delay was two-fold. First, it was because Abraham's descendents had to grow in sufficient numbers to be able to take over the land.

And second, because the sin of the present inhabitants had not yet reached the full measure of iniquity worthy of their destruction. God graciously gave them four hundred more years to repent, which they never did. They only got worse, burning their own children alive as a sacrifice to demon idols. When God later brought the Israelites back from Egypt, the minds of all the residents of Canaan had become utterly perverted beyond reformation. They were like a cancer that had to be exorcised before their perversion infected the rest of society.

ABRAHAM'S UNDERSTANDING
OF THE COVENANT

How Abraham understood this covenant is revealed in a later statement he made to his steward upon sending him to find a wife for Abraham's son Isaac:

> The LORD, the God of heaven, who brought me out of my father's household and my native land and who spoke to me and promised me on oath, saying, "To your offspring *I will* give this land"—he will send his angel before you so that you can get a wife for my son from there. If the woman is unwilling to come back with you, then you will be released from this oath of mine. Only do not take my son back there.[15]

In the light of the previous Scripture, to say, as some teachers within Christendom do, that there was no unconditional covenant made with Abraham's descendents is to accuse God of willfully deceiving Abraham. And it would be even more ludicrous to suppose that the LORD would record Abraham's wrong understanding of this covenant if in fact it was wrong. God warned that He would discipline the Israelites, but never disown them. [Note: Translators use all caps "LORD" to indicate that the original is "Yahweh," God's most solemn name which means "I AM."]

HOW ANTI-SEMITISM BEGAN

There are false teachers within the church today who would deny that the Israelites have a right to the land of their forefathers. They are known by such titles as "Dominionists," "Preterists," "Amillennialists," or "Postmillennialists."

What is common to all of these theological systems is that they allegorize all unfulfilled Bible prophecies and covenants—especially those that apply to the future of the descendents of Abraham, Isaac, and Jacob. They say that the covenants were "conditional," and therefore were canceled by Israel's rejection of the Messiah, Jesus. They teach that Israel has no future in God's plan as a distinct people and nation. They teach that the church inherited all of these covenants and promises when Israel rejected their Messiah, Jesus.

In other words, they believe that the church has now become "Israel" in place of the literal physical descendents to whom the promises were exclusively made. This is called "Replacement Theology." Augustine laid the groundwork for this teaching in the fifth century A.D. He taught that the church had become Israel and was now God's kingdom on earth. This became the rationale for the "conquistadors" to conquer and pillage the Americas in the name of the Roman Catholic Church. It also was the philosophy that set up the "Holy Roman Empire" over Europe.

This resulted in such shameful atrocities as the Crusades and the inquisitions in "the name of Jesus." These actions violated the most basic teachings of Jesus Christ. The knights of Europe under the orders of the popes slaughtered tens of thousands of innocent people, particularly the Jews.

THE NEW TESTAMENT CONFIRMS THIS TITLE DEED

In the first-century Roman Church, some Christians were inclined to turn against the Jews and think they had permanently replaced them in God's plan. This is God's answer to that error:

> For I do not want you, brethren, to be uninformed of this mystery, lest you be wise in your own estimation, that a partial hardening has happened to Israel *until* the fullness [full number] of the Gentiles has come in; and thus all Israel will be saved; just as it is written, "The Deliverer will come from Zion, He will remove ungodliness from Jacob." And, "This is My covenant with them, When I take away their sins." From the standpoint of the gospel they are enemies for your sake, but from the standpoint of God's choice they are beloved for the sake of the fathers; for the gifts and the calling of God are *irrevocable*.[16]

The Apostle Paul reveals that the present rejection of Israel is not total, nor is it final. It is only temporary *until* the full number of Gentiles is saved. Then he quotes specific promises of God that guarantee that "all Israel will be saved when the Deliverer, the Messiah Jesus, comes from Zion in the Second Coming."

The Epistle to the Romans in chapter nine carefully defines "true Israel" as the physical descendents of Abraham, Isaac, and Jacob who also believe in God's provision of salvation. They are called "the believing remnant." As it is written, "And Isaiah cries out concerning Israel, 'Though the number of the sons of Israel be as the sand of the sea, *it is the remnant that will be saved*; for the Lord will execute His word upon the earth, thoroughly and quickly.'"[17]

The practice of allegorizing these specific promises, which started with the fifth-century theologian Augustine, became the foundation of anti-Semitism in the church. Sadly, anti-Semitism spread from the church to the rest of the world.

IF THE CURSES ARE LITERAL,
THE PROMISES ARE, TOO

Moses predicted two destructions of Israel and two dispersions from their land. It is amazing that he predicted this just before they first took possession of the land.

The reason for their national destruction is given: "All these curses will come upon you. They will pursue you and overtake you until you are destroyed, because you did not obey the LORD your God and observe the commands and decrees he gave you. They will be a sign and a wonder to you and your descendants forever."[18] Moses then predicted the first destruction: "The LORD will bring a nation against you from far away, from the ends of the earth, like an eagle swooping down, a nation whose language you will not understand, a fierce-looking nation without respect for the old or pity for the young."[19] This was fulfilled by the Babylonian destruction led by Nebuchadnezzar at the end of the seventh century B.C.

Moses also predicted the second, more severe destruction and dispersion:

Then the LORD will scatter you among all nations, from one end of the earth to the other. There you will worship other gods—gods of wood and stone, which neither you nor your fathers have known. Among those nations you will find no repose, no resting place for the sole of your foot. There the LORD will give you an anxious mind, eyes weary with longing, and a despairing heart. You will live in constant suspense, filled with dread both night and day, never sure of your life. In the morning you will say, "If only it were evening!" and in the evening, "If only it were morning!"—because of the terror that will fill your hearts and the sights that your eyes will see.[20]

This terrible catastrophe took place in A.D. 70 when Titus and the Roman Tenth Legion destroyed Judah and Jerusalem and drove the survivors into exile. This dispersion lasted until it began to be reversed with the rebirth of the state of Israel in June 1948.

PREDICTIONS OF ISRAEL'S SECOND AND FINAL RESTORATION

These predictions cut to the heart of the current Arab-Israeli Conflict. They show that the "Title Deed to the land of Israel" was never revoked. It is still binding on the basis of the divine oath by which it was originally given. The Muslims absolutely reject this. So their current attempts to drive Israel out of the Holy Land are in direct defiance of God.

Moses predicts the following at the end of the same message that he made the above predictions:

When all these blessings and curses I have set before you come upon you and you take them to heart wherever the LORD your God disperses you among the nations, and when you and your children return to the LORD your God and obey him with all your heart and with all your soul according to everything I command you today, then the LORD your God will restore your fortunes and have compassion on you and gather you again from all the nations where he scattered you. Even if you have been banished to the most distant land under the heavens, from there the LORD your God will gather you and bring you back. He will bring you to the land that belonged to your fathers, and you will take possession of it. He will make you more prosperous and numerous than your fathers.[21]

It is important to note that God does not say "if" but "when" throughout this prediction. This is because God views the repentance as certain, since He will cause it to happen. It is also very clear that God addresses this promise to the believing remnant of the physical descendents of Abraham, Isaac, and Jacob—not to some allegorical offsprings in the church.

The prophet Ezekiel also speaks of this final restoration from the worldwide Roman dispersion:

This is what the Sovereign LORD says: I will deal with you as you deserve, because you have despised my oath by breaking the covenant. *Yet I will remember the covenant I made with you in the days of your youth, and I will establish an everlasting covenant with you.* Then you will remember your ways and be ashamed when you receive your sisters, both those who are older than you and those who are younger. I will give them to you as daughters, but not on the basis of my covenant with you. So I will establish my covenant with you, and you will know that I am the LORD. Then, when I make atonement for you for all you have done, you will remember and be ashamed and never again open your mouth because of your humiliation, declares the Sovereign LORD.[22]

Note that God anticipated that Israel would despise His oath and break the Mosaic covenant. He warns that He will discipline them, as they deserve. Yet despite all they will do, He still promises that He will fulfill to them the covenant made with their fathers.

There is no excuse for those who call themselves Christian to deny the clear, simple, literal statements of God's Word about the Israelites' covenant rights. The traditional prophetic view of many mainline churches that is based on unwarranted allegorical interpretations of these passages has caused great chaos and suffering to the descendents of Abraham, Isaac, and Jacob.

David Levi and Isaac Da Costa, who were Christian Biblical scholars of the nineteenth century, clearly point out a great inconsistency in the interpretation of Biblical prophecy concerning the nation of Israel by theological systems such as Preterism, Amillennialism, and Postmillennialism. "What can be more absurd," they write, "than to explain the prophecies, which foretell the calamity to befall the Jews, in a literal sense, and then those, which bespeak their future blessing, in a mystical and spiritual sense?"[23]

A SPECIFIC PREDICTION OF FINAL RESTORATION TO THE LAND

Ezekiel locates Israel's final restoration to the land and her rebirth as a nation in the "Last Days." It is imperative to note the sequence of this prophecy. It clearly shows that God will restore the Israelites to the land and cause them to be reborn as a nation *before* they repent and believe in their true Messiah:

> Therefore, say to the house of Israel, "Thus says the Lord God, *'It is not for your sake, O house of Israel, that I am about to act, but for my holy name*, which you have profaned among the nations where you went. And I will vindicate the holiness of My great name which has been profaned among the nations, which you have profaned in their midst. Then the nations will know that I am the Lord, declares the Lord. God, when I prove Myself holy among you in their sight. For *I will* take you from the nations, gather you from all the lands, and *bring you into your own land*. (emphasis added)

> *Then I will* sprinkle clean water on you, and you will be clean; *I will* cleanse you from all your filthiness and from all your idols.

Moreover, *I will* give you a new heart and put a new spirit within you; and *I will* remove the heart of stone from your flesh and give you a heart of flesh. And *I will* put My Spirit within you and cause you to walk in My statutes, and you will be careful to observe My ordinances. And you will live in the land that I gave to your fore-fathers; so you will be My people, and *I will* be your God.'"[24]

This prophecy clearly adds a new dimension to all of the pre-dictions about Israel's restoration to the land. It emphasizes that it is not being done because the people deserve it. They are returned to the land and reborn as a nation *before* they are cleansed and reborn spiritually.

The paragraph beginning with *"Then I will"* clearly marks out the sequence of events. It is only after they are returned to the land that they are brought to spiritual restoration. In every way the prophecy declares that all of this will be done by sovereign unconditional acts of God despite the unworthiness of the Israelites. God swears an oath that He will do all of this with seven sovereign *"I Wills."*

EZEKIEL'S PROPHETIC OUTLINE
OF TODAY'S EVENTS

Ezekiel lays out more clearly than any other prophet the sequence of events in the Last Days. He shows that a restored Israel is the key to all Last Days prophecy.

Ezekiel chapter 36 emphasizes the miracle of the land's resto-ration when God returns His people to it. The prophecy focuses on the desolate condition brought upon the land by the sur-rounding nations (all of them Muslim today). God warns of ter-rible judgment upon these Muslim nations who have "taken His land." The fact that it is God's land is emphasized several times.

Ezekiel chapter 37 emphasizes the miracle of returning the dis-persed Israelites from all the nations where they have been scat-tered for centuries. Ezekiel describes this miraculous national rebirth of the people in an allegory about disjointed skeletons lying in a desert full of open graves. He interprets the scattered bones as the whole house of Israel. He reveals that the open graves are the nations where the people have been scattered. The miracle of Israel's national rebirth is illustrated by all of the bones coming out of the graves and joining together. Then sinews, muscle, and flesh come upon them—and finally, breath is breathed into them. They then stand up as a mighty army. But they are still not reborn spiritually.

Ezekiel chapter 38 reveals the momentous event of history that will finally bring the Israelites to faith in their true Messiah. It will be a massive invasion against them led by a mighty nation to the extreme north. This northern commander (who can only be Russian since they are the only nation to Israel's extreme north) will lead a confederacy of people who today are all Muslim. Chief among those named is Persia, or modern Iran.

How this all turns out will be developed in later chapters. But suffice it to say, the scenario spelled out here is all in place in our current events.

The main point of these chapters is that they show that once Israel is restored, it will never be destroyed and dispersed again, even though Ezekiel does predict that Israel will go through a war so intense that all hope of survival will be lost. It is at this point that great numbers of Israelites will turn to their true Messiah, Jesus of Nazareth, and believe in Him. He will then miraculously deliver them and set up the promised kingdom of God on earth.

HOW THESE COVENANTS AFFECT TODAY

The creation of a special people with unconditional promises of an everlasting title deed to specific land in the Middle East has brought unique problems to the world.

The problem was greatly intensified, first, by their destruction and two thousand year dispersion throughout the whole world.

And second, by the fact they survived as a distinct people and returned to claim their ancient homeland again in the midst of the Muslims who have possessed it off and on for centuries.

There is one more unique problem created by these covenants that will bring the present world order to a catastrophic end. This will be the subject of a future chapter. But first, it must be established just exactly who are the inheritors of the covenants made to Abraham.

THREE

WHO IS ABRAHAM'S TRUE SON?

"God also said to Moses, 'Say to the Israelites, "The LORD,[25] the God of your fathers—the God of Abraham, the God of Isaac and the God of Jacob—has sent me to you." This is my name forever, the name by which I am to be remembered from generation to generation.'"[26]

FOR SOME READERS, this chapter's title may sound like an irrelevant question. However, Bible prophets predict that this issue will eventually become a major factor in causing the world's final conflict. So significant is this matter to Muslims that they have sought for centuries to rewrite Biblical history. They say the covenants made with Abraham were not given to his son Isaac and his grandson Jacob and then to his descendants, but rather to Ishmael and his descendants.

This ancient controversy has become more important than ever before in recent times—just as Bible prophecy predicted for the end times. Muslims have vehemently argued that neither Isaac nor Jacob were in the chosen line of descendants to whom God's covenants were confirmed. In a future chapter, I will lay out the teachings of Muslims from the Koran and Hadith about this issue—and why they dispute what the Bible clearly says. But in this chapter, I will lay out what the Bible teaches—and how it has been confirmed in history.

It is imperative to be familiar with this aspect of Biblical history, even if you don't believe in the Bible. For as we will see, it is impossible to understand the real dynamics behind the present Arab-Israeli conflict apart from understanding these facts. The reason for this is simple. Both Islam and Israel *do believe* that the Bible is the basis of what they believe about this issue. Unfortunately, the secular media and academics don't grasp this and are therefore always wrong in their analysis of this globally important issue. And I must add, both the so-called liberal and conservative politicians fail to understand the basic causes of this world-troubling issue as well. Therefore their solutions are wrong and will not work.

THE MIRACLE SON

The drama begins in the ancient civilization of Ur of the Chaldeans. A wealthy seventy-five-year-old-man named Abram and his barren sixty-five-year-old-wife, Sarai, were living in this advanced civilization when God called them to move to a far less advanced but more dangerous culture to receive the great promises outlined in the last chapter. I mention that Ur was an advanced civilization to emphasize that it took great faith to leave it and go to a far less developed civilization in which people lived inside fortified cities because of the dangers of robbers. Archaeologists have even found evidence of a form of air conditioning in ancient Ur. And to further test Abraham's faith, God commanded him to live in tents in this inhospitable country—not in the cities.

As I noted, Abraham knew that all of the promises he received required him to have a son. And since he and Sarai were childless at such an advanced age, he knew that it would take a miracle for this to happen.

When Abraham became eighty-six years old (eleven years

after God unconditionally promised to give him a son), he stumbled in his faith. He did what so many of us do—he became impatient and thought that God needed his help. He had not yet learned that one of the most important factors of true faith is "to wait" upon the LORD to fulfill His promises. So he tried to help God fulfill the promise about a son. Abraham applied the old saying, "God helps those who help themselves." But there is no such verse in the Bible. In fact, the Bible teaches the opposite. God helps those who first recognize that in themselves they are helpless to produce spiritually acceptable things. We must trust God to do in and through us things that are humanly impossible.

Waiting upon the LORD requires patient, continuing trust that He will do what He says. As Isaiah promises, "But those who *wait* on the LORD shall renew their strength; They shall mount up with wings like eagles, They shall run and not be weary, They shall walk and not faint."[27] "Waiting" means faith in the long run. It is like a distance runner, not a sprinter. The Hebrew word for "renew" means "to exchange" something. So the verse means, "Those who keep waiting upon the LORD will exchange their human strength for the LORD's strength." Now that is worth waiting for, isn't it?

This graphically illustrates how enormous the repercussions of from some of our lapses of faith can be. Abraham's lapse faith created a family feud that has troubled our world until this present hour. Indeed, it will eventually trigger Armageddon.

In his own personal circumstances, Abram's lapse of faith short-circuited God's work in his life for a very long time. It wasn't until he became ninety-nine years old (thirteen years later) that God appeared to him again and re-confirmed all the covenants. This is the occasion when God changed Abram's name from Abram, which means "father of high places," to Abraham, which means "father of many peoples or nations."[28] At that same time, God also changed Sarai's name, to Sarah, which means "the princess" because from her God promised would come kings and nations.

Shortly after this, three extraordinary individuals appeared to

Abraham. Apparently they had a heavenly bearing, because Abraham gave them the reverence he reserved only for deity. He bowed down to the ground before them and begged them to stay for dinner.

During the course of the meal, it became apparent to Abraham that the three heavenly beings were the LORD Himself. It was at this time the LORD specifically promised that about the same time next year Abraham's wife would bear him a son. Now Sarah by that time would be ninety years old, barren, and well beyond the age of childbearing. And Abraham would be one hundred years old, likewise beyond the age of having children.

As a matter of fact, when Sarah overheard this promise (she was hidden behind a curtain in the tent), she began laughing quietly to herself in unbelief. This is the point where the supernatural powers of the three men became revealed. *They* said to Abraham, "Why did Sarah, your wife, laugh?" Since she was out of sight and had not made a sound, Abraham exclaimed she didn't laugh.

Here is how the Bible records the incident:

So Sarah laughed to herself as she thought, "After I am worn out and my master is old, will I now have this pleasure." Then the LORD said to Abraham, "Why did Sarah laugh and say, 'Will I really have a child, now that I am old?' Is anything too hard for the LORD? I will return to you at the appointed time next year and Sarah will have a son." Sarah was afraid, so she lied and said, 'I did not laugh.' But he said, "Yes, you did laugh."[29]

This is a one of those wonderful times when God shows His sense of humor. God ordered them to name the miracle child, Isaac or *Yitzak* in Hebrew, which means "laughter." So every time Sarah called her son "Laughter," she was reminded that she laughed in unbelief when God promised she would bear a son.[30]

COVENANTS CONFIRMED TO ISAAC

Abraham was overjoyed when Sarah bore to him Isaac. But Isaac's birth did present some complications; I will expand on this more in the next chapter. Through his Egyptian handmaid, Abraham already had a son named Ishmael, who was technically, therefore, Abraham's first-born—a fact that is greatly stressed by the Arabs and Muslims.

When God restated to Abraham His promise that he was going to have a son through Sarah who would be his true heir, no doubt was left as to who would be the true child of the covenant:

> God also said to Abraham, "As for Sarai your wife, you are no longer to call her Sarai; her name will be Sarah. I will bless her and will surely give you a son by her. I will bless her so that she will be the mother of nations; kings of peoples will come from her." Abraham fell facedown; he laughed and said to himself, "Will a son be born to a man a hundred years old? Will Sarah bear a child at the age of ninety?" And Abraham said to God, "If only Ishmael might live under your blessing!" Then God said, "Yes, but your wife Sarah will bear you a son, and you will call him Isaac. I will establish my covenant with him as an everlasting covenant for his descendants after him.[31]

This made it very clear who was the chosen line to whom the covenants were given and through whom God would work.

Later, when making arrangements to get Isaac an approved wife, Abraham reconfirmed his understanding as to who was the chosen son:

> The servant asked him, "What if the woman is unwilling to come back with me to this land? Shall I then take your son back to the country you came from?"

"Make sure that you do not take my son back there," Abraham said. "The LORD, the God of heaven, who brought me out of my father's household and my native land and who spoke to me and promised me on oath, saying, 'To your offspring I will give this land'—he will send his angel before you so that you can get a wife for my son from there.

"If the woman is unwilling to come back with you, then you will be released from this oath of mine. Only do not take my son back there."[32]

Abraham clearly states that the land covenant belongs to Isaac. The patriarch is adamant that under no circumstances was his son to return to the land God had commanded Abraham to leave to qualify for the covenant blessings.

When Abraham made the final disposition of his estate and the blessings of the promised covenants, the Bible states, "Abraham left everything he owned to Isaac."[33]

COVENANTS CONFIRMED TO JACOB

Here is the Biblical record of Abraham's chosen descendants through Isaac:

This is the account of Abraham's son Isaac. Abraham became the father of Isaac, and Isaac was forty years old when he married Rebekah daughter of Bethuel the Aramean from Paddan Aram (That is, Northwest Mesopotamia) and sister of Laban the Aramean.

Isaac prayed to the LORD on behalf of his wife, because she was barren. The LORD answered his prayer, and his wife Rebekah became pregnant. The babies jostled each other within her, and she said, "Why is this happening to me?" So she went to inquire of the LORD. The LORD said to her, "Two nations are in your womb, and two peoples from within you will be separated; one people will be stronger than the other, and the older will serve the younger."

When the time came for her to give birth, there were twin boys in her womb. The first to come out was red, and his whole body was like a hairy garment; so they named him Esau. (Esau may mean hairy; he was also called Edom, which means red.) After this, his brother came out, with his hand grasping Esau's heel; so he was named Jacob. (Jacob means figuratively, "cheater.") Isaac was sixty years old when Rebekah gave birth to them.[34]

Talk about trouble, these boys fought each other while still in the womb—and it got worse from there.

As the boys grew up, all the makings of a family civil war were present. Isaac was crazy about Esau, because he was the "outdoorsy" type and was a great hunter. He used to bring Isaac's favorite game home and make him a spicy stew. Esau was also the warrior type. Today we would call him, "A man's man."

On the other hand, Rebekah loved Jacob. Jacob was a peaceful, contemplative type who loved to be around home. He apparently also loved spiritual things, for he sought after the blessings of the first-born, which were primarily spiritual.

In the course of events, Jacob made some lentil stew. At that time, Esau returned from a long hunt and was tired and hungry. Esau smelled the food and told Jacob, "Give me some of that red stuff, for I am famished."

Jacob capitalized on the situation and made a very shrewd deal with Esau.

Jacob replied, "First sell me your birthright." "Look, I am about to die," Esau said. "What good is the birthright to me?" But Jacob said, "Swear to me first." So he swore an oath to him, selling his birthright to Jacob. Then Jacob gave Esau some bread and some lentil stew. He ate and drank, and then got up and left. So Esau despised his birthright.[35]

This was the most expensive stew in history. Surely Esau was aware of the spiritual significance of the covenants God made with his grandfather, Abraham. If he were a believer in the God of Abraham, he would never have dealt so flippantly with such a high privilege as to be chosen by God as His representative on earth. This is why God later made this pronouncement, "Jacob I have loved; But Esau I have hated."[36]

Apparently Esau conveniently forgot about this transaction, because when it came time for Isaac to confer the rights and covenants of the firstborn, Esau expected them to be his.

But Rebekah, knowing about Esau's sale of his birthright to Jacob, helped Jacob plot a little conspiracy to make sure that he got what Esau had sold him. Near the time of his death, Isaac had gone blind. So Rebekah put Esau's clothes on Jacob to make him smell like Esau. She also tied goat hide on the back of his hands around his neck so that he would feel hairy like Esau. Then she made Isaac's favorite savory stew and had Jacob take it in to Isaac.

When Isaac smelled Esau's clothes on Jacob, hugged his hairy neck and held his hands, the father was convinced that Jacob was Esau. So Isaac swore this oath to Jacob:

See, the smell of my son is like the smell of a field which the Lord has blessed; Now may God give you of the dew of heaven, And of the fatness of the earth, And an abundance of grain and new wine; May peoples serve you, And nations bow down to you; Be master of your brothers, And may your mother's sons bow down to you.

Cursed be those who curse you, And blessed be those who bless you.[37]

Even though Isaac and Esau discovered that same day that Jacob had tricked them, the oath was still binding. All the rights of the firstborn had been irrevocably conferred upon Jacob by Isaac's oath to God. An oath made to God is binding, even though we might not think so.

Esau became enraged. So Rebekah thought up another scheme to get Jacob out of harm's way. She went to Isaac and told him that her whole life would be ruined if Jacob married one of the local women who were idol worshippers. So Isaac called Jacob in and commanded him,

You shall not take a wife from the daughters of Canaan. Arise, go to Padan-aram, to the house of Bethuel your mother's father; and from there take to yourself a wife from there of the daughters of Laban your mother's brother. May God Almighty bless you, and make you fruitful and multiply you, that you may be an assembly of peoples; And give you the blessing of Abraham, To you and to your descendants with you, That you may inherit the land in which you are a stranger, Which God gave to Abraham. So Isaac sent Jacob away, and he went to Padan Aram, to Laban the son of Bethuel the Syrian, the brother of Rebekah, the mother of Jacob and Esau.[38]

Jacob worked for his uncle Laban for twenty years. During this time, he married Laban's two daughters, Leah and Rachel, along with their maids. God blessed everything Jacob did, despite his uncle's constant efforts to cheat him. As a result, he acquired great wealth.

HOW ISRAEL GOT ITS NAME

Laban's sons became jealous of Jacob because of God's blessings to him. So they turned their father's attitude against Jacob. But Jacob still feared his brother Esau and hesitated to return to Canaan. But the Lord said to Jacob, "Return to the land of your fathers and to your relatives, and I will be with you."[39]

Something mysterious happened to Jacob along the way. He sent his family by two companies ahead of him and spent the night alone. Then a man appeared to him and wrestled with him all night. When the man did not prevail against Jacob, he dislocated his leg at the hip. Then the man said to Jacob, "Let me go, for the dawn is breaking." But Jacob said to him, "I will not let you go unless you bless me."

Then the man said to Jacob, "What is your name?" And he replied, "Jacob," which means, "cheater." At this point, an amazing thing is revealed. The man said to him, "Your name will no longer be Jacob, but Israel [Israel means 'Prince with God'] because you have struggled with God ["Elohim"] and with men and have overcome." Jacob said, "Please tell me your name." But the man replied, "Why do you ask my name?" and then he blessed Jacob. So Jacob called the place Peniel [Peniel means "face of God"], saying, "I saw God face to face, and yet my life was spared."[40]

There are enormous theological implications to this account. But simply put, the Second Person of the Godhead assumed the form of a man and condescended to wrestle with Jacob. Whenever God expresses Himself visibly or audibly, it is through the Second Person. This is the same one who later permanently joined Himself to a true human nature in the person of Jesus the Messiah.

When this incident was over, Jacob was caused to realize he had seen God face to face. He was awestruck that God had graciously condescended to be intimately close to him and had not killed him.

From this time onward, Jacob's redeemed name was "Israel." After this, God calls him Jacob when He desires to emphasize his fleshly condition. He calls him Israel to emphasize his spiritual position. The same idea is expressed when God refers to the nation as either "the children of Jacob" or "the children of Israel."

The LORD reconfirms this new name when Jacob reached Bethel in Canaan. This is the place where God appeared to him long before Jacob first fled from Esau. Jacob built an altar there. As the following passage indicates, it is at this time that the LORD gave Jacob one of His most important revelations:

> Then God appeared to Jacob again when he came from Padan Aram, and He blessed him. And God said to him, "Your name is Jacob [cheater]; You shall no longer be called Jacob, But Israel shall be your name." Thus He called him Israel.
>
> God also said to him, "I am God Almighty; Be fruitful and multiply; A nation and a company of nations shall come from you, And kings shall come forth from you. "And the land which I gave to Abraham and Isaac, I will give it to you, And I will give the land to your descendants after you."[41]

From that time onward, Israel became the name of the chosen people of God. The name *Israel* appears in 1,695 verses of the Bible, both in the Old and New Testaments. This is very important because in their zeal to replace Israel, the Muslim's most serious charge against the Jews is that they corrupted the revelation God gave them.

Divine providence again works mightily concerning this name nearly four thousand years later. On the evening of May 14, 1948, David Ben Gurion and the original founders of the modern Jewish state still could not decide what they should call it. It was at the last moment that Ben Gurion said its name shall be Israel. Thus unwittingly, prophecies concerning the nation in the later days were fulfilled—even to its name.

BIRTH OF THE TRIBAL STATES OF ISRAEL

A very essential part of this history is that Jacob had twelve sons to whom the covenants were confirmed. These sons were born to him through his wives Leah and Rachel, and their two maids, Bilhah and Zilpah. As previously mentioned, the custom of the culture of that day was that if a man's wife was either barren or became barren; she could produce legal heirs by using her maid as a surrogate mother. In this case, Jacob married them all.

It is interesting to note that when Abraham followed this custom, it was not acceptable to God. But in Jacob's case, God did accept it. Why? This can only be understood in the light of God's purpose and sovereign grace. It is clear that in Abraham's case, the motive for using the maid to produce an heir was unbelief in God's promise.

Leah gave birth to Reuben, the first-born; then Simeon, Levi, Judah, Issachar, Zebulun, and a daughter, Dinah.

Rachel's maid, Bilhah, gave birth to Dan and Naphtali.

Leah's maid, Zilpah, gave birth to Gad and Asher.

Rachel, who had been barren, finally gave birth to Joseph and the youngest son, Benjamin.

Altogether, Jacob had twelve sons who were accepted by God as the foundation of the tribal states of His chosen nation, which He would name Israel.

There was just one more addition to these tribal states. By an act of divine providence, the two sons of Joseph who were born while he was in Egypt were given an inheritance and land among this original number. Their names are Ephraim and Manasseh. And because Levi committed a particularly heinous sin in God's eyes, his tribe was not given any land. But God graciously turned this curse into blessing when He made the Levites the priests of Israel. As it is written, "Therefore Levi has no portion nor inheritance with his brethren; the Lord is his inheritance, just as the Lord your God promised him."[42]

PROVIDENCE SAVES THE NATION

Joseph soon became the favorite son of his father, Jacob. As a result, Joseph's brothers became very jealous. So when all the brothers were out hunting and came across a caravan, they sold Joseph to Egyptians as a slave. Then they told their father that Joseph became lost and was killed by a wild animal. This was a terrible, calloused sin the brothers committed. But what they meant for evil, God turned into good. By the amazing work of the LORD's providence, Joseph rose from being a slave to become second in power to the mighty pharaoh of Egypt—just in time to save all of Joseph's family from famine.

After Joseph became vice-regent of Egypt, a famine gripped the entire region of the Mediterranean Sea. God warned Joseph that this was coming, so the vice-regent prepared Egypt ahead of time for the coming calamity. When the famine hit, Jacob and his family were about to starve, so he sent ten of his sons to Egypt to buy grain, keeping only Benjamin, the youngest at home with him.

By God's providence, these brothers had to bargain for their lives with the very one they had maliciously sold into slavery. They did not recognize Joseph at first, but he knew them immediately. As I said, he was now the mighty lord and co-regent of Egypt. When Joseph finally revealed to them who he was, they were utterly terrified. They thought they were dead men.

But Joseph was inspired by God's Spirit and was full of grace toward his brothers. He viewed the whole episode from the divine viewpoint. He graciously forgave them and said:

I am your brother Joseph, whom you sold into Egypt. And now do not be grieved or angry with yourselves, because you sold me here; for God sent me before you to preserve life. For the famine has been in the land these two years, and there are still five years in which there will be neither plowing nor harvesting. And God sent me before you to preserve for you a remnant in the earth, and to keep you alive by a great deliverance.

Now, therefore, it was not you who sent me here, but God; and He has made me a father to Pharaoh and lord of all his household and ruler over all the land of Egypt. Hurry and go up to my father, and say to him, "Thus says your son Joseph, God has made me lord of all Egypt; come down to me, do not delay.

"And you shall live in the land of Goshen, and you shall be near me, you and your children and your children's children and your flocks and your herds and all that you have. There I will also provide for you, for there are still five years of famine to come, lest you and your household and all that you have be impoverished."[43]

When the sons returned with a new invention of Egypt called "wagons," and lavish provisions of food, Jacob could hardly believe it. And then when he was told that Joseph was alive and now the lord of Egypt, he was overwhelmed. When Jacob finally believed their report, God appeared to him and explained His purpose in it all:

And God spoke to Israel in visions of the night and said, "Jacob, Jacob." And he said, "Here I am." And He said, "I am God, the God of your father; do not be afraid to go down to Egypt, for I will make you a great nation there. I will go down with you to Egypt, and I will also surely bring you up (to the Promised Land) again; and Joseph will close your eyes."[44]

This began the fulfillment of the prophecy to Abraham, which I mentioned earlier, concerning the period of four hundred years in which his descendents would grow into a nation in a land that was not their own.[45] And even though they would later be made slaves, God promised He would judge that nation and cause Israel to come out with great wealth.

As for Joseph, he later made a statement that perfectly illustrates the power of a promise made in the New Testament, where we read in Romans 8: "And we know that God causes all things to work together for good to those who love God, to those who are called according to His purpose."[46] Assessing his whole experience from the divine viewpoint, Joseph told his brothers, "Do not be afraid, for am I in God's place? And as for you, you meant evil against me, but God meant it for good in order to bring about this present result, to preserve many people alive.'"[47]

You see, all things are not good. But when we trust the LORD with our problems, He works even the bad things together for good, and in the process gives us peace of mind and rest in the midst of trouble. This is the secret to a long life.

JOSEPH'S EXPERIENCES PREVIEW THE MESSIAH'S

For centuries, both Jews and Christians have recognized the parallel between Joseph's experiences and those of the Messiah.

Of course the Israelites have not fully recognized the identity of the one this symbolizes, but some rabbis who lived before Jesus was born did theorize that their must be two Messiahs that are to come. They recognized that there are two different portraits of the Messiah painted in Bible prophecy. One is a conquering king who will come in great power and glory to deliver Israel from a great holocaust and set them up in the kingdom promised to their fathers. This Messiah they called the Son of David.

The other portrait predicts the Messiah will come as a lowly servant who will suffer for the transgressions of His people. This Messiah they call the Son of Joseph because of the obvious parallels.

What is not *yet* recognized by Israel is that there is only one Messiah who comes at two different times. The first time He comes as the suffering servant. The second time as the conquering king of David's seed.

Just look at the parallels between Joseph and Jesus:

- Joseph was rejected by his brothers and sent to die at the hands of the Gentiles.
- Jesus was also rejected and turned over to the Gentiles for crucifixion.
- Joseph was received and given great honor and glory among the Gentiles.
- Jesus also has been received and honored among the Gentiles.
- While among the Gentiles, Joseph had children who were later included in the covenant blessings of Abraham, Isaac, and Joseph.
- Jesus has also been given children among the Gentiles who have been adopted into the covenants of Israel.
- When great calamity came upon the world, the only salvation for Joseph's brothers was through the very one they had rejected. He who was thought to be dead "came back to life" and saved them.
- In the same way, Bible prophecy predicts that a tribulation will sweep the whole world and only Jesus will save Israel when they turn to Him. As it is predicted, "And I will pour out on the house of David and the inhabitants of Jerusalem the Spirit of grace and supplication. They will look on me, the one they have pierced, and they will mourn for him as one mourns for an only child, and grieve bitterly for him as one grieves for a firstborn son."[48]
- When Joseph's brothers came seeking help and later acknowledged their sin, Joseph forgave and saved them and settled them in his kingdom.
- When Jesus' brothers, the Israelites, acknowledge their sin and seek Him in the last days, He is going to save them and settle them in the kingdom He promised them.

GENESIS FINALIZES WHO GOD'S
CHOSEN PEOPLE ARE

The Book of Genesis gives the complete record as to just who God's chosen people are through Abraham. Now stop and think about this for a moment. The Bible teaches as much by the amount of space given to a subject as it does by what it says.

God took only eleven chapters to record the account of mankind from his creation until the call of Abraham. This covers perhaps thousands of years. But God took from chapter twelve to chapter fifty—a period of about three hundred years—to cover the creation and establishment of His chosen people. To those who believe the Bible, this should speak volumes about the importance God places upon these people.

Genesis ends with a careful accounting of the descendents of Abraham, Isaac, Jacob, Jacob's sons, and all their families as they go into Egypt.

The many genealogies that the Bible records usually bore most readers. There are many genealogies. Almost all of these genealogies are records of the children of Abraham, Isaac, and Jacob. The important question is, why are there so many? Why such a careful record of these people—particularly if they are ultimately to be rejected and abandoned, as a Christian sect known as Preterists teach today.

More importantly on this issue, Muslims believe that the Israelites never were God's chosen people. They believe Allah sent the Prophet Mohammad to correct this falsification created by Jews and Christians. Muslims say Ishmael and his Arab descendants were cheated out of their proper inheritance, since he was Abraham's firstborn son. As we will see, the Koran teaches that "the people of the Book"[49] falsified the original revelation and made themselves the heirs of God's covenants.

THE BIBLICAL RECORD

The verse I quoted from Exodus 3 at the beginning of this chapter sets the record straight. God spoke to Moses from out of the burning bush when calling him to lead the Israelites out of Egypt:

> Say to the Israelites, "The LORD, the God of your fathers—the God of Abraham, the God of Isaac and the God of Jacob—has sent me to you."
>
> This is my name forever, the name by which I am to be remembered from generation to generation.[50]

This name is confirmed throughout the rest of the Bible. But most importantly, the Lord Jesus Christ Himself confirms it:

> But about the resurrection of the dead—have you not read what God said to you, "*I AM* the God of Abraham, the God of Isaac, and the God of Jacob?"
>
> He is not the God of the dead but of the living.[51] (emphasis added)

When Jesus corrected the Jewish Sadducee sect's denial of the resurrection, He quoted God's statement to Moses. Notice, He emphasizes that the written account is what God said to them. His whole argument to prove the resurrection is based on the Hebrew verbal construction for "continuous being." This emphasizes that God *continuously is* the God of Abraham, Isaac, and Jacob. Therefore, they must be living, since God doesn't have a living relationship with the dead. There is also inherent in this statement that God will always be in a covenant relationship with them and their descendants.

This *I AM* is the specific name that can never be applied to the church, even in a figurative sense. It is also a name that cannot be applied to the Muslims.

Why is this so important? We will see that the God of the Bible is not the God of Ishmael, Esau, Mohammad, and the Muslims. Indeed, we will see that this issue is not just some irrelevant old theological argument, but is the basis of one of the central issues that troubles our world today.

FOUR

ABRAHAM'S WILD CHILD: THE HATE BEGINS

"He will be a wild ass of a man; his hand will be against everyone and everyone's hand against him, and he will live in hostility toward all his brothers and dwell to the east of them."

—GOD'S PROPHESY ABOUT ISHMAEL[52]

SOME DECISIONS WE make in life carry consequences far beyond our comprehension. There are some things we would give anything to undo, but alas, they cannot be. What's even worse is the generational impact of our sins—that is, some consequences of our wrong choices extend themselves to our relatives for generations.

Abraham had a lapse of faith concerning God's promise to give him a son. The decision he made during this episode of unbelief resulted in such enormous consequences that they have continued through the centuries until this very hour. I am sure that if Abraham had even a small hint of the trouble that would follow, he would never have tried to help God give him a son.

This chapter details the account of how a temporary lapse of faith resulted in a catastrophe for Abraham's future descendants who inherited the covenants. The consequences have affected more than a hundred generations over a period of four thousand years.

Some of the history in this chapter will overlap with that of the last. But since this history is so critical to understanding the modern Arab-Israeli conflict, it is necessary. This chapter will emphasize Ishmael's role in this four-thousand-year-old family feud.

ABRAHAM'S LAPSE OF FAITH

Abraham turned eighty-five-years old. It had been ten years since he moved to Canaan and God made the covenants with him that necessitated his having a son. And Sarah, his wife, was still barren and becoming very impatient. Finally, she decided that since she was now seventy-five-years old and still barren, it was impossible for her to bear Abraham a son. So Sarah came up with a plan to help God:

> Now Sarai, Abram's wife, had borne him no children. But she had an Egyptian maidservant named Hagar; so she said to Abram, "The LORD has kept me from having children. Go, sleep with my maidservant; perhaps I can build a family through her." Abram agreed to what Sarai said. So after Abram had been living in Canaan ten years, Sarai his wife took her Egyptian maidservant Hagar and gave her to her husband to be his wife. He slept with Hagar, and she conceived. When she knew she was pregnant, she began to despise her mistress.[53]

Sarah decided that the LORD had prevented her from conceiving and decided He must have another plan for giving them an heir. So she assumed that the LORD needed some help. The custom for the world of that time, as I mentioned before, was for the wife to use her maid as a surrogate mother. So Abraham, whose own faith must have been wavering, agreed with Sarah's plan.

However, the plan had one big problem. It was conceived out of a lack of faith in God's ability to keep His promise. Sarah and Abraham looked at this problem from the human viewpoint

(HVP). The human viewpoint sees a problem from the stand-point of human ability. On the other hand, the divine viewpoint (DVP) looks at a problem from the standpoint of God's ability to keep His promises, no matter how impossible they may appear.

So Abraham, who should have known better, followed his wife's suggestions and had relations with her Egyptian maid. And the moment she conceived, the problems began. Naturally, the maid's attitude changed and a civil war broke out in Abraham's tents.

This situation was predictable. The Book of Proverbs warns, "Under three things the earth trembles, under four it cannot bear up: a servant who becomes king, a fool who is full of food, an unloved woman who is married, and *a maidservant who displaces her mistress.*"[54]

To make matters even worse, Sarah blamed Abraham for fol-lowing her idea: "You are responsible for the wrong I am suffer-ing. I put my servant in your arms, and now that she knows she is pregnant, she despises me. May the LORD judge between you and me."[55] Ouch!

Abraham uncharacteristically ducks the problem and throws it back into Sarah's lap. He told her, in effect: "She's your maid, you deal with her. Do whatever you want with her." And of course Sarah vented her frustration and anger on poor Hagar. She treated her so harshly that she ran away into the desert.

GOD'S PROPHECY TO HAGAR

No doubt Hagar would have died in the desert had not the Lord in His great mercy sought her out and encouraged her. The angel of the Lord[56] also gave Hagar a great promise and a prophecy about the child she would bear:

The angel of the LORD found Hagar near a spring in the desert; it was the spring that is beside the road to Shur. And he said, "Hagar, servant of Sarai, where have you come from, and where are you going?" "I'm running away from my mistress Sarai," she answered.

Then the angel of the LORD told her, "Go back to your mistress and submit to her." The angel added, "I will so increase your descendants that they will be too numerous to count." The angel of the LORD also said to her:

"You are now with child and you will have a son. You shall name him Ishmael, [Ishmael means "God hears"] for the LORD has heard of your misery.

"He will be a wild donkey of a man; his hand will be against everyone and everyone's hand against him, and he will live in hostility toward all his brothers."[57]

This was a marvelous manifestation of God's mercy. Hagar apparently was trying to follow the road across the Sinai back to Egypt. But alone on foot with no provisions, she would have died in route. Hagar, the Egyptian maid, was subjected to an affair over which she had no choice. But the LORD demonstrates that He loved her too, as He does anyone who calls out to Him and throws herself upon God's mercy. The very name that God gives her for the son she is carrying is a memorial that the LORD heard her prayer of distress. He commanded her to name him "Ishmael," which means "God hears."

A lone runaway female slave in that day was truly helpless and in danger. The LORD therefore tells her to return and be submissive to Sarah with the promise that He would bless her with descendants beyond numbering through her son. She is promised her own personal inheritance and blessing from the LORD through her son.

Because Ishmael is also a son of Abraham, God promises to bless him and make him into a great multitude of people and nations. God loves Ishmael and his descendants, even though he foreknew his wild nature that would be multiplied in his descendants. The Lord made an amazing prophecy about the kind of temperament and nature that would be in Ishmael's genes and passed on to his descendants. It is fascinating to analyze each to see how accurately it has been fulfilled in the descendants of Ishmael—the Arabs.

1. "He will be a wild ass of a man." [Note: this refers to Gen. 16:12.]

Hebrew scholars Keil and Delitzsch comment on how accurately this metaphor describes the Arab people. "The figure of a wild ass,' they write, "that wild and untamable animal, roaming at its will in the desert . . . depicts most aptly the Bedouin's boundless love of freedom as he rides about in the desert, spear in hand, upon his camel or his horse, hardy, frugal, reveling in the varied beauty of nature, and despising town life in every form."[58]

God poetically describes the nature of the "wild ass" in His challenge to Job:

Who set the wild ass free?
Who loosed the bonds of the swift ass?
Whose home I have made the wilderness,
And the barren land his dwelling?
He scorns the tumult of the city;
He does not heed the shouts of the driver.
The range of the mountains is his pasture,
And he searches after every green thing.[59]

This perfectly describes the genetic characteristics and nature of Ishmael and his descendents, the Arabs. Like the wild donkeys of the wilderness, they fiercely love their freedom and independence. They have always had a warrior's temperament.

2. "Whose home I have made the wilderness, And the barren land his dwelling." [Note: this refers to Job.] This description from Job accurately describes how the wild ass illustrates the

Arab characteristics. God predicted that the Ishmaelites would live to the east of all their brethren. God gave them the Arabian Peninsula, which is to the east of all the rest of Abraham's descendants. Philip Hitti writes about the Arab home:

> Despite its size—it is the largest peninsula in the world—its total population is estimated at only seven to eight millions. It is one of the driest and hottest countries in the whole world. True, the area is sandwiched between seas on the east and west, but these bodies of water are too narrow to break the climatic continuity of the Africo-Asian rainless continental masses. The ocean on the south does bring rains, to be sure, but the monsoons (an Arabic word, incidentally), which seasonably lash the land, leave very little moisture for the interior. It is easy to understand why the bracing and delightful east wind has always provided a favorite theme for Arabian poets.[60]

The migrant Arab is called a "Bedouin." He loves the desert and the freedom to move about the vast desert regions from oasis to oasis with the seasons—always searching after every green thing.

The Arabs call their peninsula an "island," because it is surrounded on three sides by sea and ocean—and to the north where it connects to land, the great Nafud Desert isolates it even more than an ocean.

The richest part of Arabia in ancient history was the southern coast, which thrusts out into the Indian Ocean. This area received seasonal rains and produced some of the most exotic in-demand plants of the ancient world. The much sought after fragrance called myrrh came from there. It also accumulated great wealth because its seaports were along the main trade route from Asia.

3. "His hand will be against everyone and everyone's hand will be against him." [61]

This characteristic has been dominant throughout the history of the Arabs. Hitti summarizes accurately the Arab Bedouin nature:

> The Bedouin still lives, as his forebears did, in tents of goats' or camels' hair ("houses of hair"), and grazes his sheep and goats on the same ancient pastures. Sheep-and-camel-raising, and to a lesser degree horse-breeding, hunting and raiding, are his regular occupations, and are to his mind the only occupations worthy of a man.[62]

Blood feuds have been fought between the many Arab tribes of the peninsula for centuries. Their lists of grudges against each other can go back for centuries. If an Arab is forced out of the protection of his tribe, he usually doesn't last very long.

The wild donkey reflects this very characteristic, for he groups together in small herds and is hostile with even other herds of his own kind. Similarly Arab society from its earliest history divided up into many clans. Again Hitti describes the predominant Arab social structure:

> The spirit of the clan demands boundless and unconditional loyalty to fellow clansmen, a passionate chauvinism. His allegiance, which is individualism of the member magnified, assumes that his tribe is a unit by itself, self-sufficient and absolute, *and regards every other tribe as its legitimate victim and object of plunder and murder.*[63]

There have been only a few things that have been able to unite the Arabs in all their history. The most important unifier was Mohammad and the initial impact of the Muslim religion. And over time, even the common religion could not hold the different Arab tribes together.

Then there was the common threat to their "Holy Places" posed by the Catholic crusaders. Muslim armies united to fight off the successive waves of European knights sent by the pope to liberate Jerusalem and the ancient Holy Land.

In our present era, the most powerful unifying factor of all has arisen. Nothing can unite the warring Muslim factions like their historic hatred for Jews, which has been reignited by their re-establishment of the state of Israel. To the Muslims, Israel's existence in the midst of what they consider their sacred sphere of the earth is the ultimate sacrilege. It is an insult to Allah that must be avenged and destroyed. To the Muslim, the fact that Israel has beaten them in five wars even threatens the veracity of the Koran, which promises them victory over the infidels, especially when their fight is a "Jihad to liberate their third holiest site—Jerusalem." The Jewish occupation of Jerusalem is a "humiliation" that must be avenged for the sake of the honor of Allah and the truth of the Koran. The combination of all these issues elevates religious passion to an intensity that cannot be fathomed by the Western mind.

Much more will be said on this subject later in the book.

4. "And he will live in hostility toward all of his brothers, [and he will dwell to the east of them.]"[64]

This part of the prophecy concerning Ishmael and his descendents is particularly important. Many English translations simply translate this clause as, "and he will dwell to east of all his brothers." But the Hebrew words and grammatical construction are much more complex than that translation would imply.

Hebrew scholars Keil and Delitzsch observe that the expression often translated as, "He will dwell before the face of all his brethren" (from the Hebrew פני לצ, transliterated as ["before the face of"], and which denotes in this context it is true, to the east of . . . , but the geographical notice of the dwelling-place of the Ishmaelites hardly exhausts the force of the expression, *which also indicated that Ishmael would maintain an independent standing before*

(in the presence of) all the descendants of Abraham. History has confirmed this promise. The Ishmaelites have continued to this day
in free and undiminished possession of the extensive peninsula
between the Euphrates, the Straits of Suez, and the Red Sea,
from which they have overspread both Northern Africa and
Southern Asia."[65]

According to Hebrew scholars, the expression "*in the face of*"
can also mean, "*to stand in defiant hostility toward*." The New
International Version, I believe, correctly expresses the sense of
this phrase by translating it, "and he will live in hostility toward
all his brothers." The New Revised Standard Version is an
improvement as well: "and he shall live at odds with all his kin."
However, I believe that the NIV translation better catches the
intended sense, a rendering confirmed by history to be the truest
expression of the intended meaning.

ENMITY FLASHES IN EMBRYONIC FORM

The seeds of enmity are expressed in embryonic form on the
occasion of Isaac's weaning. Abraham and Sarah threw a great
feast to celebrate Isaac's weaning. By this time, Ishmael was at
least sixteen years old and accustomed to having most of his
father's attention. So when Isaac was born and so much attention
was showered upon him, a great deal of resentment and jealousy
must have sprung up in both Ishmael and his mother. All the
ingredients for an envy-driven hatred were there.

During the celebration, the Bible reports, "Sarah saw the son
of Hagar the Egyptian, whom she had borne to Abraham, scoffing [at her son Isaac]."[66]

The Hebrew term translated "scoffing" is from the root word
"to laugh" (צחק, transliterated as [give transliteration], means "to
mock"). But in the participial form in this context it means, "making fun of, ridiculing, discounting someone's worth."

To understand the full implications of this situation, we have to put it up against the background of the promise God gave to Abraham when He announced Isaac's birth. This is what God had promised Abraham:

> Then God said to Abraham, "As for Sarai your wife, you shall not call her name Sarai, but Sarah shall be her name. And I will bless her and also give you a son by her; then I will bless her, and she shall be a mother of nations; kings of peoples shall be from her." Then Abraham fell on his face and laughed, and said in his heart, "Shall a child be born to a man who is one hundred years old? And shall Sarah, who is ninety years old, bear a child?" And Abraham said to God, "*Oh, that Ishmael might live before You!*" Then God said: "No, Sarah your wife shall bear you a son, and you shall call his name Isaac; I will establish My covenant with him for an everlasting covenant, and with his descendants after him."[67]

This God-given revelation must have certainly been made known to Abraham's entire household, including Hagar and Ishmael. And its divine authenticity was confirmed with the miraculous conception and birth of Isaac to the elderly parents.

So when Ishmael scoffed at and made fun of Isaac, he did so with the knowledge that according to divine revelation, Isaac was the chosen one. And that this was not merely a human choice based on carnal favoritism. This is why in the eyes of God Ishmael was not just mocking Isaac, but he was rejecting and ridiculing His sovereign choice. The German scholar Hengstenberg expressed the following insight, "Unbelief, envy, pride of carnal superiority, were the causes of Ishmael's conduct."[68]

This is surely the stuff of which Ishmael's "enmity" was born. Remember, *enmity* is hatred that has been nourished over a long period of time. It was just beginning to take root here. An "everlasting hatred" is the very essence of the meaning of "enmity."

GOD'S PROMISES TO ISHMAEL

The Bible makes it clear that despite the birth of Isaac, there was no lack of love for Ishmael on the part of Abraham or God. Abraham even petitioned the Lord that Ishmael could be part of the divine choice, when he said, "Oh, that Ishmael might live before You!"

And as a result, God made it clear that Ishmael would be given a great inheritance because he was also Abraham's son. God promised, "And as for Ishmael, I have heard you. Behold, I have blessed him, and will make him fruitful, and will multiply him exceedingly. He shall beget twelve princes, and I will make him a great nation. But My covenant I will establish with Isaac, whom Sarah shall bear to you at this set time next year."[69] In point of fact, the Ishmaelites were given more land and ultimately more wealth than the Israelites. This was true in their past history, not to mention the vast oil wealth of modern times. And spiritual salvation has always been open to the Ishmaelites.

But God's covenant, which concerned God's spiritual purposes to provide salvation for all mankind, was only for Isaac and his descendants. The physical blessings promised to Isaac were to facilitate God's spiritual call for the nation that would descend from him.

WHY GOD SEPARATED ISHMAEL AND ISAAC

What happened as a result of Ishmael's actions might seem too severe unless it is seen in the light of the divine perspective. When Sarah saw how Ishmael scoffed at her son, she said to Abraham (I'm sure without altogether spiritual motives), "Get rid of that slave woman and her son, for that slave woman's son will never share in the inheritance with my son Isaac."[70]

This really grieved Abraham. But in this case, God saw the spiritual necessity of separating the two. Perhaps if Ishmael had not yielded to the fleshly passions of envy and jealousy, he and his mother could have stayed on with the family. But this episode showed that he was not looking at this from the standpoint of God's sovereign purpose and choice. He was only focusing on the situation from his carnal human emotions that said, "What God gave me is not enough—I want it all." And as we will see, the Ishmaelites are still saying, "What God gave us is not enough, we want it all." And in our day, this feeling is being driven by centuries of cultivated enmity.

This is certainly a common human failure. How often I have seen even Christian ministers become ungrateful for the spiritual gifts and blessings God has given them when they become jealous of the gifts God gave others. That's always a very costly yielding to the old sin nature. The Scriptures say, "But one and the same Spirit works all these things, distributing [spiritual gifts] to each one individually as He wills."[71]

So the greatly grieved Abraham gave Hagar her freedom with provisions for her and Ishmael and sent them away. I am sure it took real faith on Abraham's part to trust that God would take care of them—because he did love Ishmael very much.

"GOD HEARS" ISHMAEL

When the provisions and water ran out, which I am sure was designed to be God's test of their faith, Hagar and Ishmael despaired. Remember the meaning of Ishmael's name is "God hears." Ishmael cried out to God, and the LORD graciously heard his cry:

> God heard the boy crying, and the angel of God called to Hagar from heaven and said to her, "What is the matter, Hagar? Do not be afraid; God has heard the boy crying as he lies there. Lift the boy up and take him by the hand, for I will make him into a great nation." Then God opened her eyes and she saw a well of water. So she went and filled the skin with water and gave the boy a drink.[72]

Hagar and Ishmael were given great privileges. This makes twice that the LORD appeared to Hagar, spoke with her, and rescued her. And this was also a gracious revelation to Ishmael. If these two did not receive God's redemption, it could never be said they had no light. How many today could truly say that God appeared and spoke with them?

The LORD never abandoned Ishmael. The Bible records, "God was with the boy as he grew up. He lived in the desert and became an archer. While he was living in the Desert of Paran, his mother got a wife for him from Egypt."[73]

Ishmael is not mentioned again until the death of his father Abraham. Then Isaac and Ishmael came together and buried their father. Apparently they then went their separate ways and did not see each other again.

ISHMAEL'S LEGACY

Ishmael had twelve sons, each of whom became a great prince, and he founded twelve nations. However, the second son, Kedar, became the most powerful and wealthy. Remember that name, for his descendants figure prominently in Arab history.

God blessed Ishmael and caused him to live 137 years. This is God's obituary for him:

> Altogether, Ishmael lived a hundred and thirty-seven years. He breathed his last and died, and he was gathered to his people. His descendants settled in the area from Havilah to Shur, near the border of Egypt, as you go toward Asshur. *And they lived in hostility toward all their brothers.*[74]
> (emphasis added)

Amazing! Exactly the same thing is said about Ishmael's descendants as was said of Ishmael himself. It is exactly the same Hebrew clause, except instead of "he," it is "they" who continued to live in "hostility toward all their brothers" and "dwelt to the east of them." And of course the brothers, against whom this hostility is aimed, are the descendants of Isaac, who lived to the west.

How that hostility became a permanent enmity is the focus of the rest of this book. Read on, for this ancient family feud is going to directly affect our lives. You will see how the prophecies of the Bible are much more relevant to our era than any mere human news

FIVE

"CURSED" BE THE TIE THAT BINDS

"Now Abraham gave all that he had to Isaac; but to the *sons of his concubines*, Abraham gave gifts while he was still living, and sent them away from his son Isaac *eastward, to the land of the east.*"
—GENESIS 25:5[75]

"So Esau hated Jacob because of the blessing with which his father blessed him, and Esau said in his heart, 'The days of mourning for my father are at hand; *then I will kill my brother Jacob.*'"
—GENESIS 27:41[76]

NEVER IN HISTORY has there been a family feud that sustained such enmity over so long a period of time. And no other ethnic violence has affected so many nations for so many centuries. The enmity of Ishmael and Esau toward Isaac and Jacob truly is supernatural. And the worst is yet to come. Indeed, as I have said so many times, the Bible predicts that the last war of the world will be triggered by a conflict over the issue of which descendents of these ancient families owns Jerusalem.

This is why it is so important to trace these peoples through history to the present day. And it is of ultimate importance to understand the root cause of the enmity toward Israel.

I believe this is the biggest single factor that is not understood by today's Western political leaders, academics, and media. And it is the reason all of their attempts to solve the Middle East conflict are destined to fail.

To my knowledge, no one has done an extensive study on the history of Abraham's greater family outside of the chosen line of Isaac and Jacob. So follow this section closely. It will throw some very important light on today's Middle East problems.

THE CURSE OF ABRAHAM'S NEPHEW

When God called Abraham, He told him very specifically, "Get out of your country, from your kindred, and from your father's house, to a land that I will show you."[77] Now the record shows that Abraham (then called Abram) only *partially obeyed* the LORD's command. For when he left Ur of the Chaldeans, his father, Terah, was in charge and went with him as far as Haran, which was only part of the way to Canaan. It appears that the LORD did not allow Abraham to even enter Canaan until after his father died in Haran.[78] God wanted Abraham to be in charge of his own household. Ancient tradition always established the eldest father as the chief of the family.

After Abraham's father died, we read in the Biblical record:

"So Abram departed as the Lord had spoken to him, and Lot went with him. And Abram was seventy-five years old when he departed from Haran. Then Abram took Sarai his wife and Lot his brother's son, and all their possessions that they had gathered, and the people whom they had acquired in Haran, and they departed to go to the land of Canaan. So they came to the land of Canaan. Abram passed through the land to the place of Shechem, as far as the terebinth tree of Moreh. And the Canaanites were then in the land. *Then* the Lord appeared to Abram and said, 'To your descendants I will give this land.' And there he built an altar to the Lord, who had appeared to him."[79] (emphasis added)

Even though Abraham was now in charge of the family, he still did not fully obey the Lord's command, for he took Lot, his nephew, with him. And Lot became the proverbial "Albatross" around Abraham's neck.

Later, when Abraham and Lot tried to live together, a range war developed between their two groups of "cowboys" and shepherds. They both had too many cattle and sheep to be sustained in the same region.

LOT'S CARNAL CHOICE

So Abraham, the senior, graciously allowed Lot first choice as to where in the land he would like to settle. Lot's choice was purely of the flesh. He chose the lush plain of the Jordan River. Here is the Bible's description:

> And Lot lifted his eyes and saw all the plain of Jordan, that it was well watered everywhere (before the Lord destroyed Sodom and Gomorrah) like the garden of the LORD, like the land of Egypt as you go toward Zoar. Then Lot chose for himself all the plain of Jordan, and Lot journeyed east. And they separated from each other. Abram dwelt in the land of Canaan, and Lot dwelt in the cities of the plain and pitched his tent even as far as Sodom. But the men of Sodom were exceedingly wicked and sinful against the Lord.[80]

There are many interesting facts revealed here. The area that is now the Dead Sea was like the Garden of Eden before God's overwhelming judgment upon the cities of Sodom and Gomorrah. The tremendous explosion that hit these two cities must have hit like a giant karate chop. This area is now a rift valley. The area in the center, where Sodom and Gomorrah were, is like a moveable stage that is between two parallel fault lines. The main fault, to which the rift valley is connected, extends from Mount Hermon in the north southward to Lake Tanganyika in Africa. The Dead Sea, which is the center of the Rift Valley, is 1,260 feet below sea level.

Standing atop Masada, I have seen some of the ruins of Sodom under the southern tip of the Dead Sea. Anyone who doubts God's attitude toward "Sodomy" only needs to look at this geographical reminder.

Lot Moves Away From Fellowship With God

Whereas Genesis 13 records that Lot first pitched his tent toward Sodom, it is later revealed that he moved into the city of Sodom and settled there in a house. From then on his troubles multiplied. We can't immerse ourselves in the things of this world and sustain fellowship with the Lord. It was apparently the influence of his wife that drove him from tents into the luxury of the city. But they paid a terrible price, as revealed in Genesis chapter 19. The people of the city were consumed with every form of sexual perversion mixed with extreme violence.

When God revealed to Abraham that He was going to destroy Sodom and Gomorrah, Abraham interceded for the wicked cities in order to save Lot and his family. God granted Abraham's desire, but not his petition. That is, He delivered Lot and his family, but destroyed the wicked cities.

God's Grace Never Fails

In 2 Peter, Lot is held up as an example of God's unfailing grace even to the carnal, out of fellowship believer:

> And [God] turning the cities of Sodom and Gomorrah into ashes, condemned them to destruction, making them an example to those who afterward would live ungodly; and delivered righteous Lot, who was oppressed by the filthy conduct of the wicked (for that righteous man, dwelling among them,

tormented his righteous soul from day to day by seeing and hearing their lawless deeds)—the Lord knows how to deliver the godly out of temptations and to reserve the unjust under punishment for the day of judgment.[81]

Lot was out of fellowship and his conduct was not righteous, but his spirit was still born again and he had the righteousness of faith that comes with receiving God's pardon for sin. Though God disciplined Lot, He never disowned him. And God delivered him because of Abraham's intercession for him.

Lot's Curse: Moab and Ammon

Now it was after this destruction and the death of Lot's wife when she turned back and yearned in her heart for the fleshly comforts of Sodom, that Lot became the father of two of Israel's greatest enemies.

Lot's two daughters feared that, since they were the only female survivors of the entire region of Sodom and Gomorrah, they would never have a husband and children. Children were like having social security for your old age in those days.

So each girl in turn made their father drunk and had sex with him. The result of this incest was the birth of two sons, Moab and Ammon. We will see that their descendants became the constant enemies of Israel and that the Bible predicts that their descendants will be part of a Muslim alliance in the war that ends this present world order—Armageddon.

ABRAHAM'S OTHER SONS

A little-considered part of Abraham's life is what happened to him after the death of Sarah, his wife. When she died, Abraham was 137 years old. After Abraham provided Rebekah as a wife for Isaac to make sure the covenant line was settled, he married another wife. He was about 139 years old by this time.

We all marvel, and rightly so, that God enabled Abraham, against nature, to have Isaac at the age of one hundred years. But here we find just how far back God turned Abraham's biological clock and restored his youth. Here is the amazing and important record:

> Abraham again took a wife, and her name was Keturah. And she bore him Zimran, Jokshan, Medan, Midian, Ishbak, and Shuah. Jokshan begot Sheba and Dedan. And the sons of Dedan were Asshurim, Letushim, and Leummim. And the sons of Midian were Ephah, Epher, Hanoch, Abidah, and Eldaah. All these were the children of Keturah.[82]

Abraham had six more sons and ten grandsons before his death at the age of 175 years.

I believe these are the people to whom the prophet Jeremiah refers in a prophetic warning to the nations that mistreated Israel. He refers to them as a part of the Arabian people, "all the kings of Arabia and all the kings of *the mixed multitude who dwell in the desert . . .*"[83]

The "mixed multitude" is no doubt descended from Abraham's other sons, who apparently mingled with the Ishmaelites in the vast Arabian Peninsula. This is supported by what the Bible says in Genesis 25. The Bible notes that, before Abraham died, he gave all he had to Isaac. Then it specifically points out that "Abraham gave gifts to the sons of the concubines which Abraham had; and while he was still living he sent them eastward, away from Isaac his son, to the country of the east."[84]

Note that it says "concubines," in the plural. Abraham only had only two concubines—Ishmael's Egyptian mother Hagar and Keturah. This would indicate that he called them all together and gave gifts to Ishmael and the six sons he had with Keturah. And then he sent them (which in context would have to mean both Ishmael and his other six sons) "eastward, away from Isaac his son, to the country of the east." As noted before, the country to the east is the land we know as the Arabian Peninsula.

THE PERPETUAL FAMILY TIE

I am sure the reason Abraham sent these family members to the east was to protect Isaac and his family. There was resentment and jealousy among all of Abraham's other sons and relatives toward Isaac. They saw only Abraham's favoritism toward Isaac, not God's sovereign choice and purpose.

This is the common factor that runs through all of Israel's relatives. *It is this enmity that developed from envy and jealousy that binds all of these family members together.*

ESAU I HAVE HATED

There are two descendants of Abraham that have been the most persistent enemies of Israel—Ishmael and Esau. As we have seen, Ishmael is the half brother of Isaac, and Esau is the twin brother of Jacob. Much was observed about Esau in chapter three, but there are some other factors that need to be noted here.

Esau and Jacob were fraternal twins. Fraternal twins are not only different in appearance, but they are also usually very different in temperament and personality. This was glaringly so in the case of these two boys.

I have fraternal twin daughters who don't even look like sisters. Their temperaments and personalities are radically different. They represent two entirely different strains of their family's genes. But thank God, they are not like these two boys—they have always loved each other.

ESAU, WHO IS CALLED EDOM

As mentioned in an earlier chapter, Esau was nicknamed "Edom" or "Red" for apparently two reasons. First, because from birth his body was covered with red hair. And second, because he called the lentil stew for which he sold his birthright, "that *red* stuff."

When Esau discovered that Jacob had tricked his father Isaac into giving him the blessing of the first born, which Esau had traded to Jacob for "red" lentil stew, Esau wept and begged for the oath to be reversed. But Isaac realized that what he had sworn before the Lord could not be reversed. Instead, as a result God made the following prophecy through Isaac about Esau's future:

> And he [Isaac] said, "Your brother came deceitfully, and has taken away your blessing." Then he said, "Is he not rightly named Jacob, for he has *cheated* [85] me these two times? He took away my birthright, and behold, now he has taken away my blessing." And he said, "Have you not reserved a blessing for me?" But Isaac answered and said to Esau, "Behold, I have made him your master, and all his relatives I have given to him as servants; and with grain and new wine I have sustained him. Now as for you then, what can I do, my son?" And Esau said to his father, "Do you have only one blessing, my father? Bless me, even me also, O my father." So Esau lifted his voice and wept. Then Isaac his father answered and said to him, "Behold, away from the fertility of the earth shall be your dwelling, And away from the dew of heaven from above. And by your sword you shall live, And your brother you shall serve; But it shall come about when you become restless, That you shall break his yoke from your neck."[86]

The LORD caused Isaac to unwillingly pronounce a sad prophecy upon Esau's future. The land where his descendants settled was not fertile—it was primarily the Arabian Peninsula. They first settled east of the Dead Sea in the mountains that extended from its lower tip southward. But eventually, almost all of them migrated and mingled with the Ishmaelites, who are the Arabs.

"BY YOUR SWORD YOU SHALL LIVE"

Like his uncle Ishmael, Esau would live by the sword. He would war and pillage to sustain his people. In this regard, consider a couple of observations from Keil and Delitzsch. First, commenting on, "Behold, away from the fertility of the earth shall be your dwelling, and away from the dew of heaven from above," they write, "This is generally the condition of the mountainous country of Edom, which although not without its fertile slopes and valleys, especially in the eastern portion, is thoroughly waste and barren in the western; so that Seetzen says it consists of 'the most desolate and barren mountains probably in the world.'"

Second, regarding, "And by your sword you shall live," they write, "The mode of life and occupation of the inhabitants were adapted to the country. . . His maintenance would be by the sword, i.e., he will live by war, rapine and freebooting [piracy]."[87]

Most important, these verses reveal that Esau was already holding a grudge against Jacob. "Is he not rightly named Jacob," Esau said, "for he has cheated me these two times?" This shows Esau was keeping count of the wrongs he considered Jacob had done to him.

HATE BECOMES "EVERLASTING ENMITY"

Once Esau realized that the inheritance and blessing had permanently been given to Jacob, he said, "So Esau hated Jacob because of the blessing with which his father blessed him, and Esau said in his heart, 'The days of mourning for my father are at hand; then I will kill my brother Jacob.'"[88]

This hatred became an enmity that permeated his descendants. They became primarily called the sons of Edom or the Edomites. They later became known as the Idumaens that produced the Herod dynasty spoken of in the New Testament. King Herod the Great, who ordered the slaughter of the infants in Bethlehem in order to kill the Messiah, was a descendant of Esau.

His son, Herod the tetrarch of Galilee, beheaded John the Baptist. They were a cunning and vicious clan. The New Testament records how they gained control over Israel for a short time under Roman sponsorship.

But perhaps the most important factor is this—there is evidence that Esau's descendants not only became part of the Ishmael/Arab race but also joined with them against Israel. They were certainly prominent among the warriors who first converted to Islam and helped spread it across the Mediterranean world.

The Bible records how Esau became part of the Arabs. When Esau observed that his father gave strict orders for Jacob not to marry any of the Canaanite women, and that the two Canaanite wives he had already married grieved Isaac, he sought to please his father. So we read, "Esau then realized how displeasing the Canaanite women were to his father Isaac; so he went to Ishmael and married Mahalath, the sister of Nebaioth and daughter of Ishmael son of Abraham, in addition to the wives he already had."[89]

A HISTORY OF EXPANDING HATE

Throughout the history of Israel, the Edomites seized every opportunity to vent their hatred against them. This is briefly illustrated by the following Biblical accounts of the Edomites' actions.

When Israel came out of captivity from Egypt, the Edomites would not even let them pass through their land. "Thus Edom refused to give Israel passage through his territory; so Israel turned away from him."[90] God graciously spared Edom despite the fact that this brought great hardship upon Israel.

God Warns Amalek

Amalek, one of the chiefs descended from Esau, has been a persistent enemy of Israel. When he fought against Israel as they came from Egypt, God made this prediction:

Then the Lord said to Moses, "Write this in a book as a memorial, and recite it to Joshua, that I will utterly blot out the memory of Amalek from under heaven." And Moses built an altar, and named it The Lord is My Banner; and he said, "The Lord has sworn; the Lord will have war against Amalek from generation to generation."[91]

Edom Becomes a Dominant Symbol of Arabs

Ezekiel predicts that God will judge "all Edom" (referring here to all Arabs) for appropriating Israel's land. This judgment comes in the last days when God miraculously returns the Israelites from all the countries where He scattered them. This prophecy refers to our time. God warns, "This is what the Sovereign LORD says: In my burning zeal I have spoken against the rest of the nations, and against *all Edom*, for *with glee* and *with malice in their hearts* they made my land their own possession so that they might plunder its pastureland."[92]

God warns Edom again about the judgment that will fall on all his descendants at the coming of the Messiah. The reason is clearly given here:

This is what the LORD says: "For three sins of Edom, even for four, I will not turn back my wrath. *Because he pursued his brother [Israel] with a sword, stifling all compassion, because his anger raged continually and his fury flamed unchecked*, I will send fire upon Teman that will consume the fortresses of Bozrah."[93]

A prophecy in the Psalms concerning the final mad attempt of the ancient descendants of Abraham's other sons to destroy Israel shows that Edom and Ishmael linked together and leading the confederacy to wipe Israel off the earth. Just look at the list of

Israel's enemies in the "Last Days." It reads like a "Who's Who" of their ancient enemies.

> Do not keep silent, O God! Do not hold Your peace, And do not be still, O God! For behold, *Your* enemies make a tumult; And those who hate *You* have lifted up their head. They have taken crafty counsel against *Your* people, And consulted together against *Your* sheltered ones. They have said, "*Come, and let us cut them off from being a nation, That the name of Israel may be remembered no more.*" For they have consulted together with one consent; they form a confederacy against You: The tents of *Edom* and the *Ishmaelites*; Moab and the Hagrites; Gebal, Ammon, and Amalek; Philistia with the inhabitants of Tyre; Assyria also has joined with them; They have helped the children of Lot. . . . Who said, "Let us take for ourselves The pastures of God for a possession."[94]

All the usual suspects are in this predicted line up of bad guys. Edom and the Ishmaelites are the primary Arab people. The descendants of Moab, the Hagrites, Gebal, Ammon, Amalek, and Philistia melted in the mixed group that were absorbed by the Arab culture and then later became converted to Islam. Today, these people make up the nations of Jordan, Saudi Arabia, United Arab Emirates, Oman, Kuwait, and Qatar. The other places named are:

- Tyre, which is now Lebanon
- Assyria, which is modern Syria
- Persia, which is modern Iran

All of these people are linked together by their common continuous enmity toward Israel.

The battle cry of all these people in five previous wars with Israel has been to wipe Israel off the map and to slaughter its people. God enabled Israel to defeat them in 1947, 1948, 1956, 1967, 1973, and 1982. But now Iran (Persia) is on the verge of producing nuclear weapons. The Ayatollah Khomeini and President Mahmoud Ahmadinejad have both declared that they will soon obliterate the state of Israel.

In the next chapter, we will examine how this ancient enmity became woven into a religion founded by a direct descendant of Ishmael. We will see how the spread of hatred toward Israel became co-extensive with the spread of this religion—Islam.

SIX

THE MUSLIM GENESIS

"From the beginning, its [Islam's] spread was accomplished through physical violence, bloodshed and war. Violence not only against non-Muslim infidels, but also against fellow Muslims. Much of Islam's spread in the world was the result of traders and Sufi missionaries, this is true. Yet the weaponry—scimitars and sabers—all through the art and symbolism of Islam, makes violence and war a central theme of Islam. . . . Mohammad both taught and practiced violence from the beginning. The phenomenal and almost unparalleled efflorescence (exponential growth) of early Islam was due in no small measure to the latent powers of the Bedouins, who, in the words of the Caliph Omar, 'furnished Islam with its raw material.'"

—ABDUL HOUSSAIN ZARIN KOUB[95]

ARAB PRE-ISLAMIC HISTORY

There is very little recorded history of the sons of Ishmael and Edom, outside of the Biblical record, prior to the birth of Mohammad and Islam. We know the names of the twelve sons of Ishmael from whom the Arabs primarily descended, but not all twelve tribal lines can be clearly traced. However, in the following passage from Genesis 25, the Bible does give a careful genealogy of Ishmael, to demonstrate that God kept His promise to him:

This is the account of Abraham's son Ishmael, whom Sarah's maidservant, Hagar the Egyptian, bore to Abraham. These are the names of the sons of Ishmael, listed in the order of their birth: Nebaioth the firstborn of Ishmael, Kedar, Adbeel, Mibsam, Mishma, Dumah, Massa, Hadad, Tema, Jetur, Naphish and Kedemah. These were the sons of Ishmael, and these are the names of the twelve tribal rulers according to their settlements and camps. Altogether, Ishmael lived a hundred and thirty-seven years. He breathed his last and died, and he was gathered to his people. His descendants settled in the area from Havilah to Shur, near the border of Egypt, as you go toward Asshur. And they lived [to the east] in hostility toward all their brothers.[96]

The second son, Kedar, is the most frequently mentioned son of Ishmael. He became the most powerful and wealthy of all his brothers.

Ezekiel confirms the sons of Ishmael as wealthy merchants who traded with the great seafaring Empire of Tyre in the fifth and fourth centuries B.C. before God destroyed it for its wickedness. Ezekiel writes, "*Arabia* and all the princes of *Kedar* were your customers; they did business with you in lambs, rams and goats."[97] This report is part of a prophecy about Tyre's destruction, which was fulfilled by Alexander the Great.

We also find some of the descendants of Abraham's other sons through his aforementioned concubine Keturah. They are mentioned in this same prophecy regarding Tyre as being part of the Arab peoples. They lived in the port cities on the southern tip of the Arabian Peninsula in what is now Yemen and Oman. Ezekiel writes, "*Dedan* traded in saddle blankets with you. . . . The merchants of *Sheba* and Raamah traded with you; for your merchandise they exchanged the finest of all kinds of spices and precious stones, and gold."[98] Sheba and Dedan are grandsons of Abraham through Keturah's second son, Jokshan.[99] Much is written about the spices produced in the southern part of Arabia. Such sought after spices as frankincense and myrrh were produced there.

Isaiah predicts that the wealth of Nebaioth (Ishmael's first-born) and Kedar will be offered to the Lord at His Second Coming when He sets up His Kingdom in Israel. In Isaiah 60:7 we read, "All Kedar's flocks will be gathered to you, the rams of Nebaioth will serve you; they will be accepted as offerings on my altar, and I will adorn my glorious temple."[100] This prophecy is very important because it indicates that descendants of Kedar and Nebaioth will continue to exist and prosper until the end of future Kingdom age. This means that a remnant of these people will repent and believe in the Messiah Jesus during the Tribulation and go into the thousand-year kingdom.

THE KORAN'S VIEW OF THIS HISTORY

According to Islamic teaching, Abraham (in Arabic, *Ibrahim*) did not stay in Canaan with Isaac and send his other seven half-brothers to the land of the East.

Muslims teach that Abraham went to Mecca, where he raised all eight sons together. Muslims also believe that it was Ishmael—not Isaac—that Abraham offered as a sacrifice on Mount Moriah until the angel stopped him. They absolutely believe that Ishmael was the chosen one of God, not Isaac. This is the basis of their denial of the Biblical covenants that are specifically confirmed to Abraham through his line of descendants from Isaac, Jacob, and Jacob's twelve sons. It is on this basis that Muslims claim all the land of Israel and Jerusalem. Christians view this as a great error because it is contrary to the specific testimony of the Lord Jesus Christ. He taught that the God of the Bible is the God of Abraham, Isaac, and Jacob—not Abraham, Ishmael, Esau, and Mohammad. The Lord Jesus confirmed this when He taught, "But regarding the resurrection of the dead, have you not read that which was spoken to you by God saying, '*I AM* the *God* of

Abraham, and the *God* of Isaac, and the *God* of Jacob.' He is not the God of the dead but of the living."[101] Jesus leaves no question about both the source of the Old Testament and just who are the heirs of His promise to Abraham. The continuous action of verb tense for I AM is the basis of why Jesus said that even though Abraham, Isaac, and Jacob died, they are still alive with God. He thus showed that He considers even the tense of verbs inspired by God in the Scriptures.

THE ARAB'S WARRING NATURE

The writer of Psalm 120 gives insight into the violent nature of the descendants of Kedar, "Woe to me . . . that I live among the tents of Kedar! Too long have I lived among those who hate peace. I am a man of peace; but when I speak, they are for war."[102] Both secular and Biblical sources describe the Arabs, especially the sons of Kedar, as a people who continuously fought. This certainly fulfills God's prophecy about the sons of Ishmael: "His hand shall be against everyone, and everyone's hand against him."

The prophet Isaiah has a number of prophetic visions of judgment concerning the nations surrounding Israel who afflicted the Jewish people. These visions are called "Oracles." The following oracle gives an insight into the character of the Arabians—particularly Kedar—in the eighth-century B.C. This oracle actually predicted the invasion of Arabia in 716 B.C. by King Sargon of Assyria. In Isaiah 21, we read:

An oracle concerning *Arabia*: You caravans of *Dedanites*, who camp in the thickets of Arabia, bring water for the thirsty; you who live in *Tema*, bring food for the fugitives. They flee from the sword, from the drawn sword, from the bent bow and from the heat of battle. This is what the Lord says to me: "Within one year, as a servant bound by contract would count it, all the

pomp of *Kedar* will come to an end. The survivors of the bow-
men, the warriors of *Kedar*, will be few." The LORD, the God
of Israel, has spoken.[103]

As indicated above, the sons of Kedar were known for being
expert archers. Kedar must have learned his skill with the bow
and arrow from his father Ishmael, for it is written of him, "God
was with the boy [Ishmael] as he grew up. He lived in the desert
and became an [expert] archer."[104] The northern Arabians fled
to the south and were weakened for over a century after this
invasion.

THE EXTENT OF ARAB TERRITORY

Keil and Delitzsch link the descendants of Kedar to the wealthy
and powerful merchants known as the Nabateans.[105] They ruled
the region known by the Chaldeans and Romans as Arabia Petra.
Petra, the capital, was a famous banking city that was built into a
natural fortress in the mountains of Edom. During the Greco-
Roman times, this kingdom covered the northern part of the
Arabian Peninsula.

Petra later became known as the "Lost City" until archeolo-
gists rediscovered it in the nineteenth century A.D. The way it
was constructed made it one of the wonders of the ancient world.

Ishmael and his descendants began in the desert of Shur and
Havilah, which was in the northwest part of the Arabian Peninsula.
From there they continued to expand southward and eastward to
extend their borders to where the peninsula touched ancient
Assyria and Babylon. As I said earlier, there is no doubt that the
Ishmaelites absorbed other people, such as the descendants of
Esau/Edom and of Abraham's sons through Keturah. But Biblical
history, supported by secular history, presents the Ishmaelites as
the dominant people called "the Arabs."

Smith's Bible Dictionary makes this observation:

> The Ishmaelites appear to have entered the peninsula from
> the northwest. That they spread over the whole of it, and that
> the modern nation is predominately Ishmaelite, is asserted
> by the Arabs . . . they mixed with other Abrahamic peoples;
> and expanded westwards to Idumaea, where they mixed with
> Edomites, etc. The tribes sprung from Ishmael have always
> been governed by petty chiefs or heads of families (sheiks and
> emirs) . . . though they have in some instances succeeded to
> those of the Joktanites.[106]

By the first century A.D., Josephus wrote that the Arabs were
"dwelling from the Euphrates to the Red Sea."[107] The climate
and terrain were so difficult that no foreign invader ever totally
conquered the Arabs. The only people to ever thrive in the vast
desert of Arabia are Arab Bedouin. And as predicted, the Arab has
prevailed in defiance of all his brothers to his west. As predicted,
Ishmael has dwelt to the east.

SEVENTH-CENTURY ARABIAN CULTURE

It is impossible to understand the Muslim religion apart from
an understanding of the Arabian culture out of which it was
born. By the time of the sixth and seventh centuries A.D., the
culture, customs, and religion of Arabia had become well established. The culture was particularly concentrated in Mecca, a
key city on the great Arabian caravan route. Virtually everything Mohammad included in the Koran and the Muslim religion can be traced to the existing culture and traditions of that
time and place.

ORGANIZATION OF ARABIAN SOCIETY
AND GOVERNMENT

The Arabians all began as nomadic tribes or clans in the deserts. They were known as Bedouins. The clan organization is the basis of the Arab Bedouin society, from its earliest days and up to modern times. The clan is led by a supreme chief called a sheik, and it is composed of many families, each of them dwelling in their own tent (or other modern-day dwelling). All members of the same clan consider each other as of one blood, submit to the authority of the sheik, and use one battle cry. Blood relationship—real or fictitious (clan kinship may be acquired by sucking a few drops of a member's blood)—furnishes the cohesive element in tribal organization.

The tent, household goods, and all personal items such as camels, horses, livestock, and weapons are individual property. But water sources, pasturage, and tillable land are the common property of the tribe.

There is a certain amount of freedom and individuality within the clan, but in all corporate clan decisions and actions, the sheik has the final word. The highest hope of a clan member is that the sheik is a "benevolent dictator."

This is why there is such an inevitable cultural collision with the West. The Arabians have no concept of a democratic government, where leaders are elected and responsible to the will of the people. Their pattern of government has always been that of a tribal chieftain, an autocratic dictator reigning over subjects. As we will see, the Islamic fundamentalist sees democracy as a threat to Islam.

VIOLENCE ENDEMIC TO ARABIAN CULTURE

Violence has been a continual fact of life for the Arabs. This is a common thread that runs through historical accounts of their culture. Philip Hitti summarized this fact well, "The raid or *ghazw* . . . is raised by the economic and social conditions of desert life to the rank of a national institution. *It lies at the base of the economic structure of Bedouin pastoral society. In desert land, where the fighting mood is a chronic mental condition*, raiding is one of the few manly occupations . . . An early Arab poet gave expression to the guiding principle of such life in two verses: 'Our business is to make raids on the enemy, on our neighbor and on our own brother, in case we find none to raid but a brother!'"[108]

How perfectly the prophecy of Genesis 16:12 about the sons of Ishmael fits this: "His hand shall be against everyone, and everyone's hand against him." Equally fitting is God's prediction concerning the other major part of the Arab people, the sons of Edom from Esau, as we read in Genesis 27, "Your dwelling will be away from the earth's richness, away from the dew of heaven above. You will live by the sword."[109] The Edomites first lived in the mountains of Seir, but over the centuries, many were forced to flee to the desert of Arabia where there is little "richness of earth or dew from heaven." Wherever they went, they lived by the sword. No wonder they responded so quickly to the call of Mohammad to convert to Islam.

It is startling that the Arabic language has almost a thousand names and synonyms for the *sword*. The only other word in Arabic that can rival that for multiple names is *camel*. Both the sword and the camel were considered essential for life in the Arabian culture. It is important to note today how many Arab nations have the insignia of the sword in their national logos. This unmistakably shows us what has always been important to an Arab.

THE ARABIAN RELIGION

The "Days of Ignorance"

Long before the founding of Islam, in what was known as the "Days of Ignorance," the Arabs lost their faith in the one true God, whom their forefathers Ishmael, Esau, and the sons of

Keturah certainly knew about. They degenerated into polytheism and worshipped "holy" rocks and trees. These objects were deemed sacred not because they were innately so within themselves but because the Arabs believed they were indwelt by *spirit beings* called "jinns" (later known as "genies").

Arabs believed then (and also in the Koran and Hadith) that "jinns" are a category of spirit creatures that are halfway between angels and man. They believe that they can be good or bad, though most are considered malicious. They can possess animals and inanimate things such as rocks, trees, wells, and so on. Jinns were adopted into Muslim theology and the Koran. Legends about jinns or genies are resplendent in Arab legends—such as the genie in the bottle.

During this period, Mecca became the most important religious center. It was a major oasis on the main caravan route from earliest times, as well as the site of the sacred Zamzam well, which Arabs believe God revealed to Abraham and Ishmael.

The Ka'abah

Mecca's greatest significance came from being the site of the special religious altar known as the Ka'abah. It is a 50-foot cubic structure of gray stone and marble. Positioned so that its corners correspond with the four points of the compass, the Ka'abah contained 360 idols—one for each of the lunar calendar days.

Most importantly, the cornerstone of the Ka'abah was the sacred Black Stone. It is a meteorite of very ancient origin. It was and is believed to have the power to absorb sin from the one who kisses it. Arabs believed that the Black Stone was a god who protected their tribes.

The Hierarchy of Gods

In the Arab pantheon of gods, there were five who were most important in their hierarchy. There were Uzza, Allat, Manat,

Hubal, and Allah. The first three were female, which formed a tritheistic relationship. On the other hand, Hubal was a male held to be the Moon deity. He is believed to have originated in Babylon.

It is Hubal that is represented in the Hilal, Islam's symbol of the Crescent Moon. The star symbol is believed to represent Uzza, the Morning Star goddess. Hubal was also believed to be the guardian of the Ka'abah.

The fifth and highest of all deities was called "Allah." He was worshipped as the supreme creator as well as the "father" of the tritheistic female goddesses.

Mecca Pilgrimage

Mecca then, with the Ka'abah, the sacred Zamzam well, and the presence of the highest deities, became the religious vortex of the Arabian Peninsula. Arabs from all over began to come on pilgrimages to Mecca—and this was long before Mohammad.

Because of the lucrative business brought by the pilgrims, possessing the guardianship of the sacred Ka'abah and Zamzam well became a prize to be sought.

Rivalry for Holy Sites Begins

From approximately 100 B.C., the Ka'abah and its sacred well were under the guardianship of the tribe known as the Beni Jurham. In about the third century A.D., the Jurham seem to have been driven out and replaced by an Ishmaelite tribe known as the Khuzaa.

Then in about A.D. 235, Fihr, the leader of another Ishmaelite tribe, the Quraysh, married the daughter of the Khuzaa tribal chief. Later, in about A.D. 420, Qusai, a descendant of Fihr, married the daughter of another Khuzaa chief of Mecca. Although he was not of the Khuzaa tribe, Qusai made himself virtually indispensable to his father-in-law, who was guardian of the Ka'abah. As a result Qusai was given the custodianship of the coveted sacred keys of the Ka'abah.

When the Khuzaa chief died, Qusai claimed custody of the Ka'abah for the Quraysh tribe. One of his first acts was to relegate the Khuzaa clan to a subordinate position. Qusai ordered the building of a semi-permanent housing around the Ka'abah. He also very shrewdly restructured the tribal social order. He instituted tribal council meetings and a hall was built near the Ka'abah for this purpose.

THE QURAYSH TRIBAL RELIGION

It was not coincidental that the Quraysh tribe from which Mohammad's family came was especially addicted to the cult of the moon god, Allah. They also witnessed the pilgrims coming to Mecca every year to worship, circling the Ka'abah seven times, kissing the Black Stone (which they considered their special tribal talisman that guaranteed their protection and blessing), and then running down to the nearby wadi to throw stones at the devil. Mohammad was destined to grow up with all of these religious traditions. So it certainly cannot be an accident that all of these religious traditions are prominent in the Muslim religion, which he supposedly got by original divine revelation.

The Quraysh Tribe Prevails

Tribal rivalries continued through the centuries. But important to our interest, the Quraysh tribe prevailed as guardians of Mecca's holy sites by the sixth century A.D. Within the Quraysh tribe, a man named Hashim married a woman named Selma, who gave birth to a son, Abdul al-Mut-Talib. Abdul had seven sons—Harith, Talib, Lahab, Jahal, Abbas, Hamza, and Abdullah.

Abdullah married Amina, who was a descendant of Qusai's brother Zuhra. Abdullah and Amina gave birth to a son whom they named *Mohammad*. And with this event, the entire history of the Arab people was about to undergo a paradigm shift.

SEVEN

MOHAMMAD: THE GREAT ENIGMA

"But even though we, or an angel from heaven, should preach to you a gospel contrary to that which we have preached to you, let him be accursed. As we have said before, so I say again now, if any man is preaching to you a gospel contrary to that which you received, let him be accursed."

—Apostle Paul[110]

"Wonderful Originator of the heavens and the earth! *How could he have a son* when he has no consort. . . . Follow what is revealed to you from your Lord; *there is no God but He*; and withdraw from the polytheists [i.e., Christians]."

—Koran, Surah 6.102, 106[111]

THE ENIGMA

The word *enigma* is defined as a "mystery: somebody or something that is not easily explained or understood."[112] This word perfectly applies to Mohammad. He is a figure of history that defies natural explanations. Indeed, apart from the acceptance of the fact that a supernatural being worked in and through him, there is no way to comprehend him.

How did an orphan become the greatest Arab leader of all time?

How could an illiterate man become the author of a book that is the pinnacle of classic Arabic—the most beautiful and majestic of all Arabic literature?

How is it possible that one who as a child was thought to be either insane or demon-possessed by his own family became the founder of the second-largest religion on earth?

How did a man who was admittedly both violent and sensual become one of the most revered religious leaders in history?

This is what I mean when I say, Mohammad is an "enigma" who, apart from the working of supernatural forces, is impossible to explain.

You can worship him as God's last and greatest prophet, or you can reject him as a false prophet—but you cannot ignore him. This one man is solely responsible for the Arabs exploding out of the Arabian Peninsula and in less than one hundred years conquering lands from the Atlantic to the borders of China and the islands of the Pacific, from North Africa to Spain and into Europe to the gates of Vienna. If the Muslim hoards had not been stopped by the Frankish king Charles Martel at the Battle of Tours in A.D. 732, all of Europe would have fallen under Islam's control.

THE BIRTH OF MOHAMMAD

Mohammad was born around A.D. 570 and died in July of the year A.D. 632. As mentioned previously, his father was from the Quraysh tribe. This tribe gained much power and influence, both because of their commercial activity in their hub at the city of Mecca, and because they were the guardians of the sacred well and the Ka'abah, with its black meteorite cornerstone. They enjoyed much prestige, influence, and profit because of the continuous religious pilgrimages Arabians made to the Meccan "holy sites."

Mohammad's father was Abdallah, the son of Abd al-Muttalib by Fatima bint 'Amr of the Quraysh clan of the Banu Makhzum. Abdallah was reputed to be quite a handsome man. Marriages were strategically calculated for political and economic goals, and Abd al-Muttalib was seeking an alliance with the Banu Zuhra (Shura) clan. Thus he secured Aminah bint Wahb as an arranged bride for his son Abdallah.

"VISITATIONS" BEGIN

The wedded couple soon became the parents of a son whom they named Mohammad. According to consistent historical witnesses, Mohammad had a strange, mystical childhood, one marked by the presence of many different guardians and "visitations of spirits and angels."

We may gain an important insight into Mohammad from a description by his mother. Muslim scholar Robert Morey writes, "Mohammad's mother, Amina, was of an excitable nature and often claimed that she was visited by spirits, or jinns. She also at times claimed to have visions and religious experiences. Mohammad's mother was involved in what we call today the 'occult arts,' and this basic orientation is thought by some scholars to have been inherited by her son."[113]

From his birth, Amina feared for the infant's health in the crowded conditions of Mecca. So she did what Quraysh mothers with means customarily did—she hired a nurse from one of the Bedouin tribes to take him out into "the healthy air of the desert."

Mohammad was entrusted to a Bedouin woman named Halima, who nursed the infant until he was two years old before bringing him back to Amina. Delighted with his healthy look, Mohammad's mother said, "Take the child with thee back again, for much do I fear for him in the unwholesome air of Mecca."[114] So Halima took him back. After two more years she returned again, but this time she was troubled. The child had experienced numerous fits, which caused Halima to think he was demon-possessed. Amina, however, pleaded with her to carry him back once more. But after Mohammad experienced subsequent epileptic fits and "spirit visitations," Halima returned him to his mother when he was five years old and refused to take him back. Mohammad always remembered Halima with great affection.

Author Robert Payne investigates in more detail the incident that caused Halima to return Mohammad. According to Halima, "Mohammad experienced the first of his 'visitations' while he was walking in a field with one of Halima's sons. He suddenly fell down shouting that 'two men in white garments' were splitting open his belly. When later asked by Halima what happened, he said 'two angels had cut open his belly searching for something.'"[115] According to Mohammad's own testimony, he experienced these sorts of 'visitations' at various times for the rest of his life.

MOHAMMAD'S EARLY TRAGEDIES

Abdullah, Mohammad's father, died before the boy was five years old, while he was still under Halima's care. About one year after he was returned to his mother, she also died. So Mohammad became an orphan at the vulnerable age of six years old. He was then entrusted to the care of his seventy-year-old grandfather and his mother's slave girl, Umm Ayan.

When Mohammad was twelve-years old, his grandfather also died. His uncle Abu Talib took him under his care and began taking him on long caravan journeys to Damascus and other great cities of the Middle East. During this time Mohammad apprenticed in the merchant trade. He continued working in the caravan trade from the ages of twelve to twenty-five years. In this formative period of his life, the travel experiences were very important. He was exposed to Christianity through encounters with various Catholic monks, who formed his erroneous ideas about the true Christian faith.

MOHAMMAD TAKES A WIFE

When Mohammad was twenty-five years old, his uncle suggested that he go to work for a woman named Khadija, a rich widow merchant in Mecca. Mohammad was hired to accompany her merchant caravan to Syria, which he did several times. Although she was forty years old, widowed twice, and had three daughters, they got married. Together they had two sons, Abdullah and Qusim, and a daughter named Fatima. Tragically, the two boys died in infancy.

As mentioned before, Mohammad exhibited mystic tendencies and was very religious from an early age. Khadija's wealth gave him the opportunity to take long retreats into the hills around Mecca for uninterrupted periods of religious meditation. However, these religious quests did not bring him the inner peace he sought. His frequent long excursions into the desert produced a "spiritual anxiety" that was reflected not just in his personality, but also in the religion he founded.

Historians have sought to analyze Mohammad's complex temperament. Sir Norman Anderson observes about this period:

> He would retire to caves for seclusion and meditation. He frequently practiced fasting; and he was prone to dreams. His character seems to have been a strange mixture. He was a poet rather than a theologian; a master improviser rather than a systematic thinker. . . . He was generous, resolute, genial and astute: a shrewd judge and a born leader of men. He could however, be cruel and vindictive to his enemies; he could stop to assassinate; and he was undeniably sensual.[116]

Robert Payne notes the contradictory traits within his nature:

> It is worthwhile to pause for a moment before the quite astonishing polarity of Mohammad's mind. *Violence and gentleness*

were at war within him. Sometimes he gives the appearance of living simultaneously in two worlds, at one and the same moment seeing the world about to be destroyed by the flames of God and in the state of divine peace.[117]

These two antithetical traits of violence and gentleness equally existing together in his soul are what made Mohammad such a complex person. He seems to have been able to exert either trait at any moment without any personal awareness of contradiction. He also held severe grudges toward those who rejected his personal religious claims, as both the Jews and the Christians learned.

Dr. Anis Shorrosh gives this interesting description of Mohammad's appearance based on eyewitness accounts:

> As an adult, Mohammad was somewhat above middle height, with a lean but commanding figure. His head was massive, with a broad and noble forehead. He had thick black hair, slightly curling which hung over his ears; his eyes were large, black and piercing; his eyebrows arched and joined; his nose high and aquiline; and he had a long bushy beard. When he was excited, the veins would swell across his forehead. His eyes were often bloodshot and always restless. Decision marked his every movement. He used to walk so rapidly that his followers half ran behind him and could hardly keep up with him.

"THE NIGHT OF POWER"—IT ALL BEGINS

In A.D. 610, when Mohammad was forty years old, he had a visitation that would come to be known as "The Night of Power." It was this extraordinary experience that finally convinced Mohammad that he was called as God's prophet and apostle. Muslims believe that Allah began revealing the true religion of Islam that night.

According to Islam, this beginning of revelation came to Mohammad in the form of "a gracious and mighty messenger, held in honor by the Lord of the Throne." The messenger appeared to him in a cave on Mount Ararat, which overlooks the Hijaz Valley in eastern Arabia in the vicinity of Mecca.

"Proclaim!" the angel commanded three times. Dazzled, Mohammad asked, "What shall I proclaim?" The angel replied: "Proclaim in the name of your Lord who created, created man from clots of blood! Proclaim! Your Lord who created the most bountiful one, who by the pen taught man what he did not know."

At this point, it is important to note that Muslim scholars believe Mohammad saw himself as more of a reformer and restorer than a founder of a new religion. Mohammad believed that he was sent to re-establish monotheism as it had originally been revealed. He believed that the original recipients—Jews and Christians—had corrupted God's true revelation. It is crucial to note that in the Koran, Mohammad calls the Jews "the people of the Book."

This fundamental belief that God's revelation had been corrupted guaranteed a collision with Judaism and Christianity. In one fell swoop, it dismisses the Bible as a book laced with lies and fraud introduced by Jews and Christians. Muslims teach that Jews—and to a lesser degree Christians—deliberately perverted the original revelation from God in order to make themselves the recipients of God's covenants and blessings.

Here are just a couple of examples of this teaching in the Koran:

O followers of the Book [Jews]! Indeed Our Apostle has come to you making clear to you much of what you concealed of the Book and passing over much; indeed, there has come to you light and a clear Book from Allah [i.e., the Koran]; With it Allah guides him who will follow His pleasure into the ways of safety and brings them out of utter darkness into light by His will and guides them to the right path. (Surah 5.15, 16)

O you who believe! Do not take the Jews and the Christians
for friends; they are friends of each other; and whoever amongst
you takes them for a friend, then surely he is one of them; surely
Allah does not guide these unjust people. (Surah 5.51)

THE MODE OF MOHAMMAD'S REVELATIONS

The mode in which Mohammad received subsequent revelations
from Allah is uniformly recorded in Muslim tradition. When
Mohammad was about to receive a revelation, he would usually
fall down on the ground, his body would begin to jerk, his eyes
would roll backward, and he would perspire profusely. His followers would cover him with a blanket during these "visitations."

The "divine visitations" occurred when Mohammad would go
into a trancelike state. When he would come out of the trance, he
would immediately begin to proclaim what had been transmitted
to him.

As we view this description today, it would seem to be an epileptic seizure. Dr. Morey makes an astute observation about this:

What must be remembered is that in the Arab culture of Mohammad's day, epileptic seizures were interpreted as a religious
sign of either demonic possession or divine visitation.

Muhammad initially considered both options as possible
interpretations of his experience. At first he worried about the
possibility that he was demon possessed. This led him to attempt to commit suicide.

But his devoted wife (Khadija) was able to stop him from
committing suicide by persuading him that he was such a good
man that he could not possibly be demon possessed.[118]

Whatever caused these trancelike states; it is clear that the
revelations received during them were from a supernatural
source. The important question here is not so much about the

method of revelation, but its source. From a Christian viewpoint, there are only two sources of supernatural: The God of the Bible and "the god of this world," who is also described as "an angel of light."[119]

TESTING SUPERNATURAL SOURCES

The Bible offers tests to prove the authenticity of a message from God. Moses, the first writing prophet from God, was given a test to prove whether a message or a prophet was truly from God:

> But the prophet who shall speak a word presumptuously in My name which I have not commanded him to speak, or which he shall speak in the name of other gods, that prophet shall die. And you may say in your heart, "How shall we know the word which the Lord has not spoken?" When a prophet speaks in the name of the Lord, if the thing does not come about or come true, that is the thing which the Lord has not spoken. The prophet has spoken it presumptuously; you shall not be afraid of him.[120]

Basically, God teaches here that the true prophet will make detailed predictions about the future that can be proven or disproven. If the prophet's words *all* came true, then the people are to heed them as the Word of God. If any part of his prophecy did not come true, the people were to stone the person as a false prophet and destroy his message.

This is why of all the books that were written in Israel's history (and there were others), *only* the ones that are genuine were preserved in the canon of Scriptures. And this was in spite of the fact that these books frequently condemned the people's sinful behavior—from the king on the throne to the peasants in the fields. Each prophet proved himself to be true by fulfilled prophecy. The Israelites had every reason to destroy these unpopular messages that even predicted the destruction of their nation for its sins. But they did not dare destroy that which was proven by fulfilled prophecies to be God's Word.

The Koran, on the other hand, has no such proofs to authenticate its divine origin. Instead, the believer is exhorted not to question its authenticity and to kill anyone who does. Blind, unquestioning belief is demanded. Today, many murders have been executed in western civilization for the crime of blaspheming the Koran.

ISLAMIC REVELATION VS. BIBLICAL INSPIRATION

The concept of how the divine message of the Koran was received is very different from how the approximately forty writers of the Bible received theirs. The Arabic word for "revelation" means *handed down*. Muslims believe that the Koran did not come "through" any man, not even Mohammad. They believe that the message came directly from Allah to the angel Gabriel, who passed it to Mohammad as a total package "intact" with no human involvement or interaction.

However, the Koran was not written down until years after Mohammad's death.

The Bible claims something very different about itself. It teaches that all Scriptures are "God-breathed" (transliteration of qeopneustoV)[121] This means that all written words of the Bible's original manuscripts have God's direct inspiration upon them. The miracle of infallible transmission took place at the time of the original composition.

The Bible further claims that it is not the product of man's interpretation of the issues with which it deals, "Above all, you must understand that no prophecy of Scripture came about by the prophet's own interpretation. For prophecy never had its origin in the will of man, but men spoke from God as they were carried along by the Holy Spirit."[122] The word translated "carried along" is a nautical term that was often used to describe the wind driving along a sailboat.

The idea is that God so moved upon specially chosen men, that they communicated what He wanted them to say, but without setting aside their individuality or background.

The Apostle Paul adds that the Holy Spirit so moved upon the minds of the writers so that what they reduced to writing was in *the very words* God desired. He writes, "Now we have received, not the spirit of the world, but the Spirit who is from God, that we might know the things freely given to us by God, which things we also speak, not in words taught by human wisdom, but in those taught by the Spirit, combining spiritual thoughts with spiritual words."[123]

THE BIBLE IS UNIQUE

The great miracle of the Bible is that some forty authors from different times and places produced a Holy Book that has one homogenous, cohesive, and consistent message. Its divine origin is stamped all over it. It does not contradict nature, history, or any proven fact of science, even though primitive men wrote it. It contains hundreds of prophecies that have all been fulfilled with 100 percent accuracy that are a matter of historical record. No other book can compare with that record.

Because the Holy Spirit combined "spiritual thoughts with spiritual words," it does not make sense to someone who is "spiritually dead." The Bible teaches that all mankind is born physically alive, but spiritually dead. This is why Jesus told a religious scholar of his day that unless a man is "born again spiritually,"[124] he couldn't understand the kingdom of God.

The Apostle Paul explains it this way, "But a natural man does not accept the things of the Spirit of God; for they are foolishness to him, and he cannot understand them, because they are spiritually appraised [understood]."[125]

The Koran does not speak on such matters as these. As a matter of fact, the Koran does not deal with such great issues as man's sin, God's absolutely righteous character, and the need for God to have a just basis upon which to forgive a hopelessly fallen man.

MOHAMMAD BEGINS TO PREACH

After the initial appearance of the angel, whom Mohammad later identified as Gabriel [*Jibril* in Arabic], Mohammad went through another period of self-doubt, depression, and thoughts of suicide.

He finally decided to commit suicide. He set out to end it all, but along the way he fell into another trance. While in this trance he had a vision in which he was told that he must not end his life because he was truly called to be God's special messenger.

KHADIJA'S KEY ROLE

It is at this point that Khadija played a pivotal role in his life. When he fully shared with her the anguish and doubt that he had about his call from God, she strongly encouraged him. She dismissed his fears of being demon-possessed as an absolute impossibility because he was such a good person. She vehemently believed that he was called of God as His prophet and apostle and kept assuring him of that.

Khadija then urged Mohammad to begin preaching the message he received from the revealing angel to his family and friends. All of his first converts were family members.

OPPOSITION AND REJECTION

When the public heard about Mohammad's new teaching, opposition started almost at once. The people of Mecca rejected and ridiculed his new message. Even some family members turned against him.

Robert Morey explains the crisis that arose in Mohammad at this point:

> In order to appease his pagan family members and the members of the Quraysh tribe, he decided that the best thing he could do was to agree with tradition—that it was perfectly proper to pray to and worship the three daughters of Allah: Al-Lat, Al-Uzza, and Manat.
>
> This led to the famous "satanic verses" in which Mohammad in a moment of weakness and supposedly under the inspiration of Satan (according to early Muslim authorities) succumbed to the temptation to appease the pagan mobs in Mecca.
>
> The literature on the "satanic verses" is so vast that an entire volume could be written just on this one issue. Every general and Islamic reference work, Muslim or Western, deals with it, as do all the biographies of Mohammad.
>
> The story of Mohammad's temporary appeasement of the pagans by allowing them their polytheism cannot be ignored or denied. It is a fact of history that is supported by all Middle East scholars, whether Western and Muslim.[126]

"YATHRIB REBUKE"

Later, when Mohammad's disciples in Yathrib (Medina) heard of these compromises with polytheism, they came to Mecca and rebuked him. After consulting with them, Mohammad reverted back to the original message of monotheism and said Allah had now forbidden worship of the three goddesses. He explained this clear contradiction by saying that Allah could "abrogate" or cancel a previous revelation. Later on, Mohammad claimed that the angel Gabriel (Jibril) appeared to him and rebuked him for allowing Satan to deceive him into condoning the Meccan's worship of the three goddesses.

This produced no end of problems for Mohammad, since

these goddesses were believed to be the "daughters of Allah." This contradicted what became the very heart of the Islamic faith: that "There is no God but Allah." The point is also problematic in view of the many Koranic verses that say Jesus cannot be the Son of God because Allah is the only God and he has no offspring. So the "revelations" Mohammad received during this time were never included in the written version of the Koran. They came to be called "the satanic verses." In our era, the ayatollahs of Iran have issued a death sentence against a Muslim named Salman Rushdie for daring to write a book about these verses. This is considered "blasphemy of God's prophet and the Koran."

MECCAN ATTACK

The people of Mecca used this situation to the fullest against Mohammad. They mocked and ridiculed him for attacking the gods of Arabia. This was especially important because of its impact on their economy. Worship of these three goddesses brought many of the lucrative pilgrim tours to Mecca. So the Meccans used Mohammad's vacillating messages attributed to Allah to mock his whole religion.

The hostility of the Meccans became so great that they drove Mohammad out of Mecca. So he fled to Ta-if. He also did not receive a good response there, so he tried to return to Mecca.

In the Koran, Mohammad claims that on the way back to Mecca, he preached to the "jinns" and converted them. The Koran says:

> Say: It has been revealed to me that a party of the jinn listened, and they said: Surely we have heard a wonderful Quran [proclamation], Guiding to the right way, so we believe in it, and we will not set up any one with our Lord: And that *He*—exalted be the majesty of our Lord—*has not taken a consort, nor a son.* (Surah 73.1–3)

This important claim is also in Surah 46.29–35 and in 73.1–28. By this revelation, Mohammad claims that even the spirits (jinns) that indwell the sacred rocks, trees, and water sources now believe his message. Note how Mohammad corrects all his previous "satanic verses" about Allah. He now proclaims that Allah never has had a "consort" such as the three moon goddesses. Reasoning from this, Mohammad then proclaimed that Allah never had a son—such as the Christian teaching about Jesus being the Son of God.[127]

When Mohammad arrived again in Mecca, he found that there was now organized hostility against him and his message. The merchants had gotten involved and were out to protect their economic interests. They rightly feared that Mohammad's renewed monotheistic attacks against the idols housed in the Ka'abah would threaten their leadership as well as the pilgrimages to Mecca and therefore their livelihood.

The animosity grew so intense against Mohammad and his followers that some Meccans sought to kill him. So he fled with some two hundred followers to Yathrib. This famous escape in A.D. 622 became known as the "Hegira."

YATHRIB BECOMES MEDINA

It took Mohammad, and his converts, about ten days to reach Yathrib. When he arrived, the oasis city extended him a lavish welcome. They greatly honored him and even changed the city's name to *Madinat-al-Nabi*, which means "The City of the Prophet." The shortened form of this name is simply "Medina."

FACTS THE WEST MUST LEARN

In Medina, Mohammad established his first Islamic theocracy. This became the model for all future Islamic rules of law and government. For this reason, it is of ultimate importance that we learn these keys to Islamic society and government. This is the reason all forms of Western democracy are considered to be against the Koran and will never be accepted.

During this period, Mohammad developed his most important Islamic doctrines. Indeed, Medina became the model for his "ideal Islamic culture" that would soon be spread to the world.

EIGHT

THE MEDINA LEGACY: JIHAD AGAINST JEWS

"And those of the People of the Book [Jews] who aided them [Meccan invaders]—Allah did take them down from their strongholds and cast terror into their hearts. So that some you slew and others you took captive. And He [Allah] made you masters of their land, their houses and their goods, and of a land which you have not yet trodden. Truly Allah has power over all things."

—THE KORAN, SURAH 33.26–27[128]

THE JEWS OF ARABIA

By around 1400 B.C., more than two thousand years before the first Muslim invasion of Palestina,[129] Israel was already established as a nation.

A civil war split Israel into two nations during the time of Rehoboam, Solomon's son. The ten tribes of the northern land known as Samaria called themselves Israel. The southern tribes of Judah, Benjamin, and Levi became known as the kingdom of Judah, from which the name *Jew* came.[130]

Assyrian Dispersion

Israel entered a continuous spiral of apostasy away from following Jehovah until He finally sent the Assyrians to destroy the northern kingdom in 721 B.C. The survivors of the ten tribes were taken away captive into Assyria.

Now why am I going into all of this? Because some of the survivors of this dispersion fled to Arabia and settled there! Arabist scholar Alfred Guillaume observes that the Israelites probably first settled in Arabia in connection with the fall of Samaria in 721 B.C. He writes, "It is not impossible that some Jewish settlements in Arabia were due to fugitives fleeing from the old northern capital of the Hebrews."[131]

BABYLONIAN DISPERSION

The southern kingdom of Judah had intermittent revivals, but finally fell into the same apostasy of the Samarian kingdom. Though the people of Judah were repeatedly warned, they did not listen. As it is written:

The LORD, the God of their fathers, sent word to them through his messengers again and again, because he had pity on his people and on his dwelling place. But they mocked God's messengers, despised his words and scoffed at his prophets until the wrath of the LORD was aroused against his people and there was no remedy. He brought up against them the king of the Babylonians, who killed their young men with the sword in the sanctuary, and spared neither young man nor young woman, old man or aged. God handed all of them over to Nebuchadnezzar. He carried to Babylon all the articles from the temple of God, both large and small, and the treasures of the LORD's temple and the treasures of the king and his officials. They set fire to God's temple and broke down the wall of Jerusalem; they burned all the palaces and destroyed everything of value there. He carried into exile to Babylon the remnant, who escaped from the sword, and they became servants to him and his sons until the kingdom of Persia came to power. The land enjoyed its Sabbath rests; all the time of its desolation it rested, until the seventy years were completed in fulfillment of the word of the LORD spoken by Jeremiah.[132]

This is one of the many amazing prophecies in the Bible. Even the number of years the Jews would be held captive against their will was predicted by the prophet Jeremiah and fulfilled to the letter. The Babylonian destruction itself was predicted 150 years before it happened by Isaiah the prophet:

Then Isaiah said to Hezekiah, "Hear the word of the LORD Almighty: The time will surely come when everything in your palace, and all that your fathers have stored up until this day, will be carried off to Babylon. Nothing will be left, says the LORD. And some of your descendants, your own flesh and blood who will be born to you, will be taken away, and they will become eunuchs in the palace of the king of Babylon."[133]

The Bible records that not all of the Jews were taken to Babylon. A few were left in Judea to maintain the land, and some were able to flee to Egypt or Arabia. In 1949, after the birth of the state of Israel, Israelis rescued the Jews of Yemen from the wrath of the Muslims. In an amazing surprise airlift that became known as "the wings of eagles," all of Yemenite Jews were taken to Israel. These Jews trace their origins in Arabia back twenty-five hundred years, which was the time of the Babylonian invasion.

ROMAN DISPERSION

The greatest flood of Jewish refugees came as a result of the initial Roman destruction of Jerusalem and Judea in A.D. 70 and in the period of some 150 years afterwards. During this time, the

Romans fought off different Jewish guerilla-style insurgencies that tried to take Jerusalem back. The Jewish resistance was finally totally crushed. Some poor survivors stayed on in Israel. Others fled.

Guillaume is certain that "in the first and second centuries A.D., Arabia offered a near asylum" to the Jews who were victimized by the "utterly ruthless" Romans.

"Yathrib" (Medina) Established by Jews?

Historian Joan Peters[134] quotes a vital insight by Bernard Lewis:

> The Arabian land considered by many to be "purely Arab," in the very land that would spawn Islam many centuries later, numbers of Jewish and Christian settlements were established. Both Christians and Jews helped develop Aramaic and Hellenistic culture. The chief southern Arabian Christian centre was in Najran, where a relatively advanced political life was developed. Jews and Judaized Arabs were everywhere, especially in *Yathrib* later named Medina. They were mainly agriculturists and artisans.[135]

An amazing fact is revealed here and confirmed by other historical sources. The second holiest city in the Islamic world may have been first established as a community by Jews! Whatever the case, Jews certainly played a large role in developing Yathrib. How often do we hear or read about this in history? The story of widespread Jewish settlement in pre-Islamic Arabia is certainly one of the world's best-kept secrets.

The First Palestinian Refugees

"Thus," writes Joan Peters, "evolved the flight of the first 'Palestinian refugees'—the Judeans, or Jews." I believe it is extremely important to understand how the early Jewish settlements in Arabia got there. These Jewish refugees are seldom discussed, yet understanding what happened to them is critical to understanding today's Middle East crisis.

You may ask, why is this important to know? Because the pattern of action that developed toward the Jews in Arabia established the Islamic tradition that has been followed wherever Islam has spread!

Before Mohammad's time, the comparative wealth of Yathrib (Medina), thanks to the hard-working, industrious Jewish refuges, attracted many pagan Arabs. They came for the jobs, the markets, and the commercial opportunities.[136] In subsequent chapters, we will see this pattern first established in Yathrib repeated in nineteenth- and twentieth-century "Palestine."

It is important to note that Judaism was very popular in parts of Arabia just before the birth of Mohammad. Guillaume writes,

At the dawn of Islam the Jews dominated the economic life of the Hijaz (the sacred eastern section of Arabia that contains Mecca and Medina). They held all of the best land. . . . At Medina they must have formed at least half of the population. There was also a Jewish settlement to the north of the Gulf of Aqaba. . . . What is important is to note that the Jews of the Hijaz made many proselytes (or converts) among the Arab tribesmen.[137]

Guillaume suggests that the prosperity of the Jews was due to their superior farming abilities and technology. So the first "Palestinian refugees"—the Jews—quickly became large landowners and controllers of Arabian finance and trade. This success no doubt led to the Jews becoming something of a stumbling block to their envious Arab neighbors—especially in Medina, or Yathrib; as it was then called.[138]

Enter Mohammad

It was into this historical context that Mohammad launched his ministry. As noted in the last chapter, Mohammad's zealous crusade against polytheism made him increasingly unpopular in his hometown of Mecca. When townsmen tried to kill him, he and his disciples fled to Yathrib.

Not surprisingly, the Jews of Yathrib did not accept Mohammad's claim to be a prophet of God. He tried very hard to win the Jews over by representing himself as only a teacher of the creed of Abraham. He even adopted the Jewish Sabbath, some dietary laws, and initially required prayer toward Jerusalem rather than Mecca.[139]

Believe or Be Beheaded

The Jews, however, were not deceived and refused to acknowledge him as anything but a false prophet. This infuriated Mohammad, who wrote into Islam a perpetual doctrine against Jews and then initiated an action that would become his standard pattern—the sword. He marched against this particular Jewish tribe and besieged their village. When they surrendered and came out one by one, they were beheaded. So the first Muslim massacre was executed on the Jews. The pattern of "confess Islam or face the sword" was established in this action.

Mohammad was anxious to spread Islam beyond Medina. After the Jews, who not only rejected but also opposed him, were dealt with, he began to train his disciples as warriors and developed a new strategy for defending Medina. He had them dig a long deep trench along the side of the city where the Meccans were expected to attack.

The Battle of the Trench

Although simple by modern standards, this strategy was totally innovative in seventh-century Arabia. Unable to get beyond the trench, the Meccan army laid siege to Medina.

Some of the surviving Jewish citizens within the city seized this opportunity to attack Mohammad's army from behind. He had to divide his army to deal with a two-front battle. But a sand storm suddenly struck and forced the Meccans to pull back. Then the Muslims turned their whole army upon the Jews and slaughtered them.

The Battle of the Trench is commemorated as one of the most decisive and critical battles in the formative stages of Islam.

The Critical Battle of Badr

At the wells of Badr, near the coast of the Red Sea, Mohammad's three-hundred-man army was caught off guard by a superior three-to-one force from Mecca. Although outnumbered, the Muslims defeated the Meccans.

Mohammad claimed that his victory was due to thousands of angels, led by Jabril (Gabriel), who fought for them.

I mention this battle as significant because if Mohammad's army had lost, or if Mohammad had been killed, it would have ended the Muslim movement. The victory gained both converts as well as prestige among the Arabs and other people of the region.

"QURAYSH MODEL" OF MECCAN CONQUEST

Three years after the Battle of Badr, a ten-thousand-man Meccan army again laid siege to Medina, but the Quraysh tribe of Mecca was not able to conquer the city. On the other hand, Mohammad was not yet strong enough to defeat the Quraysh tribe, so he signed a ten-year treaty of non-aggression with Mecca. However, by A.D. 630, barely a year later, Mohammad had built up a strong army. He ignored the treaty and stormed Mecca by surprise, quickly conquering the city. At last he made himself ruler of the city of his birth.

Mohammad's first act was to establish Mecca as the holiest city of Islam. John Noss writes:

> One of his first acts was to go reverently to the Ka'aba; yet he showed no signs of yielding to the ancient Meccan polytheism. After honoring the Black Stone and riding seven times around the shrine, he ordered the destruction of the idols within it and sanctioned the use of the well Zamzam and restored the boundary pillars defining the sacred territory around Mecca.[140]

Mohammad then proclaimed the Ka'abah as "Haram" (forbidden to non-Muslims). Islam now had two capitals—Medina the political, and Mecca the religious.

Since that time, Muslims have quoted the "Quraysh Model" as justification for deceptive treaties. This model means: "Negotiate 'peace' with your enemy until you become strong enough to annihilate him." This is the justification Chairman Yasser Arafat quoted in Arabic to the Muslim world when he signed the Oslo Agreement. Muslims believe that no infidels really understand what the Quraysh Model means—and for the vast majority of non-Muslims, that is a correct assumption.

WHY JEWS WERE PERSECUTED

Mohammad and his disciples treated the Jews much more severely than any other "unbelievers." Why? "They had irritated him by their refusal to recognize him as a prophet, by ridicule and by argument," explains Guillaume. "And of course their economic supremacy was a standing irritant."

Guillaume continues, "Their leaders opposed his claim to be an apostle sent by God, and though they doubtless drew some satisfaction from his acceptance of the divine mission of Abraham, Moses and the prophets, they could hardly be expected to welcome the inclusion of Jesus and Ishmael among his chosen messengers."[141]

Mohammad decided that these non-believers—these skeptics—right there in his own homeland had to be eliminated if he was going to fulfill his imperial ambitions. So Mohammad decreed a deadly Islamic law: "Two religions may not dwell together on the Arabian Peninsula."

ARABIAN HOLOCAUST

After issuing this decree, Mohammad wasted no time in enforcing it. He went after all the Jewish communities of northern Arabia. He systematically slaughtered them all. First the Quraiza tribe was exterminated. Then Mohammad sent messengers to the Jewish community at the oasis of Khaibar, "inviting" Usayr—their war chief—to visit Medina for peace negotiations.

"Usayr set off with 30 companions and a Muslim escort," writes historian Norman Stillman. "Suspecting no foul play, the Jews went unarmed. On the way the Muslims turned upon the defenseless delegation, killing all but one who managed to escape."[142]

Mohammad then attacked and destroyed their whole community.

Mohammad justified this treachery by saying, "War is deception." War practiced according to this Muslim doctrine was not just deception, it was a literal hell—even with the primitive weapons of the seventh century. The complete annihilation of the two Arabian-Jewish tribes, with every man, woman, and child slaughtered, is, according to the late Israeli historian and President Itzhak Ben-Zvi, "a tragedy for which no parallel can be found in Jewish history."[143]

Parenthetically, in the West's current war against Islamic fundamentalist terrorism, it would be good for the leaders to remember this "Islamic tactic of warfare." According to this "religious" doctrine of Islam, what Muslims say does not have to be true—after all, to them, "War is deception." And the end justifies the means.

A HERITAGE OF BRUTALITY

As an example of the enormity of Islamic brutality and barbarity, after another Jewish town surrendered to the Muslims, approximately one thousand men were beheaded in one day. The women and children were sold into slavery.[144]

Elsewhere, as the attacks on the Jews continued, some managed to survive. Under a new Islamic policy, non-Muslims or "infidels" were permitted to maintain their land so long as they paid a 50 percent tribute for their "protection."[145]

"Thus the Jewish *dhimmi* evolved—the robbery of freedom and political independence compounding the extortion and eventual expropriation of property," writes Peters. "Tolerated between onslaughts, expulsions and pillages from the Arab Muslim conquest onward, the non-Muslim *dhimmi*—predominantly Jewish but with Christians too—provided the important source of religious revenue through the 'infidel's' head tax. He became very quickly a convenient political scapegoat and whipping boy as well."[146]

THE "IRRESISTIBLE APPEAL" OF ISLAM

As noted earlier, the Bedouin was raised to fight, raid, and pillage. It was endemic in his genes. As historian Philip Hitti wrote, "The raid is raised by the economic and social conditions of desert life to the rank of a national institution. *It lies at the base of the economic structure of Bedouin pastoral society. In desert land, where the fighting mood is a chronic mental condition,* raiding is one of the few manly occupations. An early Arab poet gave expression to the guiding principle of such life in two verses: 'Our business is to make raids on the enemy, on our neighbor and on our own brother, in case we find none to raid but a brother!'"[147]

And now comes Mohammad, who tells them they can fight, raid, and pillage in the sanctified service of Allah—and keep the booty as well. Their fighting is now raised to the level of a "holy war" in the cause of Allah. In fact, an old Arabic word was dusted off and given new meaning—*Jihad*, Holy War."

Guillaume explains how this new policy of repression and confiscation led to Islam's growing appeal among the nomadic Arab tribes:

> Much of the wealth of the country which had been concentrated in the hands of the Jews had now been seized by the Muslims, who were no longer indigents but wealthy landowners, men of substance, owning camels and horses and their own weapons. . . . Mohammad's fame spread far and wide, and the Bedouin flocked to him in thousands.[148]

The fact that the plunder of Jewish people directly led to the explosive growth and popularity of Islam among the Arabs is supported by Islamic historian Ali Dashti, who writes, "The immediate step which secured the economic base and strengthened the prestige of the Muslims was their seizure of the property of the Jews at Yathrib."[149]

THE PRECEDENT OF PREY

The betrayal and killing of the Jews at Medina, the massacres of the Nadhir and Kainuka tribes, and the dispossession of property by Muslims set up what Joan Peters rightly calls "the precedent of prey"—a pattern that would be repeated again and again. The agrarian and merchant Jews lucky enough to escape death would be plundered and exploited by the nomadic Arabs. Islam not only gave them an excuse for such oppression, *it commanded it.*

"It is likely that among the Jewish refugees fleeing from Arabia were numbers of Jews whose 'Palestinian'—or Judean—ancestors had fled from the Romans," writes Peters. The "Judeans," Peters continues,

> . . . returned to seventh-century Palestine, joining their Jewish brethren who had never left. Ironically, the Jewish refugees return coincided with the introduction of the Arab conquerors from the desert; the very invaders who had forced themselves in and the Jews out of their homes in Arabia would now plunder Judah-Palestine in the identical pattern. And the Jews who inhabited many towns of "Palestine" uninterruptedly would one day in the twentieth century be forced out as the Arabian Jews had been—by slaughter or expropriation and terrorizing. The towns would then, in the later twentieth century, be touted as "purely Arab Palestinian areas since time immemorial," just as the Arabian Peninsula had come to be perceived as "purely Arab," when in fact the holy Arab Muslim city of Medina had been originally settled by Jews.[150]

IMPERATIVE HISTORY YOU WILL RARELY HEAR

If you think over this correction of history, it is truly remarkable. Talk about myths. The Arab Muslims have spun the mother of all myths with their claim that "Palestine has always been Arab—from time immemorial."

All over the world today—from Georgia to Azerbaijan to Serbia to India to Sudan and Eritrea—long-forgotten ethnic tensions resulting from historical injustices and memories are on the rise. Is it any wonder, given the enormity of the atrocities against the Jews, that Israelis would be just a little suspicious of today's experts who are quick to say, "The past is the past"? No wonder

Israeli Prime Minister Benjamin Netanyahu says, "It isn't the size of Israel that bothers the Muslims; it is the existence of Israel."

Until this vital history is fully explored in a truthful and open way, there is no hope of rectifying the Middle East's historical injustices. "The Medina Legacy" established a pattern of institutionalized Islamic anti-Semitism that is at the very root of today's Middle East crisis. Without addressing that reality, there is no hope of understanding, let alone settling, the conflict. And the current idiotic handicap of "political correctness" that has been placed on all things Islamic only hinders the crucial historical facts from being discovered and understood.

[NINE]

INSTITUTIONALIZED ANTI-SEMITISM

"The power struggle between Israel and the Arabs is a long-term historical trial. Victory or defeat are for us questions of existence or annihilation, the outcome of an irreconcilable hatred."

— AL RIYADH SAUD, SAUDI ARABIAN LEADER

"The war is open until Israel ceases to exist and until the last Jew in the world is eliminated."

— HAMAS LEADER[151]

HOW ENMITY BECAME A RELIGIOUS DOCTRINE

What began as rivalry between brothers degenerated into a family feud. Then it evolved into an everlasting, irreconcilable enmity.

There were some cases of reconciliation between the Arabs and Jews of Arabia in the centuries just before the birth of Mohammad. The Jews were not loved, but they were accepted. Some Arabs who lived by Jewish communities even converted to Judaism.

Joan Peters notes concerning this period, "It was the Prophet Mohammad himself who attempted to negate the positive image of the Jew that had been prevalent earlier."[152]

Hatred of Jews in Islam is justified as a religious cause. Islam literally resurrected the ancient enmities and jealousies of the sons of Ishmael, Esau, and Keturah toward the Jews and enshrined that malevolence into a basic doctrine of their religion.

Though the information in this chapter may be a bit overloaded with facts, it is absolutely essential to understand if we are to see through the double-speak and outright fabrications set forth by Muslims in negotiations over Palestine with Western diplomats.

Beginning with Mohammad and continuing to this day, Islam contains an inherently anti-Jewish character. Despite myths to the contrary, this characteristic has meant centuries of horror for all non-Muslims (especially Jews)—or *dhimmis*, as they are called—unfortunate enough to be forced to live in an Arab land.

It should be noted that the historic anti-Jewish attitude of Islam has multiplied a hundred-fold since the birth of the modern Jewish state of Israel in 1948.

The Exponential Spread of Jew-Hate

Before Mohammad and Islam, endemic hatred for Jews was largely confined to the Arabs and the Arabian Peninsula. But after hatred for the Jews became enshrined in the Koran and the sacred traditions of Islam, wherever Islam has spread, hatred for the Jews has spread with it.

Here is a graphic illustration. Muslims in Indonesia are not Arabs, neither have they had much contact with Jews, nor have they a natural relationship to "Palestine." But they hate Jews because it's part of their religion and faith.

The same can be said of the Muslims of Afghanistan, Pakistan, Chechnya, and so on. They are not Arab, but they caught their hatred of the Jew like a super-contagious disease.

The Deification of Seventh-Century Arab Culture

The Muslim religion actually froze the seventh-century Arab culture of Mecca and Medina in time and raised it to the level of "divine revelation" on how all people should live for all time. The modern concept of "Jihad" primarily has to do with forcing this culture upon the whole world—either by conversion or conquest.

In a profound, almost mystical sense, Mohammad is the product of seventh-century Arab culture, and Islam is an expression of his perceptions of that culture. In addition, a major part of his character was marked by hatred for the Jews; Mohammad never forgave them for rejecting him and his claim of being God's prophet. Without question, that hatred is woven into the Koran.

A modern example of just how profoundly Arab society today is tied to the seventh-century is provided by the return of the Ayatollah Khomeini to Iran in 1979. As soon as he took over, he ripped the people away from the twentieth-century advancements they had incorporated into their lives, and he dragged the country back to seventh-century Arab culture. Thousands who did not comply were executed. Others escaped with only the clothes on their backs. And once again, the Jewish community experienced an all-too-familiar pattern: Those who had settled in Iran during the Shah's tolerant reign fled for their lives.

To the Muslim fundamentalist, everything about Western culture is evil. Not because everything about Western culture is sinful in a moral sense, but because it is different from Arab culture. This is why they hate democracy—there is no precedent for it in Arab culture and in the Koran from which that culture sprang.

Religious-Cultural Imperialism

Islam is nothing less than a religious-cultural imperialism that is determined to subject the entire planet to Islamic rule. This is why Mohammad divided the world into two spheres:

- Dar al-Islam—The land of peace
- Dar al-harb—The land of war

Mohammad believed that the Muslim is in a perpetual state of *Jihad*—"holy war"—with all countries in the Dar al-harb sphere. The true follower of Mohammad believes that Allah has willed Muslims to subject Islamic culture and law upon the whole world—either by conversion or by the sword.

Islam believes this doctrine is especially applicable to all of the Middle East, which Muslims claim as the center of their world. Furthermore, they believe that any land that has been captured and held by Muslim forces in the past is sacred. But the myths built around Jerusalem and Palestine makes this area second only to Mecca and Medina as a most holy place.

A remnant of Jews has always continued to dwell in Jerusalem and Palestine in spite of the dangers and difficulties. But when Jews began to return there in growing numbers at the end of the nineteenth century, Muslims were greatly alarmed.

And when the Jews declared a state in Palestine in 1948, the Islamic world called it *Al Nabka*—"the catastrophe." The continuing presence of the Jews in Jerusalem is now regarded as the ultimate blasphemy to Muslims. It is viewed as a desecration of the "Third Holiest Place in Islam"—an insult to Allah that must be removed and cleansed at any cost.

As we noted earlier, Israel's victories over the "armies of Allah" in five major wars have even placed faith in the Koran in jeopardy, for it promises the forces of Islam victory in "holy wars." Some devout Muslims fervently believe this is something that must be avenged for the sake of the Koran's veracity. Nothing can cleanse this insult to Allah but an ultimate military defeat of Israel.

Religion, Culture, and Land

Islam views the possession of land in a way very different from other religions. As noted above, once Islamic culture is established in a land, it is considered sanctified to Allah. It becomes *Dar al-Islam*—the land of peace. When an invader takes it away, all Muslims are obligated to take it back for Allah, no matter what the sacrifice or how long it takes.

This is why the Muslim forces fought the Christian crusaders of Europe for three centuries over "the Holy Land." But now since 1948, the Jew has invaded, and the ancient enmity toward all Israelites makes this "occupation" an utterly intolerable sacrilege. Muslims call Israel "a cancer in the heart of Islam that must be removed."

Western civilization just does not understand this basic thinking of Islam. Western media particularly doesn't have a clue as to what motivates the Muslim—or what strategies he will use to attain what he views as his duty to Allah. This is why so many in the press swallow Muslim propaganda "hook, line and sinker." As we will see, the modern Arab myths spun about the "legitimate rights of the Palestinian refugees" and "Israel's occupation of Palestinian territory" are based on monstrous distortions of history.

As Mohammad taught: "War is deception." And he set the example for negotiating peace with your enemy until you are strong enough to annihilate him." Remember "the Quraysh Model." This was the ten-year peace treaty Mohammad signed with the Quraysh tribe of Mecca, which he broke within a year and destroyed them. This is how he conquered Mecca and made it the holiest site in Islam—through treachery.

Rise of the "Khaliph Rasul Allahs"

Mohammad's death in A.D. 632 was unexpected and sudden, leaving Islam with no plan of succession. The fact that Mohammad had no male heir made the problem much more difficult. This left inevitable problems that later resulted in major conflicts within the Muslim religion.

My purpose here is not to trace the details of this phase of Islam, but rather to note that these internal conflicts resulted in the formation of the Shi'ite and Sunni sects. Basically the Shi'ites believed the *Khaliph Rasul Allah*, or the "successor of the Messenger of God," had to be in the bloodline of Mohammad.

The Sunni sect held the majority opinion. They believed that any worthy member of the faithful was eligible, though some of these added that it was preferable that he should be of the Quraysh tribe.

The First of "the Divinely Guided Ones"

Mohammad's first four successors, or *Khaliphs*, are known collectively as the "rashidun," or "the Divinely Guided Ones." They each knew "the Prophet" personally and worked with him to build and spread Islam. Thus their credentials were as unique as their thirty years of rule (A.D. 632–662). Their accomplishments were nothing short of extraordinary by anyone's measure.

After some controversy, Abu Bakr Sedeik (A.D. 632–634) became the first to possess the title of Khaliph Rasul Allah. This title represented the temporal authority of the Prophet and the holder's responsibility as defender of the faithful. Since Mohammad was "the last, or Seal, of the Prophets," the Khaliph was not the spiritual head of the House of Islam but rather the secular "commander of the faithful."

Bakr's khaliphate magnified, if it did not create, a schism that endures to this day via the geo-religio-political division of the Shi'ite and Sunni sects.

When the Shi'ites' choice, Ali, was not chosen as Khaliph, a violent struggle erupted that continues until this present day. Ali ibn Talib was not only Mohammad's first cousin and adopted son, but he was also married to Mohammad's only surviving child— his daughter Fatima. If you think this is irrelevant ancient history, just remember that Sunni Iraq fought a bloody war with Shi'ite Iran over this issue during the entire decade of the 1980s.

In the Muslim Middle East, events that happened centuries

ago are still as relevant as those that happened yesterday. A grudge based on an event that occurred a thousand years ago can erupt today into a savage war against the "descendants of the offender."

Only two issues in history have really united the Sunnis and the Shi'ites. The first was the long war against the Christian crusaders in the Middle Ages—the second is the mutual hatred of Jews and the desire to destroy the state of Israel. It's truly amazing, but after Iraq and Iran inflicted over a million casualties on each other, they "kissed and made up" because of the mutually perceived threat of the U.S. led invasion of Iraq.

Bakr's short two-year khaliphate was spent reuniting the tribes of Arabia, most of which immediately revolted after Mohammad's death. He had the help of an amazing military leader named Khalid ibn-Walid, who became known as "the Sword of Allah."[153]

Omar, "The Second Founder of Islam"

Omar ibn al-Khattab, by prearrangement, succeeded Bakr and reigned from A.D. 634–644. He is very important to understand, because he devastated the Christian world with a vengeance.

Historian George Grant offers these descriptions of Omar:

A stern giant of a man with a long dark beard and a full, brooding countenance. He wore coarse, frayed garments and always carried a whip in his right fist in order to enforce righteous humility among his men. He had little appreciation for the accomplishments of Byzantium and was single-minded in his desire to bring the empire to its knees.

According to the Shah Nemeh, a contemporary chronicle of caliphs and kings, Umar (Omar) despised the Christian infidels for their "half-faith" and yearned to force their confessions, creeds, and liturgies into extinction.[154]

Omar was driven as one empowered by a "supernatural spirit," which probably explains his amazing career. Under his "inspired leadership" the united tribes of Arabia exploded from the peninsula. They charged in every direction, conquering and occupying all they encountered.

The exploits of Walid, "the Sword of Allah," are particularly important to this book. In A.D. 635, Walid crossed the border of Persia and subdued the village of Hira. He then made an incredible forced march across the Syrian desert to join forces with another Muslim army that was near Jerusalem. In short order, although out-numbered two to one, Walid led his forces in a series of brilliant cavalry charges that cut the Byzantine defenders to pieces.

Walid quickly conquered the territory generally known as Palestine. By the fall of A.D. 635, Walid reached the very gates of Damascus, having decimated the opposition along the way. After a six-month siege, the Muslims captured the ancient city of Damascus.

Jerusalem's First Fall to Islam

In the fateful month of August, A.D. 635, the Muslim armies captured Jerusalem.

Khaliph Omar came into the city on a February day in A.D. 638 and personally proclaimed the Temple Mount one of Islam's holiest sites. He built a wooden mosque over the great rock on the Temple Mount. However, Muslims believe a story that differs from the history recorded in the Biblical record. They believe the Temple Mount is the site where Abraham built an altar on which to sacrifice *Ishmael*. The Bible clearly states the altar was built to sacrifice Isaac, not Ishmael. God's choice of Isaac over Ishmael is an essential part of the entire Biblical revelation concerning His plan for mankind's redemption. It is also the basis for the centuries-old feud between the two races that sprang from Ishmael and Isaac.

Muslims developed the legend that this rock is the very

foundation stone from which Allah created the earth and the place where Adam made atonement after his fall. Most importantly, the Muslims believe Mohammad ascended to heaven from here on his horse named Barak that miraculously sprouted wings. This is the Muslim basis for designating the Temple area the third holiest site of Islam.

Chuck Missler quotes Steve Runciman concerning Omar's triumphant entry to Jerusalem:

> On a February day in the year A.D. 638 the Khaliph Omar entered Jerusalem, riding upon a white camel. He was dressed in worn filthy robes, and the army that followed him was rough and unkempt; but its discipline was perfect. . . . Omar rode straight to the sight of the Temple of Solomon. . . . Omar was shocked at the filth and rubble that lay strewn about the Temple Mount. Because the holy sight had been neglected he made the Christian Patriarch (Sophronius) grovel in the muck. Afterward Omar set about clearing the sight. He then built a wooden mosque on the temple mount."[155]

Omar's Amazing Conquests

During the short nine years of Omar's khaliphate, the Muslims went from a regional kingdom on the Arabian Peninsula to become an Islamic world-empire. Grant comments on this amazing fete:

> Before his death in A.D. 644 [Omar] had spread the dominion of Islam from the Euphrates across the North African Littoral. He had conquered all of Iraq, brought the Persians to the brink of collapse, controlled the southern Mediterranean coastline, and put Christendom on the defensive at every turn. In addition, he left his successors a tumultuous momentum that gave them expansive new conquests in Spain, Sicily, Crete, and Italy.[156]

Most important to our focus, Omar's conquests brought under his brutal control Jewish communities that had lived for hundreds of years in the areas he conquered. Those who were not killed received the status of something only slightly less terrible—they became "dhimmis," which I mentioned before.

Most of the Christian Byzantine civilization was also conquered, and the survivors suffered a fate similar to that of the Jews. Historic churches were converted to mosques. Priceless Christian art was obliterated. Everything Christian was destroyed. Everything that referred to Jesus as the Son of God was removed. In its place, the Muslims posted ornate signs that read, "All praise be to Allah who never had a son."

Islam's "Benevolent Law" for "Dhimmis"

It was under Khaliph Omar that the laws regarding non-believers were firmly established by Muslims. As dhimmis, Jews were forbidden to touch the Koran. They were forced to wear distinctive clothes and a yellow badge (Christians had to wear blue). They were not permitted to perform religious practices in public, not allowed to own or ride a horse, and were required to bury their dead without any public expression of grief.

As an expression of gratitude for being allowed to live among Muslims, dhimmis were expected to pay special confiscatory taxes prescribed by the Koran—usually at least 50 percent of all earnings. (Tax-wise, it sounds much like America's current taxes.)

Here is an example of "Islamic justice" for the Jewish dhimmis. "Islamic religious law decreed that, although the murder of one Muslim by another Muslim was punishable by death, a Muslim who murdered a non-Muslim was not given the death penalty, but only the obligation to pay 'blood money' to the family of the slain infidel," writes author Joan Peters. "Even this punishment was unlikely, however, because the law held the testimony of a Jew or a Christian invalid against a Muslim, and the penalty could only be exacted under improbable conditions—when two Muslims were willing to testify against a brother Muslim for the sake of an infidel."[157]

This kind of blatantly ruthless double standard in Islam has continued through the centuries—enforced to varying degrees of cruelty depending on the character of the Muslim ruler and the country. Under the best of circumstances, life was intolerable and filled with indignities. *In the worst of circumstances, Jews and Christians lived every moment of every day in fear for their very lives.*

Jews dwelling in Muslim-ruled lands all lived under the terrible law of the dhimmi. As Islam spread, Jewish communities were swept into the storm. Those who weren't killed lived lives of humiliation and terror.

What Moses predicted centuries before about the Israelites became a terrifying reality:

> Moreover, the Lord will scatter you among all peoples, from one end of the earth to the other end of the earth. . . . Among those nations you shall find no rest, and there shall be no resting place for the sole of your foot; but there the Lord will give you a trembling heart, failing of eyes, and despair of soul. So your life shall hang in doubt before you; and you shall be in dread night and day, and shall have no assurance of your life.[158]

It is true that Jews were persecuted in other cultures as well, but the Muslims raised it to the level of a religious sacrament.

Slavery and Dehumanization

The practices that started then continue to this present day. Here are a few examples of some of the ancient Jewish communities, and how they have continued to our present era.

Yemen

Life for Jews has always been particularly demeaning. In Yemen, for example, Jews were treated like subhuman slaves, forced to clean the public latrines and clear the streets of animal carcasses without pay on the Sabbath day.[159]

A particularly horrible Yemenite law decreed that fatherless Jewish children under thirteen be taken from their mothers and raised as Muslims. "Children were torn away from their mothers," according to historian S. D. Goitein. "To my mind this law, which was enforced with new vigor about 50 years ago, more than anything else impelled the Yemenite Jews to quit that country to which they were very much attached. The result was that many families arrived in Israel with one or more of their children lost to them . . . some widows were bereaved in this way of all their offspring."[160]

Persecution in Yemen was consistent and extreme over the years. Stoning Jews continued as an age-old custom right up until most Yemenite Jews left for Israel in 1948. They had lived there for twenty-five hundred years.

Babylon and Iraq

Jews had a long history of residence in Babylon until the Muslim conquest in the year A.D. 634. Later, the heavy taxes were imposed, synagogues were razed, and, ultimately, entire communities were slaughtered.

In the modern era, after Israel became a state, Iraq came down on Iraqi Jews with a pent-up fury. There was a long history of persecution in this region, but this was horrific. More than 123,000 Iraqi Jews fled to Israel in terror between 1949 and 1952 alone. Many were killed in riots. Those who fled left with nothing but the clothes on their backs—thankful they escaped with their lives. They left behind wealth and property that their families had accumulated over some twenty-five hundred years. Most of these families could trace their origins in Iraq back to the Babylonian captivity in the days of Daniel the prophet.

Egypt

Prior to 1948, the Jewish community in Egypt lived in relative peace and harmony compared to the plight of Jews in the neighboring Muslim nations. Even so, their lives were filled with constant uncertainty. Humiliations, property confiscations, and physical atrocities happened daily at the whim of the Muslim neighbors.

Beginning in 1940, spurred by Nazi propaganda and the growth of the Zionist movement, many Jews were killed in anti-Jewish riots. Egypt even passed laws that all but prohibited Jews from being employed. The government confiscated property, and after the 1947 vote to partition Palestine, Jewish homes were looted and synagogues destroyed.

In one ten-day period in 1948, 150 Jews were murdered or seriously wounded in Egyptian bloodletting. As soon as a ban on Jews leaving the country was lifted in 1949, some twenty thousand fled Egypt, mostly for Israel, with only the clothes on their backs.

Admiration for Hitler

Egypt's Gamal Abdel Nasser openly declared in 1964, "Our sympathy was with the Germans. The president of our Parliament, for instance, Anwar Sadat, was imprisoned for his sympathy with the Germans."[161]

In the 1970s, a prominent Egyptian writer was, once more, helping to stir up the old blood libels against Jews. Anis Mansour assured his readers that the medieval lie that Jews sacrificed children and drank their blood was historically true and that "the Jews confessed." Because of this, he said it was perfectly appropriate to persecute "the wild beasts." Another time he wrote: "People all over the world have come to realize that Hitler was right, since Jews . . . are bloodsuckers . . . interested in destroying the whole world which has . . . expelled them and despised them for centuries . . . and burnt them in Hitler's crematoria . . . one million . . . six million—I would that he had finished it!"[162]

Mansour is hardly regarded as some kind of renegade nut in Egypt. In 1975, he represented the nation at the fortieth International PEN (writers) Conference in Vienna. Upon his return he charged that "the Jews are guilty" for Nazism, and that they "have only themselves to blame."[163]

Syria

Egypt was just a walk in the park in the twentieth century compared to Syria, which was a living hell for Jews. The smoldering enmity against Jews that has always been in Syria burst into a roaring fire with the advent of Zionism. Damascus became the headquarters of anti-Jewish activities and feasted on Nazism.

During World War II, the Jewish quarter in Damascus was raided several times because of ridiculous rumors that Churchill and Roosevelt had agreed to make Syria into a Jewish state.

Israelis have told me on many occasions that the most vicious enemy in the whole Middle Eastern neighborhood is Syria—and that's a rough neighborhood. Today, Damascus is host to offices of virtually every Islamic terror organization on the planet.

Jew-Hating Taught from Infancy

Not only do Muslim families teach their children from the cradle to hate Jews, but Islamic educators also interweave this message of hatred into their class instruction.

Today, Muslim governments have official policies against Jews actually written into public school textbooks. For example:

- "The Jews in Europe were persecuted and despised because of their corruption, meanness and treachery" —Jordanian history textbook, from 1966 onward.
- "Israel was born to die. Prove it" —Instructions in a Jordanian high school.
- "The Jews . . . live exiled and despised since by their nature they are vile, greedy and enemies of mankind" —Syrian junior high school textbook.
- "We shall expel all the Jews from Muslim lands" —A fifth-year elementary school syntax exercise in a Syrian textbook.
- "The Arabs do not cease to act for the extermination of Israel" —An Egyptian junior high school grammar exercise in a textbook.
- "Israel hopes to be the homeland of the Jew, and they have the stubbornness of 4,000 years of history behind them. But Israel shall not live if the Arabs stand fast in their hatred. She shall wither and decline. Even if all the human race, and the devil in Hell, conspires to aid her, she shall not exist" —A ninth-grade Egyptian text.

Official Anti-Jewishness

"The anti-Semitic literature published by the Arabs since World War II has been voluminous, and is continually increasing, despite the almost total evacuation of the Arab world's Jews," writes Peters. "The virulence of this literature is disturbing, but even more significant is the official or governmental origin of the publications—not from an extremist fringe, which might be lightly dismissed, but from Arab governments, including those called 'moderate.'" [164] The examples below are all too typical of the anti-Semitism in the Arab press:

- *El-Ahram*, a leading daily with more than 700,000 readers, carried a book review of *The First Terrorists* in which the critic, Abd El-Muneim Qandil, asserted March 3, 1987: "I lower my pen in respect to the author who presents proof from Israeli books to the malice of the Jews who wish to kill all male newborns and pregnant women in order to uproot the Palestinians. . . . The author speaks about turning facts upside down . . . such as their claim that the gas chambers used by Hitler to get rid of people infected by plague were especially built to burn Jews alive."

- *El Masa*, a daily of 100,000, reported April 21, 1987: "Jews distributed a 'ridiculous lie' after the Second World War concerning the Holocaust. They started with the claim that 100,000 Jews were exterminated but later reached the figure of 8 million. Jews are inflating these numbers in order to achieve bigger help from the USA. . . .We can expect, therefore, that very soon the number of Jews killed by the Nazis will reach 10 million."

- *Sawt El-Arab*, a daily with a large circulation, wrote on March 15, 1987: "Israel sells to Egypt seeds, plants and cattle infected with diseases in order to destroy the local agriculture."

- *El Mukhtar El-Islami*, a monthly religious publication, states in April 1986: "The Jews were responsible for World War II. They initiated this war in order to crush Nazi Germany, which was the last obstacle before Jewish domination of the world. Europe was indeed destroyed and Zionist strategy had its victory. The Jews were also behind the murder of President Abraham Lincoln."

- *El-Nur*, a weekly publication of the Muslim Brotherhood, circulation over 100,000, said October 22, 1986: "We wait for the moment that all Jews will gather in Palestine and that will be the great day for enormous massacre."

- *Sawt Filastin*, a semi-official weekly published for Palestinians, published in August 1987, the fifth anniversary of the Sabra and Shatilla massacre: "Deception and treason are basic components of Jewish character. Jews always used tricks and plots to spread terror and death all over the world."

■ *El-Tawhid*, a fundamentalist Islamic monthly, stated in February 1987: "The children of Israel are 'garbage allied with Satan, purulence causing pain and infection, a deposit of germs.'"

Many more examples like these could be quoted here, but these illustrate the irrational hatred that is constantly spread against the Jew in the Muslim world. If anything, anti-Semitism has gotten far worse in the twenty-first century.

Christians Are Also Increasingly Targeted

That this hatred is spreading around the world is illustrated by the 9/11 attack on the United States is evidence this hatred is spreading around the world. Islamic fundamentalists see the United States as the world center of the Judeo-Christian-based world order, which they believe is the greatest threat to true Islam. They believe we must be destroyed and replaced with an Islamic-based world order.

Just as the Jews were driven out of Muslim lands, Christians are now targeted for persecution. Here are just a few examples of anti-Christian persecution occurring throughout the Islamic world.

■ Indonesia, which has the largest Muslim population of any country in the world, is systematically killing and terrorizing Christians. More than five hundred churches have been burned and hundreds of Christians killed. People have fled certain areas in fear for their lives.

■ Muslims of the Sudan have systematically slaughtered Christians in Eritrea and Ethiopia. Thousands have been killed, and millions have been driven into exile, resulting in tens of thousands dying of famine.

▪ In Egypt, Muslim fundamentalists have forced Christians to stay inside their mud hovels for months at a time due to the intensity of persecution. Churches have been burned, Christian shops looted and destroyed, and Christians have been killed. One Coptic Christian said, "Life for Christians is over. Now we must figure out how to get out alive." Coptic Christians, who number seven to eight million of Egypt's fifty-six million people, belong to one of the oldest denominations in Christendom.[165]

Because "Christian U.S. soldiers" have stayed in Saudi Arabia to defend it against Iraqi invasion, Osama Bin Laden has declared this protection as the ultimate sacrilege. To him and his al Qaeda, our mere presence on Saudi soil constitutes an invasion of sacred Islamic land and desecrates the most holy places of Islam.

This is clearly expressed in Bin Laden's "Fatwa," which declared a Jihad against all Americans. The terror leader writes, "For over seven years the United States has been occupying the lands of Islam in the holiest of places, the Arabian Peninsula, plundering its riches, dictating to its rulers, humiliating its people, terrorizing its neighbors, and turning its bases in the Peninsula into a spearhead through which to fight the neighboring Muslim peoples." For this and equally "serious crimes," Osama concludes, "We—with God's help—call on every Muslim who believes in God and wishes to be rewarded to comply with God's order to *kill the Americans* and plunder their money whenever and wherever they find it. We call on Muslim ulema [believers], leaders, youths, and soldiers to launch the raid on Satan's U.S. troops and the devil's supporters allying with them, and to displace those who are behind them so that they may learn a lesson."[166]

The Koranic Verses

You, like most westerners, must be asking, "Where does this kind of hate come from?" We have seen how the hate started in the tents of Abraham and grew in the deserts of Arabia. But the constantly flowing spring that feeds and nourishes this hate is the Koran itself. The Muslim holy book pulls no punches in its denunciations of both Jews and Christians. I will close with just a few examples out of many that could be cited. Later we will examine this issue in more detail. The following verses were taken from an English translation of the Koran on an Islamic Web site:

> "Certainly you will find the most violent of people in enmity for those who believe to be the Jews and those who are polytheists [Christians]." —Surah 5.82

> "So when the sacred months have passed away, then slay the idolaters wherever you find them, and take them captives and besiege them and lie in wait for them in every ambush."
> —Surah 9.5

> "O you who believe! Do not take the Jews and the Christians for friends; they are friends of each other; and whoever amongst you takes them for a friend, then surely he is one of them; surely Allah does not guide the unjust people." —Surah 5.51

> "Abasement is made to cleave to them [Jews] wherever they are found, . . . and they have become deserving of wrath from Allah, and humiliation is made to cleave to them; this is because they disbelieved in the communications of Allah and slew the prophets unjustly; this is because they disobeyed and exceeded the limits." —Surah 3.112

"And you will most certainly find them [Jews] the greediest of men." —Surah 2.96

"And when there came to them [Jews] a Book from Allah (Koran) verifying that which they have . . . they disbelieved in him; so Allah's curse is on the unbelievers. Evil is that for which they [Jews] have sold their souls—that they should deny what Allah has revealed, out of envy that Allah should send down of His grace on whomsoever of His servants He pleases; so they have made themselves deserving of wrath upon wrath."

—Surah 2.89–90

"Those who disbelieve in Our communications, We shall make them enter fire; so oft as their skins are thoroughly burned, We will change them for other skins, that they may taste the chastisement; surely Allah is Mighty, Wise." —Surah 4.56

"Of those who are Jews [they are those who] alter words from their places and say: We have heard and we disobey . . . but Allah has cursed them on account of their unbelief." —Surah 4:46

"Shall I inform you of him who is worse than this in the retribution from Allah? Worse is he [Jews] whom Allah has cursed and brought His wrath upon, and of whom He made apes and pigs, and he who served the Satan; these are worse in place and more erring from the straight path." —Surah 5.60

With this kind of institutionalized anti-Semitism justified by their sacred religious book, their religious traditions, and the example of Mohammad himself, is it any wonder that nearly all the Jews living under Muslim rule gladly fled and left their possessions behind in 1948?

And is it any wonder that today's leaders of Israel are not anxious to rush into granting statehood to the Palestinians? The current Palestinian demands would make the borders of Israel indefensible. Israeli concerns are especially understandable since the Palestinians cannot stop their vicious terrorist attacks for even a week. Israel is being asked to give irreplaceable land and defensive positions for nothing more than the Muslim's promises of peace. And given what we know about the "Quraysh model" and Mohammad's declaration that "war is deception," that is a suicidal choice.

Maybe Israel's leaders have concluded that Muslims today really believe the Prophet Mohammad's words that, "war is deception." Who in their right mind would want to gamble the survival of their nation on that kind of "peace partner"?

TEN

THE OTHER PALESTINIAN REFUGEES

"Over the last 40 years, the countries of the Middle East and North Africa have undergone radical transformations which, among other things, have brought about the near extinction of Jewish communities after 2,000 to 3,000 years of existence."

—BAT YE'OR[167]

"The Jews always did live previously in Arab countries with complete freedom and liberty, as natives of the country. In fact, Muslim rule has always been tolerant . . . according to history Jews had a most quiet and peaceful residence under Arab rule."

—HAJ AMIN AL-HUSSEINI[168]

THE UNTOLD REFUGEE STORY

If you read about the Middle East problem in the newspaper today or listen to the discussions on the news, you can't help but be bombarded by analysts suggesting that the key to peace is resolving "the "Palestinian refugee issue." Well, prepare to be shocked. There is another virtually untold side of the Middle East refugee story.[169]

Joan Peters put it so well in her monumental work, *From Time Immemorial*:

For every refugee—adult or child—in Syria, Lebanon or elsewhere in the Arab world who compels our sympathy, there is a Jewish refugee who fled from the Arab country of his birth. For every Arab who moved to neighboring lands, a Jew was forced to flee from a community where he and his ancestors may have lived for 2,000 years.[170]

The world seldom if ever hears about the more than 800,000 Jewish refugees who fled Arab terror and hatred and settled in Israel as a result of the Muslim fury at the 1948 establishment of the state of Israel. Perhaps it is because every single one of those refugees was accepted, resettled, and provided for by the young struggling Jewish state without question or hesitation. There never has been a Jewish refugee camp in Israel or anywhere else.[171] On the other hand, Palestinians have never been accepted and settled in Muslim countries. They have been deliberately kept in miserable conditions so as to keep their hatred against the Jews and Israel at a fever pitch.

Exodus, Phase II

Here are some indisputable facts. In 1948, there were more than 850,000 Jews living in the Arab world. Today, there are fewer than 29,000. Where were those Jewish dhimmi communities in the Arab world? Before Israel was reborn, between 125,000 and 135,000 Jews lived in Iraq; 75,000 lived in Egypt; 30,000 lived in Syria; 55,000 lived in Yemen; 8,000 lived in Aden; 265,000 lived in Morocco; up to 140,000 lived in Algeria; 105,000 lived in Tunisia; 5,000 lived in Lebanon; and some 38,000 lived in Libya.[172]

Where are all of these Jews now? What happened to them? Where are their properties and financial resources? Why are they never mentioned in the "Palestinian Refugee debate" that keeps being trumpeted in the United Nations and the liberal media?

"The Arab world has been virtually emptied of its Jews, and the fledgling Jewish state would bear the burden of its hundreds of thousands of Jewish Arab-born refugees almost in secret," explains Peters. "So unknown and undisclosed are these Arab-born Jews and the plight they have faced—the camps, squalor, uprooting, loss of property and security, discontent, unemployment and what they sensed to be neglect of their problems in Israel—that in countless conversations outside the Middle East with academics or professionals, from university graduates to blue-collar workers, including Jews as well as non-Jews, when the question of the 'Middle East refugees' is raised, almost without exception the response is, 'You mean the Palestinians—the Arabs, of course.' It is as though the sad and painful story of the Arab-born Jewish refugees had been erased, their struggle covered over by a revision of the pages of history."[173]

Why the Cover-Up?

Why isn't this story reported? Why isn't it chronicled? Why isn't it remembered? If Arab nations are responsible for expelling Jews in approximately the same numbers as the much-publicized Arab refugees displaced after the creation of Israel, why isn't the obvious solution a simple population exchange? Nowhere is the enormity of the Muslim myth swallowed by the West more graphically illustrated than in this issue.

Note also that there is absolutely no moral equivalence in this situation, *for the Jews did not drive out the Palestinian refugees*. The Palestinians were not threatened and killed to terrorize them into leaving. In many cases they were begged to stay. No! They were ordered to leave "temporarily" by the combined Muslim armies who promised to annihilate the Jews and their new state, and to give them the booty left by the Jews.

On the other hand, the Jews living in Arab countries were terrorized, killed, and driven out with nothing but the clothes on their backs. Their properties and assets were all confiscated. Those who escaped were thankful just to be alive.

The Jews were received and immediately repatriated into the new fragile state of Israel. They were given aid and jobs to the best of the ability of the struggling new country.

The Palestinians were deliberately forced into refugee camps by their fellow Muslims and not permitted to integrate in any way into the society of their unwilling hosts. Their own people didn't even try to help them; instead they prevailed upon the United Nations and gullible Western charities to supply the refugees' needs. They have been kept in these camps for more than sixty years—like an unhealed wound by their own people—just to be used as political pawns by Muslim negotiators to charge their plight as "Israeli aggression."

Some Popular Muslim Mythology

Many myths have been spun to suppress the facts about the Jewish immigration from Arab lands. Some of these have already been exploded in earlier chapters. But let us rehearse again some of the myths that actually teach the exact opposite of the actual, demonstrable truth:

Myth #1: The Arabs have nothing against Jews in general and "lived in peace and harmony with them" until the creation of the Zionist Movement and the consequent creation of the state of Israel in 1948.

Myth #2: Alienation with the Jews *began* in large part because Israel is almost entirely made up of European Jews who displaced indigenous Arab peoples in Palestine.

Myth #3: The key to resolving the Middle East crisis is to stop "Israeli aggression and occupation of Arab lands" and to create an independent Palestinian state.

Myth #4: Israel's U.S.-supplied military juggernaut has practiced continuous aggression against the neighboring, basically peaceful Muslim nations who are only trying to right a terrible wrong forced upon them by the West.

These myths have worked like magic for the Muslim propagandists for decades, but especially in the negotiations that have resulted from the Oslo Agreement.

Terror of a Dhimmi's Life

While there has been much mythology about how the Arab refugees in the Middle East became refugees; there is little doubt about why Jews in Arab nations left their homes and their belongings to flee for their lives. Anyone who takes the trouble to investigate will discover that the facts of history easy to find.

"Clearly," writes Joan Peters, "the massive exodus of Jewish refugees from the Arab countries was triggered largely by the Arabs' own Nazi-like bursts of brutality, which had become the lot of the Jewish communities."[174]

In the 1947 debates over the rebirth of Israel, Egypt's delegate to the United Nations General Assembly quite openly threatened the very lives of the Jews living in Arab countries: "The lives of one million Jews in Muslim countries would be jeopardized by partition," he blatantly warned.[175]

In fact, even the small handful of Jews still living in Arab lands do not remain by choice. In terms of both percentages of population and in real numbers, fewer Jews have chosen to live in Arab nations than chose to live in Hitler's Germany between 1933 and 1939.[176]

Why the contrast? Why did Jews leave everything behind to

flee Arab lands between 1948 and the present, while two-thirds of Germany's Jews, despite official anti-Semitic policies, stuck it out?

"Arab-born Jews realized that the Arab threats would be carried out, because they had lived as second-class—dhimmis—with reminders of pogroms in their own or their families' past experiences, whereas the German Jews felt themselves 'assimilated,' part of the German mainstream," explains Peters. "They expressed initial 'disbelief' that any such bigotry as the Nazis' could be more than a cruel political joke." No such illusions, however, were held with regard to the Arabs.

The big difference between the 1930s Germany and the situation beginning in 1948 was that Jews now had a place to go—Israel.

Imagine you're a Jew living in an Arab land and you hear the following report on the radio: "The Jews in the Arab countries have not respected the defense that Islam has given them for generations. They have encouraged World Zionism and Israel in every way in its aggression against the Arabs. . . . The Congress hereby declares that the Jews in the Muslim countries whose ties with Zionism and Israel are proved shall be regarded as fighters against the Muslims, unfit for the patronage and protection which the Muslim faith prescribes for adherents of peaceful protected faiths."

If you lived within range of Radio Amman in 1967, you would not have had to imagine such a broadcast. This was an actual report and typical of many others heard on Arab radio and television throughout the Middle East.[177]

"Arab propagandists and sympathizers have persisted in the charge that Israel is a foreign outpost of Western civilization, the intruding offspring of Europe inhabited by European survivors of Nazi brutality. In actuality, more than half of the people in Israel today are Jews or offsprings of Jews who lived in Arab countries and have fled from Arab brutality; Israel's present population consists mainly of refugees and their descendants from two oppressions, European-Nazis and Arab."[178]

"Collective Amnesia"

For some reason, the whole world has swallowed the sometimes-unbelievable products of the Arab propaganda machine. As Egyptian-born author Bat Ye'or sees it, "Even in Israel there is a kind of 'collective amnesia' with regard to the awesome contribution played by the Arab Jew in the history of the Jewish state."[179]

"The fact that the Zionist struggle was active mainly in Europe and America, and the fact that ignorance has prevailed concerning the dhimmi condition and its after-effects (insecurity, fear and silence), have led to Zionism's being viewed as an exclusively Western movement," Ye'or writes.

> The constant obfuscation of the Oriental dimension of Zionism has helped to foster the image of Israel as a colonial state of Western origin—even perceived as a reaction to Nazism. In this way Israel is defined within an exclusively Western framework, in contradiction to the realities of history, geography and its demography. Without in any way denying the specific dynamics of European Zionism and its essential achievements, nothing can change the fact that the fate of Palestine and its Jewish population was determined by the laws of jihad and its ulterior consequences. It is the historical amnesia specific to Oriental Jewry that has caused Zionism to be interpreted as an exclusively European movement, even though it is the stream in which all the currents of a nation, dismembered by exile, converge and unite. This shortcoming is in part responsible for the difficulty of dialogue with those who attribute the present situation of the Palestinian Arab refugees to European and Nazism, whereas it is the consequence of a much more ancient tragedy. Only when the history of the dhimmis will have been taken into consideration will solutions be found to satisfy the rights of each party in conformity with historical realities.[180]

Incredible Irony

Modern media invented a perfect term for what the Muslim nations have done with the history of dhimmis—*turnspeak*—which means, "a cynical inverting or distorting of facts, which for example, makes the *victim* appear to be the *oppressor*." Arab propagandists have used *turnspeak* to perfection in perpetuating the myth of "displaced" and "terrorized" Arabs in the Jewish-settled area of Palestine-cum-Israel.

The record shows that the migrant Muslims who traveled from other Arab lands to areas of Palestine that were reclaimed and developed by the Jews came to get jobs. It was *afterward* that Muslims began to claim "Jews displaced them from land that had been in their families for hundreds of years."

I agree that there have been some colossal injustices inflicted on the people of Palestine. Only it wasn't the Jews who committed them, but the Muslims, who sought to drive the Jews out of a tiny plot of land that was only a fraction of what was originally mandated to them by the League of Nations. As we will see, when the map of the Middle East was completely redrawn after the fall of the Turkish Ottoman Empire in 1917, and Arab states were created from the stateless remains of the Ottoman occupation, a certain section was mandated to the Jews as a homeland. I hope that everyone reading this book will clearly see, that no matter how small the Jewish state was made, it was still too big for the Muslims—*because it isn't the size of Israel that matters to the Muslims, it is the existence of Israel.*

A Rule of Hatred

The most cynical myth of all, however, is the lie that Jews enjoyed freedom, liberty, and kind treatment while dwelling in Muslim-ruled lands before the rise of Zionism. Here are some facts from impartial observers on how the Jews, or dhimmis, were treated:

In their Holy Land, the Jews as well as Christians suffered long from harsh discrimination, persecution, and pogroms. According to the British Consulate report in 1839, *"the Jew's life was not much above that of a dog."*

In truth, *"Arab" terrorism in the Holy Land originated centuries before the recent tool of "the Palestinian cause was invented."* In towns where Jews lived for hundreds of years, those Jews were periodically robbed, raped, in some places massacred, and in many instances, the survivors were obliged to abandon their possessions and run. As we have seen, beginning with the Prophet Mohammad's edict demanding racial purity—that "Two religions may not dwell together . . ."—the Arab-Muslim world codified its supremacist credo, and later that belief was interpreted liberally enough to allow many non-Muslim dhimmis, or infidels, to remain alive between onslaughts in the Muslim world as a means of revenue. The infidel's head tax, in addition to other extortions—and the availability of the "non-believers" to act as helpless scapegoats for the oft-dissatisfied masses—became a highly useful mainstay to the Arab-Muslim rulers. Thus the pronouncement of the Prophet Mohammad was altered in practice to: two religions may not dwell together equally. That was the pragmatic interpretation.[181]

In the early seventeenth century, a pair of Christian visitors to Safed [Galilee] told of life for the Jews: "Life here is the poorest and most miserable that one can imagine." Because of the harshness of Turkish rule and its crippling dhimmi oppression, the Jews "pay for the very air they breath".[182]

Reports like these could be multiplied. The audacity of Haj Amin al-Husseini's claim that the "Jews always did live previously in Arab countries with complete freedom and liberty, as natives of the country" and that, "in fact, Muslim rule has always been tolerant . . . according to history Jews had a most quiet and peaceful residence under Arab rule," is shown to be a cynical lie.

This simply shows that Haj al-Husseini learned a lot from his visit to Nazis Germany. Adolf Hitler, whom he greatly admired, developed the propaganda tactic of "the Big Lie."

One thing is certain, Jewish dhimmis were never treated with kindness and never had anything approaching freedom. They were continually persecuted, brutalized, and given the most degrading and humiliating treatment.

The monstrous myth "that there was no problem for the Jews living peacefully with the Muslims until the rise of Zionism and the founding of the state of Israel" is a classic example of Muslim "turnspeak" and the cynical hatred that motivated it. The Muslim idea of humane, peaceful treatment for Jews is to have them subjected to the status of second-rate citizens; to be available as taxable assets; to be scapegoats for whatever leadership failure or calamity that comes along; and to be objects to hit, kick, rape, rob, or murder whenever Muslims just need to let out their aggressions and frustrations.

The Real Refugees

The Jews who lived in Muslim countries of the Middle East are in fact more truly refugees than the much-publicized "Palestinian refugees." It is supremely important to again review the facts. Here are the contrasting conditions of how the two groups became "refugees."

The Palestinians were not driven out of the Palestinian territory by Jewish threats and acts of terror. They left at the urging of their own fellow Muslims who promised them it would be for only a short while. The reason for the Palestinian "exodus" was to facilitate the Muslim annihilation of the state of Israel and the massacre of the Jewish people. When the Islamic onslaught failed, the Palestinians were never accepted in new lands or repatriated to their brother Muslim countries. Instead, this displaced population has been deliberately kept in the harshness and squalor of refugee camps "to keep their flames of hatred toward the Israelis white hot."

The Jews who resided in Muslim lands for centuries were driven out by savage acts of terrorism and massacres. Those who were able to leave alive were not allowed to take anything with them. All of their assets were seized. However, in contrast to how Muslims treated Palestinian refugees, all Jewish refugees were immediately received and repatriated by Israel with the help of financing from Jewish people abroad.

ELEVEN

THE "TURKEYFICATION" OF ISLAM: THE ENORMOUS IMPACT OF THE OTTOMANS

"The Palestinians who are today's refugees in the neighboring countries know all this—that their present nationalist exploiters are the worthy sons of their feudal exploiters of yesterday, and that the thorns of their life are of Arab, not Jewish origin."

—ABDEL RAZAK KADER[183]

FROM THE CRUSADES TO THE OTTOMAN TURK EMPIRE

Many great movements of history took place during the time-frame from the last Crusade in A.D. 1291 to the fall of the Ottoman Empire in 1917, a period that affected both the Islamic Empire and the Christian West.

THE LAST EUROPEAN CRUSADE

The eighth and final European Crusade was led by the king of France. It ended in A.D. 1291 with the fall of the last Christian stronghold in the Holy Land—the port city of Acre (*Akko* in Hebrew). There would not be another European attempt to liberate the Holy Land for five hundred years. And oddly enough, another French ruler, Napoleon Bonaparte, would launch it. He arrived there in 1798. After defeating Egypt and all resistance in Palestine except the garrison at the fortress of Acre, Napoleon had his artillery loaded aboard the French fleet and shipped to him at Joppa. Interestingly, the great general's noble quest failed because he suffered his first defeat in battle at Acre in 1799.

NAPOLEON AND GOD'S PROVIDENCE

By God's providence, Napoleon's canons were captured from the French fleet while being transported from Alexandria to Joppa. British Admiral Nelson intercepted and defeated the French fleet, captured Napoleon's artillery, and brought the guns ashore at Acre without Napoleon's knowledge. Napoleon arrived at Acre only to face his own deadly artillery. Some of his best and bravest soldiers were lost at this unlikely battleground before he finally gave up and left. I have closely examined some of Napoleon's cannons that are still on display at Acre. Bible prophecy and God's hand were in this. Napoleon had promised his Jewish financier's that he would capture the Holy Land and reestablish the state of Israel. But this would have been completely out of sync with God's predicted timetable. The Hebrew prophets predicted that God would bring back the scattered sons of Israel and cause the state of Israel to be reborn only in the "Last Days," shortly before the coming of the Messiah to set up the promised Kingdom of God. Napoleon's effort to restore the nation of Israel was 150 years too early. And so, one the greatest generals of all time suffered his first defeat as a result.

Mongol Invasion of Muslims

The Mongol tribes became united under a chief called Temujin in A.D. 1206. He was renamed Ghengis Khan, which means

"Supreme Ruler." He charged across the Eurasian Steppes and over the Caucasus Mountains to take on the Muslim empire.

The formidable Mongol cavalry and fierce warriors were virtually unstoppable. By 1258, the "golden horde," led by Ghengis Khan's grandson Hulagu Khan, destroyed both the Abbasid Khaliphate of Baghdad, as well as the Seljuk Sultanate in Asia Minor.

The Mongols posed a tremendous threat to Asia, the Middle East, and Europe. They were finally defeated by the Muslim Mamelukes at the battle of Ain Jalut in A.D. 1260.[184]

The greatest significance of all this to my theme is that these events created the circumstances for the rise of the Muslim Ottoman Turks to take control of the Middle East from the Arabs.

The Origin of the Ottoman Turks

Robert Goldston chronicles the events that set the stage for the Ottomans:

> After the Mongols had passed, a young Turkish mercenary named Othman [Uthman] gathered some of the shattered Seljuks forces together and began to impose order amid ruin. Othman slowly extended his martial law through Asia Minor. After many years of struggle he created the only kind of state feasible amid the wreckage left by the Mongols—a military dictatorship of which he became the first sultan.[185]

In A.D. 1288, Uthman, the first sultan of all Turks, founded the Uthman Muslim Dynasty. It soon became known by its variant name—the Ottoman Empire. They called their leaders sultans instead of khaliphs.

For the next six centuries, thirty-seven descendents of the house of Uthman, or Ottoman, ruled over the empire. It became one of the largest and richest in history. Of particular importance to our interests are three of these sultans.

Sultan *Mehmed al-Fatih* ("The Conqueror") ruled from A.D. 1451 to 1481. He was a brilliant, well-educated man who was conversant in Turkish, Arabic, Persian, and Greek literature. He loved poetry. He could also converse in Serbian and Italian. He had an insatiable thirst for literature about Alexander the Great, the Caesars, and the Roman legions. It was no doubt his study of all available literature about war and all things associated with it that enabled him to field one of the finest armies in history. He established a military tradition that remained after him.

Mehmed's greatest importance is that he conquered the eastern capital of the old Roman Empire and the center of Byzantine Christianity—Constantinople. It was renamed Istanbul and made the capital of the Ottoman Empire. A steady transfer of Islamic power began, and Istanbul became the great center of Islam.

Sultan *Salim al-Yavuz* reigned from A.D. 1512 to 1520. Although he ruled for only eight years, he added more territory to the Islamic empire than any other sultan. But most importantly, Salim conquered the Holy Land and Jerusalem for the Ottomans in 1517. They would hold control of this territory until British General Allenby liberated it four hundred years later in December 1917.

Under Sultan *Suleiman "the Magnificent,"* who ruled from A.D. 1520 to 1586, the Ottoman Empire reached its zenith of power and glory. During this time, the empire extended northward to include all of Greece, modern Bulgaria, Romania, Hungary, and all of the Balkans in what was modern Yugoslavia. They ruled the entire Mediterranean coast from Egypt to Morocco; they ruled the Sudan and all of Middle East, including Arabia; and they ruled the territories of Syria, Persia, Afghanistan, and India. Twice they nearly conquered Vienna.

It was Suleiman that rebuilt Jerusalem and its ancient walls that exist to this day. But from Suleiman's reign onward, the Ottoman Empire began a slow but steady decline. The following sultans became more interested in the size of their harems than the state of their kingdom. The empire drifted from Koranic dynamism to corrupt despotism.

The Ottoman Empire's Impact on the Middle East

Robert Goldston notes a very important development within the Muslim world of this time:

> The Ottoman Turks were not and never considered themselves to be, part of the Arab world. [They were] a cosmopolitan regime whose rulers looked upon all peoples—Bulgarians, Egyptians, Greeks, Syrians, Romanians, Persians, Lebanese, Jews and Arabs—as subject nations to be governed from, and for the benefit of, the Turkish homeland in Asia Minor. To Arabs, as to Europeans, the Ottoman Turks were essentially foreign masters.[186]

It is most important to understand what resulted from the Ottoman's attitude toward the lands and peoples they controlled: *Ottoman rule literally obliterated the state identities and boundaries of the Middle East. For the next four centuries, there were no nation-states such as Syria, Lebanon, Iraq/Babylon, Arabia, Persia, and so on.* They were simply territories ruled by Ottoman viziers from major regional cities.

"Palestine," for instance, included what is now known as Syria, Lebanon, Jordan, and Israel and was ruled from Damascus. There were no independent Arab nations and no defined boundaries.

Remember this well, for when the British liberated the area from the Ottoman Turks, no Arab had any claim on of a specific land or state that was more valid than the Jews' claim. As a matter of fact, the Jews were the only people who had a ratified mandate for a specific land from the League of Nations.

Britain Seeks to Secure the Land Bridge

Around the middle of the nineteenth century, the sultan was desperately trying to halt the slide of his empire into oblivion. There were internal threats, and there was concern over the military expansionism of Russia. At this time, long before they teamed up with czarist Russia in an alliance against Germany and Turkey, Britain and France were interested in maintaining the Ottoman Empire for geo-strategic reasons and began applying pressure on Istanbul.

The British had an almost inordinate fear of either Russia or Germany controlling the "strategic land bridge" that connected the continents of Europe, Asia, and Africa. That "bridge" begins in the north at the Bosporus Straights at Istanbul and extends southward through Turkey, Syria, Lebanon, Israel, and the Sinai—ending at the Suez Canal. The British rightly believed that it was absolutely necessary to control this area. If the land bridge fell into the hands of a hostile power, it would threaten Britain's vital link to its most important colony—India.

Relief for Dhimmis

Though the Ottoman Turks were not Arabs, they were infected with the old Arab hatred of Jews and Christians through the Koran and the Muslim traditions. They applied the Islamic dhimmi laws with a calloused cruelty.

Fortunately, because of the continuous European influence, from 1847 through about 1880, there was a brief relaxation of the institutionalized and legalized repression against Jews and Christians in the Ottoman Empire, especially in the Holy Land.

Here are excerpts from some observations noted by a Polish traveler in Palestine around A.D. 1850:

> O brothers of Israel, how can I convey to you the harshness of the yoke of exile that our brethren living in Palestine suffered

prior to the year 1847: Even were I to relate everything, would it be credible? It was a great danger for Jews to venture even a few yards outside the gates of Jerusalem because of the Arab brigands. They were accustomed to say Ashlah Yahudi, that is: "Strip yourself, Jew," and any Jew caught in such a predicament, seeing their aggressiveness and weapons, would strip, while they divided the spoil between them and sent him away naked and barefoot. They call this spoil: Kasb Allah, that is, Allah's reward.

Moreover, the seven-hour journey from Jerusalem to Hebron was fraught with danger even with a large caravan, and all the more so was a trip to smaller towns. To this day it is customary to recite a thanksgiving prayer when arriving safely at a town from another. If a Jew encounters a Muslim in the street and passes on the latter's right, the Muslim says ishmal that is, "Pass on my left side." If he touches him or bumps into him, and especially if he stains his clothing or shoes, then the Muslim attacks him cruelly and finds witnesses to the effect that the Jew insulted him, his religion and his prophet Muhammad, with the result that a numerous crowd of Muslims descend upon him and leave the Jew practically unconscious. Then they carry him off to jail, where he is subjected to terrible chastisement.

There are many more such sufferings that the pen would weary to describe. These occur particularly when we go to visit the cemetery and when we pray at the Wall of Lamentations, when stones are thrown at us and we are jeered at.[187]

More Restrictions on Jews

Though reforms made life slightly more tolerable for the Jews and Christians in the Holy Land, the local Muslims resented the edicts from Istanbul and often disregarded them. In addition, the reforms were not long lasting. Faced with a budding Zionist movement urging the return of Jews to Palestine, Istanbul repealed the reforms and enacted even more restrictive laws against Jews.

In 1887, a law was passed forbidding Jews to immigrate into Palestine, to reside there, to buy land, to restore houses, or to live in Jerusalem. It applied only to Jews but not to Christians or Muslim immigrants.[188]

Palestinians from Bosnia-Herzegovina

At the same time, to counteract the effect of Jewish emigration between 1847 and 1880, Ottoman authorities began an affirmative action program to resettle mostly European Muslims in Palestine. While the Arabs often make much of the European heritage of many of Israel's Jews—even calling them "foreign invaders"—the truth is that many of today's so called Palestinians have European roots that go back no more than a generation or two.

During the latter stages of the receding Ottoman Empire, beginning in the late 1870s, Muslim refugees from the lost Islamic provinces of Europe streamed into Palestine. "The Ottoman government settled these emigrants in troubled regions, thereby tightening its control through a policy of Muslim colonization," writes author Bat Ye'or. "In 1878 after annexation of *Bosnia-Herzegovina* by Austria, *Bosnian Muslim colonists arrived in Macedonia and on the coastal plain of Palestine.*"[189]

Ottoman Desolation of Holy Land

The Holy Land under the Ottoman Turks suffered more devastation in four hundred years than in the previous fifteen hundred years. By the nineteenth century, the ancient canal and irrigation systems were destroyed. The land was barren and filled with malaria-ridden swamps. The hills were denuded of trees and brush so that all of the terraces and topsoil were eroded away, leaving only rocks.[190]

Mark Twain writes his observations from his visit to the Holy Land in 1867: "Stirring scenes . . . occur in the valley [of Jezreel] no more," wrote Mark Twain as he described the Holy Land he visited in 1867. "There is not a solitary village throughout its whole extent—not for 30 miles in either direction. There are two or three small clusters of Bedouin tents, but not a single permanent habitation. One may ride 10 miles hereabouts and not see 10 human beings."[191]

How accurately Mark Twain described the exact conditions predicted by Ezekiel and other prophets about the land Holy Land in the Last Days—just before the Lord would began to return His people to it.

Curse of the Turk "Effendis"

Because of the horrible condition of the land in the late-nineteenth century, most Muslim inhabitants of the Holy Land were only too eager to leave if a buyer for their property could be found.

Perhaps the greatest factor in the final desertification of Palestine was the practice of the landlord class—the *effendis*—exploiting the Muslim peasants who worked the fields. In some cases, the peasant farmer would have to pay 200 to 300 percent interest to buy seeds.[192]

When the debts would reach an unbearable level, the Muslim peasant farmer would simply pack up his meager belongings and join a band of Bedouins. The land then was left without workers and became despoiled.

The steady pattern: No one really cared for the land. The absentee Ottoman effendi landlords cared only about profit and seldom left the luxury of Istanbul to even check on the land.

AMAZING JEWISH RECLAMATION

From the 1880s through 1918, the Jews returning to Palestine faced a harsh life in a barren, Malaria-infested land. But still they came. And by the turn of the century, Jewish villages dotted the countryside. A few years later, Jews represented a majority of the population in Jerusalem. There was new life in Haifa, Safed, and Tiberias. In 1909, the first modern all-Hebrew city was founded on the sands of the Mediterranean—Tel Aviv.

Far from being run off the land, the Muslim population benefited greatly from these developments. Very quickly, opportunities arose for three Arab groups:

- The landless population looking for work
- The people indebted to the absentee landlords
- The effendis themselves, who were selling land to the Jews at astronomical prices[193]

"EFFENDIS" SOW SEEDS OF MIDDLE EAST CRISIS

The effendis collected taxes for the Turkish administration and controlled the populace from seats of power on governing councils. But, before long, many of them began to see their little feudal empires threatened by the growing influence of the Jews. So, effendis resorted to the age-old tactic that always worked in Muslim history—make the Jews the scapegoats.

"It was in 1909, at the time when leading effendis felt their grip over the lives and fortunes of their erstwhile prey was getting too loose, that effendi Ruhi Bey al-Khalidi warned that the Jews would 'displace the Arab farmers from their land and their fathers' heritage. . . . The Jews were not here when we conquered the country,'" writes historian Joan Peters. "It mattered little that the effendi's argument was false. It served his group's long-range economic interests, and at least some of his misstatements would be swallowed whole by a surprisingly large part of the world for the better part of a century."[194]

Peters continues:

> Those few "Arab effendi" families . . . who had been dispossessing and then continuing to exploit the hapless peasant-migrant in underpopulated Palestine would become threatened by the spectacle of "dhimmi Jews" living on the land as equals, tilling their own soil and granting previously unknown benefits to the Arabic-speaking non-Jewish worker. The Jews would undoubtedly upset the "sweets of office" which had been accruing to the effendis. Thousands of peasant-migrants would be emigrating to reap the better wages, health benefits and improvements of the Jewish communities. Although the effendis would charge scalper's prices for land they sold to the Jews, at the same time they would lose thousands of their former debtors who saw an escape from the stranglehold of usury and corruption prevalent in Palestine for generations. In short, in "Palestine," the greatest exploitations and injustices against the peasant-migrant Muslims were committed against them by their "brother" Muslim effendis.[195]

The Jews became a victim of their own success. The more they restored the land and made it fertile, the more Muslims were attracted from nearby Muslim countries and flocked to Jewish-settled areas for jobs. These same poor Muslims who benefited from Jewish-created jobs later charged that the Jews had stolen land that had been in their families since time immemorial. This remains one of the most colossal lies of history. Yet the West has swallowed the lie hook, line, and sinker. This lie will eventually lead to Armageddon.

THE EFFECT OF WORLD WAR I ON PALESTINE

During World War I, it became clear to the Zionist leaders—Chaim Weizmann, Zeev Jabotinsky, and Aaron Aaronson—that working through the Ottoman Empire, now at war with its one-time protector Britain and the allied powers, was a no-win situation.

"Each independently came to the conclusion that Jewish restoration could be built only on the ruins of the Ottoman Empire," explains author Samuel Katz. "Each in his own way sought to provide Britain and her allies with help to win the war."[196]

The Jews' alliance with Britain during World War I, which was critical to the allies' success in the Middle East campaign, was not without heavy risks for the Jews. By this time, there was a considerable Jewish population in Palestine under Turkish rule. Every one of these lives would be in great peril if the Jewish people were to be perceived as anti-Turkish.

"Fear of Turkish reprisals . . . was overcome, however, by a more powerful emotion—the urge to national regeneration," writes Katz.[197]

What exactly did the Jews contribute to the successful allied war effort? A Jewish legion was formed to fight within the British Army for the liberation of Palestine. A Jewish auxiliary unit, the Zion Mule Corps, took part in the Gallipoli campaign. Jewish battalions comprised of volunteers from Britain, the United States, Canada, and Palestine took part in Gen. Allenby's ultimate liberation of the Holy Land. Meanwhile, in Palestine, Aaronson organized the Nili group, an indispensable intelligence service operating behind Turkish lines for the British.[198]

THE LAWRENCE OF ARABIA
MYTH'S TERRIBLE EFFECT

Movie fans might ask at this point: "Well, what about Lawrence of Arabia? Wasn't the Arab revolt key to the liberation of the

Middle East from the Turks?" To get at the truth on this issue, you have to forget the magnificent movie that was so beautifully acted by Peter O'Toole, Anthony Quinn, and Omar Sharif. It was great entertainment, but nothing close to the truth.

No folks—once again, Hollywood has helped perpetuate a gross myth on the public with its glorification of the young British army officer T. E. Lawrence and his largely fabricated Arab revolt.

Stunned by their early military disaster on the shores of Gallipoli, some British diplomatic and military leaders got the brilliant idea of bringing vast areas of the Arab-speaking world, now under Ottoman rule, under British control after the war. They envisioned "a federation of semi-independent Arab states under European guidance and supervision . . . owing spiritual allegiance to a single Arab prelate, and looking to Great Britain as patron and protector."[199]

THE BRITISH SET UP THE MIDDLE EAST CRISES

The British were about to get a lesson in the age-old Arab trait— "Promise an Arab a centimeter and he will demand a kilometer."

Another gross British miscalculation had to do with the Muslim religious power structure. The sherif of Mecca did not have the same kind of authority and control over Islam that the pope exercises over the Roman Catholics Church. Yet the British plan to control the Arabs after the war depended on this basic assumption. In fact, the Turks had destroyed the Arab Caliphate centuries before—so the British had no central authority with which to deal. There was only a bunch of warring tribes all wanting to get the best deal in the great land-grab following the collapse of the Ottoman Empire.

Britain's first step in achieving its glorious imperial ambition was to enlist the Arabs in their fight against the Turks. The first contact was with Hussein ibn-Ali, sherif of Mecca. Hussein was promised much of Arabia and vast amounts of gold and arms if he would lead a revolt against the Turks.

A key player in what followed was Lawrence, an ambitious and imaginative officer who dramatized and embellished his own heroics in the desert. It was this bit of self-aggrandizement that helped create the myth that the Arabs played a key role in the British Middle East campaign.

Indeed the one significant contribution of the Arab revolt was the capture of Aqaba. But Lawrence did not lead this campaign. It was led by Auda abu Tayi, the sheikh of the Howeitat tribe (played by Anthony Quinn in the movie). Lawrence was permitted by Auda to ride along with the Bedouin army. But by the time Lawrence returned to British headquarters, he was claiming a personal military triumph.

Nevertheless, it was not until 1955 that British writer Richard Aldington ultimately exposed the Lawrence myth, including the "key role" played by Arabs, as totally false.

THE BRITISH FOREIGN OFFICE USES THE MYTH

Even though the English knew the Lawrence affair was a myth, the British Foreign Office used it for their own purposes. They pursued their imperial dreams for the Middle East based on a policy of befriending and rewarding the Arabs, which was based entirely on the myth. This erroneous policy ultimately laid the groundwork for the Muslims to claim more and more of the land that was originally given to the Jews for a homeland by the League of Nations at the Conference of San Remo in 1921–22.

Even though the general staff of the British army knew that the Arab revolt contributed little to their victory, *they allowed the British Foreign Office to negotiate with the Arabs on the basis that they had earned the right to have independent states under their control.* And all of this based on the myth of "their great contribution to the war effort."

This policy caused enormous problems later when the Arabs pressed demands upon the British to stop Jewish immigration to Palestine. Incredibly, on the basis of the Lawrence of Arabia myth, most British Foreign Office officials thought they owed this favor to the Arabs. In fact, many Jews went to Hitler's gas ovens because of the immigration restrictions implemented on the basis of this myth.

The allied victory in World War I and the liberation of the Holy Land made it possible for the Jews to shake off the vestiges of dhimmi oppression and second-class citizenship in their own homeland. But in spite of their contributions to that victory, the Jews would face a myriad of problems that would lead to the Middle East crisis we see today. And we can thank the Middle East section of the British Foreign Office for the chaos that would follow.

TWELVE

ENGLAND AWAKENS TO BIBLE PROPHECY

"Where is your Christianity if you do not believe in their Judaism? On every altar . . . we find the table of the Jewish law . . . All the early Christians were Jews . . . every man in the early ages of the Church by whose power or zeal or genius the Christian faith was propagated, was a Jew. . . . If you had not forgotten what you owe to this people, you as Christians would be only too ready to seize the first opportunity of meeting the claims of those who profess their religion. . . . I will not take upon me the awful responsibility of excluding from the legislature those who are of the religion in the bosom of which my Lord and Saviour was born."

—BENJAMIN DISRAELI, BRITISH PRIME MINISTER[200]

TO FULLY APPRECIATE the miracle of Israel's rebirth in the modern world, it is necessary to have an understanding of the motivations of its on-again-off-again sponsor—England.

England has had a long fascination with the Holy Land, dating back to the earliest days of Christianity in Britain. Though we have Biblical records of how the Gospel was established in Rome and Spain by Paul and Peter, we have only extra-Biblical accounts of how the Gospel was first brought to Britain. The most reliable accounts contend that it was Joseph of Arimathea that first evangelized the British Isles. So an Apostle who had seen the risen

Lord Jesus and had first hand knowledge of Him founded the British Church. There is evidence that the Gospel spread very early to all of the Isles.

In search of their spiritual roots and, perhaps, their sense of nationality, the British spent several hundred years trying to conquer the Holy Land by brute military force in the name of Christianity. Generation after generation of England's best and brightest young men were sacrificed in a series of bloody Crusades determined to re-capture Jerusalem and the Holy Land.

THE IMPACT OF LITERAL INTERPRETATION

But it wasn't until the seventeenth century and the early stirrings of the Puritan movement that attitudes toward the Jews began to change. For more than fifteen hundred years, most Christians were led to believe by the Church that Israel's special covenants with God were revoked and given to the Church because of rejecting Christ. However, one of the major contributions of the sixteen-century Reformation, was the recovery of the literal or "normal" interpretation of the Scriptures. This especially impacted the Puritans. But it took awhile for the theologians to begin to apply literal interpretation to Bible prophecy, as Jesus and the Apostles had done. As soon as Christian interpreters did, Israel and the Jewish people were seen in an entirely new light. In England, the Puritans were the first to diligently study Bible prophecy using the literal method of interpretation. Because of this, the Puritans began to understand the special relationship that exists between the Jews and their promised land.

In 1948, the Jewish state was physically reborn, due in large measure to the spiritual vision of British students of prophecy and the resulting Bible conferences they held that influenced the whole nation—including even members of Parliament.

In 1649, Jews were officially forbidden from residing in England, even though they had already been there some 350 years. But two English Puritans, Joanna and Ebenezer Cartwright, got the idea to petition the government to repeal the ban and sponsor an effort to transport European Jews to the Holy Land for the purpose of restoring the nation of Israel.

"That this Nation of England, with the inhabitants of the Netherlands, shall be the first and the readiest to transport Israel's sons and daughters in their ships to the Land promised to their forefathers, Abraham, Isaac and Jacob for an everlasting inheritance [is our purpose]," they wrote.[201]

The Puritans took the Bible seriously—both the Old and New Testament. They were quick to see that the prophecies regarding the Second Coming of Christ all presupposed a reborn-Jewish nation comprised of people who had been scattered into "every nation throughout the world."

England As Way Station

As I said, there were no Jews in England after 1649 when they were driven out. So as a pre-requisite to the ultimate fulfillment of prophecy— the rebirth of Israel—the British Puritans believed it was first necessary to bring Jews back into England from Holland. Many Jews who had fled Spain and Portugal had settled and flourished in Holland.

But why bring Jews to England? Even the Puritans were not yet totally free of the prejudices and misguided ideas Crusaders had developed about the Jews. So they believed Jews first had to be converted to Christianity before England could take them to the Holy Land to fulfill the prophecies. The Puritans failed to see that prophecies like Ezekiel's clearly show that the Israelites would not fully come to faith in their true Messiah until *after* the state of Israel was miraculously reborn.

As Barbara Tuchman explains it: "The movement was not for the sake of the Jews, but for the sake of the promise made to them. According to Scripture the kingdom of God for all mankind would come when the people of Israel were restored to Zion. Only then would the world see the advent of the Messiah or, in Christian terms, The Second Advent."[202]

The Puritans saw the return only in terms of an ethnically Jewish nation converted to Christianity. Therefore, the Jews must first come to England. The Puritans were certain that Jews exposed to Puritan teaching in England could be persuaded that Jesus was their Messiah. After all, the Puritans reasoned, they were fluent in Hebrew and the Old Testament traditions and rituals. How could they fail?

The Puritans' Use of the Old Testament

The English Puritans, a people who shared with the ancient Hebrews the experience of persecution, were indeed captivated by the Old Testament.

"They baptized their children by the names not of Christian saints but of Hebrew patriarchs and warriors," wrote historian T. B. Macauley. "They turned the weekly festival by which the church had from primitive times commemorated the resurrection of the Lord, into the Jewish Sabbath. They sought for precedents to guide their ordinary conduct in the books of Judges and Kings."[203]

Imagine that! In England in the mid-seventeenth century names like Mary and John were considered passé, while Old Testament favorites like Enoch, Amos, Obadiah, Job, Seth, Eli, Esther, and Rebecca were all the rage! No Old Testament names were overlooked. There are records of English Puritans of the day named Zerrubabel, Habakkuk, and even Shadrack, Meshach, and Abednego.[204]

These were serious Bible scholars. Some of them were said to rise at 3 or 4 a.m., eat a raw egg and study the Scriptures until evening. Not surprisingly, it was in this sober Christian environment that believers began to understand the prophecies of the End-times, especially those concerning Israel.

Jews Share the Vision

The Jews of the mid-1600s also began to think the time was right to live out that old hope: "Next year in Jerusalem." Manasseh ben Israel, a respected rabbi in Amsterdam, became convinced that the first step toward the fulfillment of the rebirth of Israel was emigration to England. Like the Puritans, he believed the Jewish Diaspora had to reach every nation before the return to the Holy Land began.

Partly because he was caught up in the prophetic fervor, and partly for strategic and economic reasons over his war with Holland and Portugal, Oliver Cromwell exhorted his Parliament to aid in the restoration of the Jewish nation. He reasoned, "Truly you are called by God as Judah was to rule with Him and for Him. You are at the edge of the Promises and Prophecies."[205]

The Parliament, however, did not agree. Members couldn't have agreed, because it was not yet God's time. The rebirth of Israel was still several centuries away. It had to happen in concert with a whole predicted scenario, and that was not yet present.

However, all was not lost. Though Parliament refused to go along with Cromwell's whole program, the ban of Jewish emigration to England was tacitly disregarded. England proved a haven for Jews during and after England's war with Spain in 1656.

"There first stirrings in Puritan England of interest in the restoration of Israel were unquestionably religious in origin, born out of the Old Testament reign over the mind and faith of the party in power during the middle years of the seventeenth century," writes Tuchman. "But religion was not enough."

No practical results would have come out of the Puritans' sense of brotherhood with the children of Israel, or out of their ideals of toleration, or out of their mystical hopes of hastening the millennium, had not political and economic expediency intervened.

Cromwell's interest in Manasseh ben Israel's proposal was dictated by the same factor that dictated Lloyd George's interest in

Chaim Weizmann's proposal ten generations later: namely, the aid that each believed the Jews could render in a wartime situation. And from Cromwell's time on, every future episode of British concern with Palestine depended on the twin presence of the profit motive, whether commercial, military or imperial, and the religious motive inherited from the Bible."[206]

The Next Attempt

The great British scientist Sir Isaac Newton (A.D. 1643–1727) was one of those visionaries who initially got the literal interpretation of prophecy moving. He was one of the first scholars to study prophecy as something other than just a collection of allegories, symbols, poems, and meaningless metaphors that had already been fulfilled in past history. After a lifetime of study in Bible prophecy, he predicted, *"About the time of the End, a body of men will be raised up who will turn their attention to the prophecies, and insist on their literal interpretation in the midst of much clamor and opposition."*

As one of those who has been part of the fulfillment of this prediction, I can testify that there is plenty of opposition to the insistence that Bible prophecy is going to be literally fulfilled— and sooner than you think!

No doubt the far-reaching revival of interest in prophecy that occurred at the beginning of the nineteenth century greatly affected the general population of England. Even some of the aristocracy who later became high government officials were deeply affected. This revival was the direct result of the previous turn to literal interpretation of the Bible that began with the Reformation under Luther and spread to the Puritans. It took longer for this method to be applied to prophecy, but by the early eighteen hundreds, it was in full bloom.

Many annual camp meetings were set up to pursue and learn about Bible prophecy. Such articulate luminaries in this movement as John Darby and Sir Robert Anderson spoke to large crowds about the sudden coming of Jesus Christ for His church. They also linked the return of God's ancient people to the Holy Land as an indispensable part of the final scenario of predicted events. They not only believed in a literal rebirth of the state of Israel, but also insisted that God's purpose for the Jews as a people and a nation, which was promised throughout the Old Testament, would then be fulfilled.

Lord Shaftesbury and Lord Albert Lindsey

In an earlier chapter we discussed how England intervened with the sultan in 1840 on behalf of the Jews already living in the Holy Land. The decision to prod the Turks toward a more humane treatment and acceptance of the Jews was inspired by Anthony Ashley Cooper, the seventh Earl of Shaftesbury, another Englishman who believed deeply in the promises of the Bible and their literal meaning.

Besides promoting the restoration of Israel, this Bible-believing Christian is also credited by historians with pushing through Parliament laws that dramatically improved working and living conditions for the wretched poor of England. In fact, that is what Lord Shaftesbury is most remembered for. But he also worked diligently on behalf of those he called reverently "God's ancient people."[207]

Belief in the Second Coming of Jesus Christ "has always been a moving principle of my life, for I see everything going in the world subordinate to this great event." He told his biographer. He confidently believed on the basis of the Scriptural evidence that the return of the Jews was indispensable to the Second Coming.[208]

But Shaftesbury, like his contemporary evangelicals and his seventeenth-century Puritan forebears, still believed that the Jews must be converted before Israel could or would be reborn.

He believed Israel should be restored under the aegis of the Anglican Church. He foresaw the day when a converted Jew would preside as the consecrated Anglican bishop in Jerusalem. This effort, obviously, did not meet with a great deal of success.

Interestingly, Lord Shaftesbury and his contemporaries were persuaded of the important role of the Jews in restoring Israel by the books of Lord Albert Lindsey, who wrote eloquently about how the barrenness and decay of the Holy Land was due to the "removal of the ancient inhabitants."[209]

Lord Lindsey wrote, "The Jewish race, so wonderfully preserved, may yet have another stage of national existence opened to them, they may once more obtain possession of their native land. The soil of Palestine still enjoys her Sabbaths, and only waits for the return of her banished children, and the application of industry, commensurate with her agricultural capabilities, to burst once more into universal luxuriance, and be all that she ever was in the days of Solomon."[210]

Shaftesbury and other British evangelicals of his day were also influenced by the Frenchman Napoleon Bonaparte, who, in 1798, had pledged to conquer Palestine and "restore the country to the Jews." He of course, failed, as I explained in a previous chapter.

Not for Naught

The efforts of these men of vision were not fruitless. England took up the cause of restoring Israel once more in the early twentieth century. But Lord Balfour's declaration would not have been possible without the strong Biblical case that had been made for Israel by British Christians in the eighteenth and especially the nineteenth centuries.

Following Lord Shaftesbury, another Englishman became taken by the idea of restoring Israel. Benjamin Disraeli, who would one day rise to become prime minister, was one of the most provocative figures in British history. A Jewish convert to

Christianity, he was more concerned with the world's debt to the Jews than the Jews' future in the world. In 1878, Disraeli recaptured Cyprus for Britain and purchased Suez—both geographically speaking a mere stone's throw from the Holy Land. Disraeli knew that it was just a matter of time.

Meet Lord Balfour

The next British leader to catch the vision for restoring the state of Israel was Arthur James Balfour, who, as England's foreign minister, signed the famous Balfour Declaration that mandated the recreation of the Jewish state. He, too, believed religion and civilization in general, owed Judaism "an immeasurable debt, shamefully ill repaid."[211]

Freshly deposed as prime minister in 1906, Balfour set out on a personal mission. Having met Chaim Weizmann, the leader of the Zionist movement who would one day be Israel's first head of government, Balfour saw an opportunity not only to bring the Holy Land back to life but also, as he put it, to do "something material to wash out an ancient stain upon our own civilization."[212]

His motivations were made even clearer in a speech he delivered to the House of Lords in 1922:

> This is the ideal which chiefly moves me . . . that Christendom is not oblivious to their [Jews'] faith, is not unmindful of the service they have rendered to the great religions of the world, and that we desire to the best of our ability to give them the opportunity of developing in peace and quietness under British rule, those great gifts which hitherto they have been compelled to bring to fruition in countries which know not their language and belong not to their race.[213]

While Lord Balfour's motivations were clear, the motives of the others who were responsible for the mandate and what followed were more suspect. The World War I campaign in the Middle East was the paramount concern. And the Jews had much to offer—strategically and militarily.

In 1917, Britain's Palestine policy was being shaped by many hands—from Cabinet ministers to bureaucrats. But, nevertheless, on October 13, the Cabinet authorized the foreign secretary to issue the Balfour Declaration that promised the Jews a homeland after the war.

A few days later, the *London Times* published a story about a celebration by the British Zionist Federation. "Its outstanding features," said the *Times*, "were the Old Testament spirit which pervaded it and the feeling that, in the somewhat incongruous setting of a London theatre, the approaching fulfillment of ancient prophecy was being celebrated with faith and fervor."

"It was appropriate that it should be so," concludes author David Fromkin. "Biblical prophecy was the first and most enduring of the many motives that led Britons to want to restore the Jews to Zion."[214]

In the next chapter, however, we will see how those good motives were hijacked on the way to Jerusalem.

THIRTEEN

BRITAIN'S BETRAYAL: THE SELLOUT OF THE JEWS

"This land is capable of supporting a large population if irrigated and cultivated scientifically. . . . The Zionists have as much right to this no-man's land as the Arabs, or more.
— Arnold Toynbee[215]

"If we must have preferences, let me murmur in your ear that I prefer Arabs to Jews."
— Anthony Eden, British secretary of foreign affairs[216]

ELEMENTS OF BETRAYAL

Of all the injustices perpetrated against the Jewish people in the Holy Land, the worst is the way their land has been continually reduced from its original mandated seize. As we have seen, historical evidence shows that during the four centuries under Ottoman control, the Holy Land reached its ultimate state of desolation.

During that period, the absentee landlord effendis practiced such calloused usury and taxation on the poor Arab's who attempted to farm the land that they all were eventually overwhelmed with debt and fled the land. By the beginning of the nineteenth century, every report from officials and visitors described a land virtually absent of any settled people. Remarks such as these call attention to the terrible condition of the land, and speak of hardly any living souls inhabiting the vast desolation that lay between the few villages and towns.

True history also reveals there has continually been a sizable Jewish remnant living in the Holy Land despite the Roman destruction of Israel in A.D. 70 and the final crushing of Jewish rebellions in the second century A.D. Amazingly, as we jump forward to the eighteenth and nineteenth centuries, the number of Jews living in Jerusalem actually exceeded the number of Muslims.

Another very important factor we saw in previous chapters is that the Arab-Muslim world of the nineteenth-century Middle East was totally wiped clean of national entities. All semblances of independent states and nationalism were crushed during the centuries of harsh Ottoman occupation of the Arabs. All that was left were tribal sheikdoms that warred with each other constantly, and the small Arab Hashemite Kingdom of the Hedjaz region that controlled Mecca and Medina.

Whence Cometh the Palestinians?

There never was any such thing as a Palestinian state—much less a people known as "Palestinians." The few Arabic-speaking people that lived there thought of themselves as "Ottomans," "Turks," "Southern Syrians," or simply as "Arab people," but never as "Palestinians." The migratory Bedouins who seasonally moved through the area never had any claim to the land.

The Jews who began to come to the Holy Land in earnest during the mid-nineteenth century bought land from the all-too-willing-to-sell Ottoman effendis and the few local owners, who also were delighted to sell the desolated lands for enormously inflated prices.

Jews Become "Victims" of Their Success

At the price of Herculean labor and the loss of many lives to malaria, the Jews began to reclaim the land and make it flourish. This is when a significant number of poor Arab-Muslim people flocked to the land the Jews had settled, to find work and a better standard of living. Becoming victims of their own success, little did these Jews realize that these migrant Arabs they were helping would later claim that the Jews had "stolen their land that had belonged to their families from time immemorial." Most of these so-called Palestinian refugees couldn't even establish to the UN officials sent to help them that they had lived in Palestine more than two years before fleeing in 1948 to allow the Arab armies to annihilate the new state of Israel.

The Balfour Declaration

This was the condition of the Middle East the British Parliament knew. It was because of full knowledge of all these conditions that Lord Balfour and other members of the British Parliament thought it not an invasion of Arab-Muslim land to set forth the propositions contained in the Balfour Declaration. The motto of the British forming committee was, *"A people for a land, for a land without a people."* Furthermore, the League of Nations concurred with the declaration for all the same reasons. As we have noted in this and in previous chapters, apart from a few villages and towns, the land was an utter desolation devoid of people. No one could live in it until the returning Jews almost miraculously restored it.

It was because of the above facts that the actual Balfour Declaration of 1917 was a rather simple statement. A simple statement was thought all that was necessary. It committed Britain to work toward the establishment of a Jewish homeland in the vast wasteland of the area designated as the Palestinian territory. It reads:

> His Majesty's Government view with favor the establishment in Palestine of a national home for the Jewish people, and will use their best endeavors to facilitate the achievement of this object, it being clearly understood that nothing shall be done which may prejudice the civil and religious rights of existing non-Jewish communities in Palestine or the rights and political status enjoyed by Jews in any other country.

With its passage in the Parliament, Lord Balfour expressed the Parliament's general feelings, saying, "We hope that the 'small notch' of Palestine being given the Jews would not be 'grudged' by the Arab leaders."

Now look at the map (No. 1) on page 184, and see what Lord Balfour referred to as "a small notch" of Palestine. This map shows the borders specifically designated for a Jewish National Homeland by the Balfour Declaration in 1917.

On January 4, 1919, a formal agreement on this mandated Jewish homeland illustrated by map No. 1 was signed in London. The signatories were: His Royal Highness the Emir Feisal ibn-Hussein, representing and acting on behalf of the Arab Kingdom of Hedjaz, and Chaim Weitzmann, representing and acting on behalf of the Zionist Organization.[217]

The Balfour Declaration was the end product of a great many debates and compromises within the British government but, without question, reflects the unequivocal goal at the time. Later, all kinds of ridiculous interpretations were placed on the declaration, but representatives of all sides clearly and unambiguously understood at the time: A Jewish state was to be established as soon as Jewish immigration and development was sufficient in the barren wilderness of Palestine.

Map 1

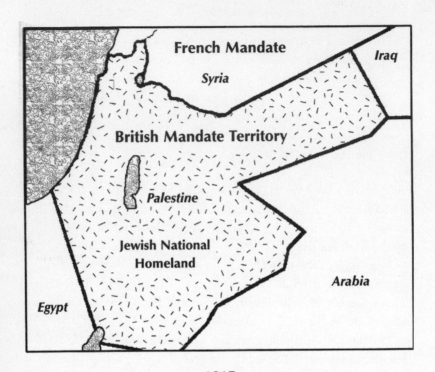

1917

The Jewish National Homeland

The Balfour Declaration

The League of Nations Mandate

The boundaries of this new nation were codified and approved unanimously by the League of Nations five years later (1924) with Britain being given authority over the entire Middle East, from the Mediterranean to the borders of India. The territory that would become the state of Israel—then variously referred to as "Palestine," "Western Palestine," "South Syria," or even as part of Turkey—extended east and west of the Jordan River from the Mediterranean to Arabia and Iraq, and north and south from Egypt to Lebanon and Syria. On today's map, that would include most of the Arab nations of Jordan, southern Lebanon, and the Sinai. (See map No. 2 on page 186)

At the same time, independent Arab statehood was being granted to Syria, Iraq, and Saudi Arabia. With this giant landmass being turned over to Arab control, Lord Balfour hoped that the "small notch" of Palestine being given to the Jews would not be "grudged" by Arab leaders. The land originally given here was considerably bigger than today's Jewish state, even if you include the territories Israel captured in June 1967. There is some evidence to show that Arab leaders were initially satisfied with their acquisition and unquestioning as far as the status of Jewish Palestine.

In a letter to then-Colonial Secretary Winston Churchill from Col. T. E. Lawrence in January 1921, Lawrence it stated that Emir Feisal, the man who had led the Arab revolt, had "agreed to abandon all claim of his father to [Western] Palestine," if Feisal got Iraq and Eastern Palestine as Arab territories. (See copy of letter in Appendix A) In fact, Emir Feisal had written in his own hand a letter agreeing to exactly this in a 1919 meeting with Zionist representative Chaim Weizmann. (See Appendix B)

Furthermore, in an agreement worked out between Chaim Weizmann, leader of the British Zionist movement, and Feisal, both sides pledged the "closest possible collaboration" and "most cordial goodwill" in working out the details of the creation of the

Map 2

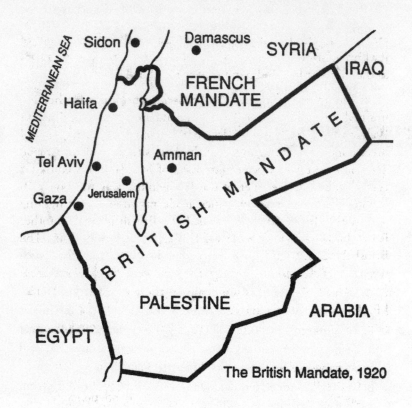

The British Mandate, 1920

modern Arab states and Israel.[218] (See complete copy of Agreement in Appendix C).

The Arabs probably felt magnanimous at the time because they had just come out of having nothing of their own during the many centuries of the Ottoman occupation. Then suddenly Britain hands them an enormous gift of land and sovereign states for doing virtually nothing to earn it. This is why Lord Balfour could not imagine that they would "begrudge the small notch of land" the Jews were being given.

Britain Gives Away 75 Percent of the Jew's Mandated Land

It wasn't long, however, before Abdullah, brother of Feisal ibn-Hussein, decided he should have Transjordan as his kingdom. He protested to the British, who unilaterally decided to carve out of the Jewish Palestine mandate 75 percent of its territory, the area then known as Transjordan, and hand it over to Abdullah.[219]

The main reason Abdullah, who was a Hashemite, was in Transjordan was because the tribe of Ibn Saud and his fanatical sect of Wahabi Muslims had just driven the Hashemite tribe out of Mecca and Medina. The Hashemites had been custodians of those holy sites for centuries, but now the Wahabis were in charge of Mecca and Medina and all of Arabia.

Feisal, the ruler of the Hashemites, was the one with whom the British Foreign Office made promises for fighting against the Turks. Abdullah argued that the British gave his brother Feisal Ibn-Hussein both Syria and Iraq, but had given him nothing. So the British Foreign Office scrambled to give Abdullah the major part of the land they were bound by League of Nation mandate to give to Israel. Now recall, this was all done on the basis of the T. E. Lawrence myth that said they had significantly helped Britain defeat the Ottoman Turks in the Middle East.

The League of Nations mandate for Palestine remained unchanged even though Britain had unilaterally altered its map and its purpose," explains Joan Peters. "The Mandate included Transjordan until 1946, when that land was declared an independent state. Transjordan had finally become the de jure Arab state in Palestine just two years before Israel gained its Jewish statehood in the remaining one-quarter of Palestine; Transjordan comprised nearly 38,000 square miles; Israel, less than 8,000 square miles."[220] (See map No. 3 on page 189)

How Britain Violated Its Mandate

When Britain gave Transjordan to Abdullah, it specifically violated Article 5 of the mandate given by the unanimous approval of the League of Nations at the San Remo Conference July 24, 1922. (See complete document in Appendix C)

Article 5 stated, "The Mandatory [Britain] shall be responsible for seeing that no Palestine territory shall be ceded or leased to, or in any way placed under the control of, the Government of any foreign Power." Abdullah was a foreign power and certainly not part of the Zionist organization to whom Transjordan had been given.

The local British officials of the Foreign Office grossly violated the main reason for Britain being given the mandate by the League of Nations. They were specifically charged *only* with facilitating the immigration of Jews to Palestine to populate and settle the land that had been granted as a Jewish homeland. Britain had express instructions *not* to allow or facilitate more immigration of Arabs into the land mandated for the Jewish homeland.

As the following details will show, the British did exactly the opposite of what they were mandated to do. They increasingly restricted Jewish immigration while opening the floodgates to Arab immigration.

Map 3

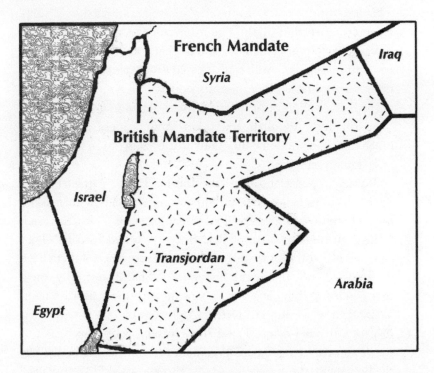

1921

35,000 square miles of the Jewish National Homeland were given to Arabs (80% of their promised land was lost).

The Real Palestinian State

This historical footnote to the Arab-Israeli conflict should shatter another Muslim myth. The modern-day state known as the Royal Kingdom of Jordan was and is clearly and literally an independent Palestinian-Arab state located geographically on most of the land once called Palestine. Its population is mostly made up of the former migrant Arab farmers who began to call themselves "Palestinians." Abdullah and other Arab leaders admitted as much just prior to launching their war of aggression against the new state of Israel in 1948.

Western Media thought that former Prime Minister Ariel Sharon was just being sarcastic and evasive when a newsman asked him, "If he would give the Palestinians a state." He answered, "There already is a state of Palestine—it's called Jordan." That sounded preposterous to the reporters, because most of them have no knowledge of that area's history. But Sharon not only knew that history well, he is a living eyewitness to the reasons Chaim Weizmann was willing to forfeit 75 percent of Israel's mandated territory. It was because Feisal Ibn-Hussein, acting on behalf of the Arab people, signed an agreement that this would be used as the homeland of any migrant Arabs, also known as "Palestinians," that might be displaced by the mandated Jewish homeland.

"Palestine and Transjordan are one, for Palestine is the coastline and Transjordan the hinterland of the same country," said Abdullah. His prime minister, Hazza al-Majali, went even further: "We are the army of Palestine . . . the overwhelming majority of the Palestine Arabs are living in Jordan."[221] This confirms that the Arabs recognized Jordan as a homeland of the so-called Palestinians.

East and West Palestine

It is the forgotten concept of "Eastern" and "Western" Palestine that is at the root of another Arab myth. Because as we have seen already, most of the Palestinian population was "excluded from the new state of Israel not by force but by where borders were drawn on the map by the British, false assumptions have been perpetuated on the world. This is at the root of why people generally accept the idea that Jews forced Palestinians out of their homeland. As we have seen in earlier chapters, the settled Muslim population in what became the Jewish state only began growing after the time Jewish emigration began in the 1880s through 1948. The evidence repeatedly shows that the migrant Arab workers came to Palestine seeking jobs after the Jews began to reclaim the land.

As Peters, who conducted a first-hand population study in the region, puts it: "The 'unprecedented' sudden 'natural' increase among Arabs of Western Palestine after centuries of static population figures was intriguing. That extraordinary increase was represented as a countrywide 'phenomenon.'"[222]

The purpose of Peters' original study was "to determine whether in fact there was a large-scale displacement of Arab natives by Jews in Western Palestine before and at the time of the November 1947–1948 war of Arabs against Jewish independence." Peters admits that when she began the investigation her sympathies were with the "Palestinian refugees." She expected to find evidence of Israeli aggression against helpless Palestinians and of Jewish occupation of Palestinian family lands.

Peters was astonished at the evidence she found. She writes, "What the calculations indicate is that, rather than a situation in which a teeming Arab people, present 'from time immemorial,' was forced off or excluded from its land, the situation is almost the exact opposite . . . the Jews, whose presence attracted Arab migrants, and the Jews' land, earmarked as their Home, was usurped by the arrival of these Arab in-migrants from outside Jewish-settled areas."[223]

More Falsehoods Discovered

Peters also found in her original population investigation:

- Even the earlier conservative estimates of Muslim population in the Jewish-settled areas of Palestine had been grossly exaggerated.[224]
- Arabs indeed migrated from the depressed areas of the region to those places where they could gain greater economic advantage in the Jewish-settled areas.[225]

Overlooking the Obvious

So, why was this factor of "explosive Arab population growth" not investigated or at least considered before? It was simply because the British never attempted to count Arab in-migration or illegal Arab immigration. They only quantified Jewish immigration into the Holy Land, and they did this with scrupulous zeal for details. Furthermore, Peters found, the population was never accurately identified by location or analyzed according to Jewish and non-Jewish areas.

Amazingly, the false assumptions in subsequent generations have been that "all Palestine was Jewish-settled" and "Jewish-settled Palestine was all Arab Palestine." Most of the British Foreign Service could never get it through their heads that the Jews came to a land that was an utter desolation and almost entirely barren of settled people of any kind. But some influential British Foreign Service officers did not care what the facts were. They just didn't like Jews.

So what made the British turn a blind eye toward this kind of one-sided population movement? Clearly, within the British

Foreign Service there were men who wanted to see the idea of a Jewish state fail. For the sake of their own imperial ambitions in the Middle East, they preferred working with the Arabs rather than with the more troublesome, independently minded Jews.

Underlings Secretly Reverse Foreign Policy

When British Gen. Edmund Allenby walked reverently into Jerusalem, leading his army of liberation on December 9, 1917, he was set to institute a military government. Unfortunately, virtually the entire staff of Ronald Storrs, the governor of Jerusalem, was riddled with army officers who did not believe in the principles of the Balfour Declaration. Without authorization, they reversed on the field the official policy of their government and sabotaged the mandate given their country by the League of Nations. Had this been discovered and investigated at the time, it would have been considered a crime at best and treason at worst. These men betrayed the official policy of their government.

One example of this group's illegal action was when Gov. Storrs decided to placate the spiritual leader of the Muslims of Jerusalem, Haj Amin al-Husseini, the grand mufti of Jerusalem. You will recall from earlier in the book that al-Husseini stayed for a couple of years in Nazi Germany as the special guest of Adolf Hitler, learning how to deal with "the Jewish Problem." The Grand Mufti Husseini, to whom Yasser Arafat was related, used a subtle blend of religious rhetoric, threats, terror, and very real physical violence to get his way. And, as much as he used the British, those pro-Arab Foreign Service officers also tried to use him.

Britain Enacts Harsher Restrictions on Jews

From 1920 on, partly as a result of anti-Jewish terrorism, British policy focused almost exclusively on limiting the immigration of Jews into Palestine. For the Arabs, a different set of rules applied.

"In actuality, British restrictions against Jewish emigration were harsher and more discriminatory than even those of the Turks."[226]

There were dissenters among the British officers' corps—men who were disgusted by the seemingly official tolerance of Arab violence against Jews. They were ridiculed by their colleagues and often reassigned. They were overruled because an even-handed approach might alienate the Arab leaders and jeopardize Britain's tenuous imperial plans for Arabia.

The Infamous White Papers

By 1930, the British began to rationalize and justify their anti-Jewish policies in Palestine with a series of papers—first being the "Hope-Simpson Report." Prompted by the 1929 Arab massacres of Jews and other disturbances, it concluded that the best way to prevent further bloodshed was to limit Jewish immigration and land purchases even more. The report admitted that illicit Arab immigration had, in fact, crowded out many opportunities for Jewish refugees in their designated national homeland. But its solution was to deny any more Jewish settlement.[227]

Now that was a splendid display of justice—stop further bloodshed by punishing the victim and rewarding the criminal. It doesn't take a rocket scientist to figure out that the Arabs would be encouraged to pour on more violence to ultimately get the Jews removed from Palestine altogether "in order to avoid more bloodshed."

The Passfield-White Paper

Shortly after the "Hope-Simpson Report," came the infamous "Passfield-White Paper" of 1930, which mandated that Jewish emigration would be suspended and that landless Arabs would be given property to cultivate. In the future, the "White Paper" stated, a resumption of Jewish immigration would depend on an improvement in the Arab employment picture. In effect, the Jews were now being relegated to a permanent minority status, subject only to the future whims of decidedly pro-Arab British officials.

Keep in mind that under League of Nations mandate, Britain was charged only with facilitating the immigration of Jews, not Arabs. And also bear in mind that the British were seeking to give to those migrant Arabs things that their own Arab brothers had never considered giving them. But the whole process— per usual in the Middle East—was turned upside-down by British administrators who had little or no knowledge of the region's history. Not that it would have made any difference to most of them.

Israel "Downsized" Again

By 1937, the situation in Palestine had deteriorated greatly and the British conducted another of "their many studies." The "Royal Commission Report," somewhat more evenhanded than its predecessors, at least acknowledged the primary purpose of the mandate was to facilitate the creation of a Jewish homeland. But it also came to the conclusion that the original mandate for the homeland would have to be downsized significantly and partitioned into one Jewish state and one Arab. (See map No. 4, i.e., the Partition into a Jewish and an Arab State in the territory mandated to the Jews.)

So the Arabs once again succeeded in slicing off another piece of the mandated land that was originally given to the Jews by the League of Nations. Never mind that the Arab Muslims had been given 98 percent of the Middle East land liberated from the Ottoman Turks. Glaringly apparent in the history of this era is this familiar theme: If Israel owned even one square meter of land in the Holy Land, it would still be too much for the Arabs to bear.

Accessories to Mass Murder

It is particularly striking that the illegal Arab immigration into Palestine continued and the British continued to place roadblocks in the way of Jewish immigration—even at a time (1937–38) when wholesale persecution of the Jews by the Nazis was under way in Poland and Germany. At this point in history, Hitler was eager to permit Jews to emigrate, but no nation in the world was willing to accommodate their vast numbers, including the United States, which was in the Great Depression.

"I can only hope and expect that the other world, which has such deep sympathy for these criminals [Jews], will at least be generous enough to convert this sympathy into practical aid," Hitler mocked in a 1938 speech. "We on our part, are ready to put all these criminals at the disposal of these countries, for all I care, even on luxury ships."228

In spite of this clear and apparent danger posed to the Jews by Hitler, Britain refused to allow anything more than "very limited" immigration into Palestine.

In fact, a year later in the 1939 "White Paper," they completely reversed the intent of the Balfour Declaration and the League of Nations mandate. They had the audacity to announce that Britain had no intention of facilitating the re-creation of the Jewish state. And why? Because, the British Foreign Service said, "This would be contrary to our [England's] obligations to the Arabs."229

Lost Honor! Lost Empire!

Talk about lack of honor and character. I believe that these very actions are responsible for God destroying the British Empire. Shortly after the end of World War II, the mighty world empire of Great Britain became a memory. Remember, God promised Abraham and his descendants, "I will bless those who bless you, and curse those who curse you."

These actions also guaranteed that Hitler's gas ovens would be full. It is not overstating the case to say that the British policy of appeasement of the Arabs was the direct cause of hundreds of thousands of Jews going to the gas chambers. The British version of their "final solution"—outlined in the 1939 "White Paper"— would limit Jewish immigration to ten thousand a year for five years, at which point it would be terminated unless the Arabs of Palestine were willing to accept more! Is there anyone stupid enough to think they ever would accept more when they wanted only to annihilate the ones who were already there?

The leader of the Arabs in Palestine was our old friend Haj Amin al-Husseini, who had by now been appointed by the British as grand mufti of Jerusalem. Since the early 1930s, he had made no secret of his close affinity for the Nazis and their final solution for the Jews. He kept a copy of Hitler's *Mein Kampf* next to his Koran.

Haj Amin was in fact a pathological murderer who masterminded the killing of Arabs as well as Jews. He secretly fomented the anti-British, anti-Zionist riots of 1936–1939. When this became known, he had to flee Palestine, escaping through Iraq to Nazi Germany where he became a confidante to Hitler. He also organized Muslims from Bosnia to fight alongside the elite German Waffen SS troops.[230]

Britain's Most Shameful Hour

The anti-Jewish attitude among the British had reached a zenith. After the latest restrictions on Jewish immigration were announced, the British cabled their ambassador in Berlin and instructed him to ask the Germans to discourage Jews who might think of illegally traveling to Palestine! That was like pleading with the hangmen not to let their victims escape.

Let me say here that it is not fair to characterize British policy as reflecting the will of all Englishmen. In fact, quite a few outspoken leaders harshly criticized their country's betrayal of the

Jews. Winston Churchill, for one, saw it clearly as a continuation of Neville Chamberlain's policy of appeasement.

Nevertheless, the strict limits on Jewish immigration remained throughout the war. And by 1945, over six million Jews had been systematically murdered in Europe. Only fifty-one thousand had been permitted to immigrate to Palestine. Incredibly, however, at the same time, the British continued to wink at illegal immigration into Palestine by the Arabs.

The Turning Point

This was the thanks from the British that the Jews got for their loyalty and patience and long-suffering. But the issuance of the "White Paper of 1939" sparked a new attitude among some of the Zionists. Now the Jews, while fighting alongside the British against the Nazis, would also defy British attempts to isolate and neutralize the Jews in Palestine.

It was only through this newfound Jewish militancy—an antidote to the pressure constantly exerted by the Arabs upon the British—that Israel was reborn in 1948.

Had the British followed their own declaration and the League of Nations mandate they were honor-bound to implement, the rebirth of Israel would have happened a lot sooner.

Had the British enforced their own laws against the effendis' usury, extortion, and exploitation of the Arab peasantry instead of defending Muslims' anti-Jewish incitements, the rebirth of Israel would have happened a lot sooner.

Had the British had the good sense to allow more Jews to immigrate to Palestine, the Nazi Holocaust might have been avoided.

The Price of Britain's Betrayal

Great Britain received a terrible punishment in World War II. London and other major cities were bombed and ravaged by

Hitler's Luftwaffe. Before England's infamous treatment of the Jews and the betrayal of the mandate, "the sun never set on the British Empire."

Even though the Allies won the war, the British Empire came to an end. Britain is only a shadow of its former glory. I don't believe this is a coincidence. I believe it was a direct result of the British betrayal of the Jewish people and the Jewish nation. The God of Abraham, Isaac, and Jacob still keeps His Word: "I will curse those who curse you."

And now, the United States is the main party pushing Israel into a further reduction of the land originally allotted to it. The Obama Administration has adopted the most anti-Israel policies of any American president in history. We are foolishly pushing Israel to accept a Palestinian state filled with Muslim terrorists who believe it is their duty to Allah to destroy Israel.

President Obama continues to favor the Muslims and to give them more advantages than ever before. We have learned to not listen to what he says, but to watch what he does.

The new borders now being pushed upon Israel will make it indefensible by conventional military means. Once those borders are established, Israel will have only one assurance that they will not be attacked—"the promises of the Muslims." No one in his right mind would base his survival on those empty words. History and the doctrines of Islam teach the folly of relying on such an assurance.

In the interest of short-term peace, we are courting nuclear war. Israel already has the "Samson Option" plan in place in case the Muslim armies overrun them. This "Option" will vaporize the Arab capitals with thermonuclear warheads. I will have much more to say about this in the final chapter.

Are we in the U.S. not presently doing the same thing the British did—only worse? Let us pray that our leaders will not continue this insane policy. For the God of Israel will certainly keep His Word—but this time against us, the United States of America.

The rapid disintegration of the once mighty British Empire is an object lesson in recent history that should not be ignored.

It is a fearful thing to defy the Word of the living God. If you don't believe that, buckle up. You will soon find out.

FOURTEEN

ISRAEL:
A MIRACLE NATION

"This is what the LORD says, he who appoints the sun to shine by day, who decrees the moon and stars to shine by night, who stirs up the sea so that its waves roar—the LORD Almighty is his name: 'Only if these decrees vanish from my sight,' declares the LORD, 'will the descendants of Israel ever cease to be a nation before me.'"

—JEHOVAH, THE GOD OF ABRAHAM, ISAAC AND JACOB[231]

"We shall never call for or accept a negotiated peace. We shall only accept war—Jihad—the holy war. We have resolved to drench the lands of Palestine and Arabia with the blood of the infidels or to accept martyrdom for the glory of Allah."

—ABDUL AZIZ IBN SAUD (Founder of Saudi Arabia)

THE MIRACLE OF ISRAEL'S SURVIVAL

The original birth and founding of the nation of Israel was a miracle. Its deliverance from Egyptian bondage was a miracle. Its restoration from the Babylonian/Persian captivity was a miracle. Its rebirth in June 1948 was a miracle.

Its continued survival through four all-out wars—1948–49, 1956, 1967, and 1973, all of which were launched by the combined might of Islam for the express purpose of annihilating Israel and its people—is a miracle. Do you begin to see a pattern here?

It has been a colossal miracle that the race of Israel has survived. It is equally as great a miracle that the modern state of Israel has survived. Many people have tried to explain the miracle of Israel's modern survival in purely natural terms—but frankly, it takes more faith than I've got to explain it that way.

The Muslims say that it's because Israel has been furnished with so many modern weapons by the U.S. But the Soviet Union, France, China, and so on, have also furnished the Muslims with modern weapons. The Muslim forces always outnumbered the Israelis at least 4 to 1. They have had more modern tanks, aircraft, missiles, and artillery.

It is certainly not because Israelis are individually more courageous. Arab-Muslim soldiers are as brave as any in the world. Militarily speaking, there is only one advantage that stands out for the Israelis; they fight more with their reason than with their emotions. And they fight more as a unit than do the Muslims.

EXAMPLES OF MODERN MIRACLES

1967 Six Day War

An Israeli friend of mine was a young flight leader in the Israeli Air Force during the 1967 Six Day War. He related to me the extremely difficult battle plan they had to execute at the beginning of the war.

They had to coordinate multiple flights of fighter-bombers so that they all arrived on target at the same time. If timing and navigation were off, the whole war could have been a disaster. Israel's outgunned and outnumbered forces had to seize air supremacy at the very beginning to have any chance at all.

Multiple flights of jet fighters screamed toward multiple targets from multiple directions at supersonic speed. The planes flew so low that some were taking in spray from the ocean and others were just above the sand dunes. They had to maintain absolute radio silence, so no timing coordination or course corrections with each other were possible.

This is my friend's account:

I glanced out of the cockpit to glimpse the Nile River streak by underneath. I pulled up lightly to get over a bridge. I was flying so low that I nearly hit the mast of an Egyptian fishing boat. Just three hours before, I was on my honeymoon. A helicopter picked me up off the roof of the hotel. I still remember waving goodbye to my beautiful new bride as she stood on the hotel roof in her negligee.

I went over the battle plan in my mind. The great pyramids of Egypt flashed by off my starboard wing. I looked over my shoulder—all the young pilots were in tight formation behind me. I glanced at my airspeed indicator—Mach .85. I reminded myself, "Must keep just under the sound barrier so as not to set off alarms." We were counting on the populace thinking we were Egyptian fighters on maneuvers. "One thing for sure," I thought, "at this speed and low altitude, they will never be able to identify the planes. We are gone before they know we are there."

I checked my watch again. "Will we all arrive at the same time?" I wondered. "Will one of the squadrons hit a base early and alert the other bases to launch their fighters?" We had timed the strike to hit just after the Egyptians early morning patrols. "They would be having morning tea about now," I thought.

"Oops! There is my landmark." I instinctively pulled the stick back hard and went into a vertical climb to line up for attack. "Are we on time? Where are the other squadrons?" I rolled my fighter so that I could see. To my amazement, the other two attack units that had come in from different directions were all climbing in the vertical staring back at me. "Amazing! We had all arrived at the same precise moment."

I pulled over the top and rolled into a screaming dive right down the center of Egypt's main fighter base just outside of Cairo. There before me was the pride of the Egyptian Air Force parked in neat rows on the airport tarmac. I lined up and delivered my two 500 kg bombs. Three MIG 21s exploded in fireballs. I whipped my plane around in a tight turn for another pass. My little Mirage fighter's delta wings dug in hard against the g-forces. A large Tupelov bomber filled my gunsight. I fired a quick burst from my two 30 mm canons and it exploded in flames. In minutes, every aircraft on the Egyptian base was destroyed. The Egyptian base was in such chaos that not one shot had been fired at us.

As we turned and streaked across the Sinai for home, I thought, "What a way to enter a war. Less than four hours ago, I held my bride in my arms. Now I have just completed the first mission of a desperate war that will determine the survival of Israel."

My friend had not yet learned how great a victory the Israeli Air force had just completed. Virtually the entire combined air forces of Egypt, Jordan, and Syria were destroyed on the first day. Every airfield was hit at approximately the same time. Reconnaissance photos showed that at every airfield in Egypt, almost every warplane had been hit dead center. The absolute necessity of achieving air superiority was accomplished.

In six days the outnumbered Israeli Defense Forces destroyed the best of the combined Muslim armies of the Middle East.

There are some who would say this happened because of superior training. My friend believed that played a part—but he also believed that Israel's God must have been with them.

1973 Yom Kippur War

I interviewed a tank commander from the crack Golani Brigade about what happened in the first hours of the Yom Kippur war on the Golan Heights.

On October 6 1973, all Israeli soldiers that could be spared were home on leave for Israel's holiest day of the year, Yom Kippur. Only a bare minimum force was on duty. Suddenly, at dawn, the entire Syrian border erupted with artillery fire. Fourteen hundred top-of-the-line Soviet-built tanks charged forward. Another one thousand tanks were in reserve. The Syrians had a new anti-tank missile that wreaked havoc with the Israel's tanks.

The Israeli Air Force streaked in low to attack the Syrian ground forces, trying to stop the onslaught. Baruch watched in horror as plane after plane was blown out of the sky. The Soviets had designed a new Surface-to-Air Missile (SAM) for intercepting low-flying planes. Israel had no countermeasures for it. This same missile wreaked havoc with the Israeli Air Force both in the Sinai and on the Golan Heights.

By noon, the Golani tank force had been cut to pieces. Baruch[232] commanded the last three remaining tanks. They took up position at a critical crossroad for a fight to the death. They knew that they were all that stood between the Syrian army and Galilee. The thriving city of Tiberius lay helpless in the path of the Syrian juggernaut. Syrians are infamous for their barbaric treatment of Israeli prisoners—Baruch shuttered at the thought.

When the Syrian commander could see only three tanks blocking his way, "He said it's too easy—this must be a trap." So he ordered his forces to stop for lunch while they analyzed the situation. He reasoned the Israelis were for all purposes already beaten.

During the lunch break, reinforcements were able to rush to the front and furiously beat the Syrian forces. By a miracle of God, they got no further into Israel—though the fighting continued to be horrific. The tough Israeli tank commander, who had not been religious, attributed this whole episode to God's protective care over Israel.

The final victory in the Yom Kippur War was actually a greater miracle than the 1967 Six Day War, but the cost in lives and weapons was horrific.

ISRAEL ALMOST DEFEATED

The Yom Kippur war was not like the Six Day War or any of the previous wars with the Muslims. This time the Arab armies scored unprecedented and stunning initial victories. Israeli casualties were the highest yet seen. Hardened and confident combat units were so outnumbered and outflanked they were fleeing in disarray. Israel lost more than five hundred tanks and forty-nine aircraft in the first three days alone.

I interviewed Randy Cunningham, who was America's leading Vietnam ace at the time. He told me that he was one of the pilots in our Mediterranean fleet that shuttled aircraft from U.S. carriers to Israel to replace their heavy losses. He said that as soon as he landed, the Israelis started refueling and arming the plane while painting a Star of David over the U.S. insignia. That's how critical the situation was.

In the Sinai, the modernized Egyptian forces used new missiles and electronic defenses to blast their way to the eastern bank of the Suez Canal. Israeli counterattacks by three tank divisions were repelled.

THE NUCLEAR HOLOCAUST THAT "ALMOST WAS"

Early on October 8, Defense Minister Moshe Dayan called Golda Meir and said, "This is the end of the Third Temple. The situation is desperate—everything is lost. We must withdraw. Arm the 'doomsday weapons,' I am initiating the 'Samson Option.'"[233]

The Samson Option is a continuously practiced plan that will be put into action if the Muslim forces overrun Israel. If the plan is put into action, every Arab capitol will be vaporized in a thermonuclear mushroom cloud. Only now, ballistic missiles launched from land and submarines will deliver most of the warheads. Aircraft will be held in reserve for back-up strikes if needed.

SEIZING VICTORY OUT OF DEFEAT

The Muslim leaders realized after the Yom Kippur War that another strategy had to be adopted. The leaders surmised that Israel had to be weakened by reducing its borders to an indefensible size. Only then could they overwhelm the hated "Zionist entity" and annihilate it.

The Muslim world also realized that they had to work toward matching both Israel's nuclear arsenal and missile delivery systems. They wanted to become able to attack with all kinds of weapons of mass destruction—chemical and biological as well as nuclear. So missile development, along with nuclear development, became top priority for nations like Pakistan, Iraq, Libya— and now Iran and Syria.

New Kind of War

In the meantime, Israel is facing a new kind of threat that is potentially more dangerous than the military threats of the past. The Arab world has succeeded in framing the debate over the Middle East as a struggle between "the downtrodden Palestinians" and the powerful, heavily armed Israelis. Somehow they have convinced the world that Israel, with six million citizens, is bullying the Muslim nations of the Middle East, which have some two hundred and forty million citizens. The Islamic world has also covered over the fact that there are over a billion Muslims worldwide that are sympathetic to the "Palestinian" cause.

The new weapons of conquest are carefully crafted propaganda slogans like, "Land for peace!" "The legitimate rights of the Palestinians!" "End the Israeli aggression!" "End the 'occupation' of Palestinian land!"

These familiar pieces of propaganda have been all too readily taken up and spread by a Western media that have little concern for the facts of history in this region.

The shocking tragedy is that some Israelis, like the late Prime Minister Yitzak Rabin and Foreign Minister Shimon Perez, played along with these myths, even they knew they were not true. They led Israelis, who were understandably tired of war, along with them into the folly of the Oslo Agreement. They decided that peace, no matter the risks, was worth a try.

More and more Israelis are willing to be deceived into turning over lands in Judea, Samaria, Gaza, and the Golan Heights to the Palestinians in exchange for their "promises of peace." The vast number of recent Jewish immigrants does not have the same awareness of the dangers facing Israel from her neighbors as the *Sabras* (native-born Israelis) who have fought through most of the previous wars.

The Oslo Agreement set up a suicidal process that could lead to the destruction of Israel, according to independent objective military and intelligence experts.

Minimum Territory for Survival

Back in 1967, when the level of military technology and sophistication available to the Arab states was much lower than now, a Pentagon study found that Israel, at a minimum, needed control of the Golan Heights, the land east of Jerusalem to Jordan River, the central West Bank territory of the Jordan River, and part of the Sinai, including Sharm e-Sheikh.

More recently, intelligence expert Joseph de Courcy concluded, "The absolute minimum territory Israel requires to deter war is the territory it is controlling today."[234] This conclusion was drawn from an extensive report made by two prestigious military think tanks.

THE PUSH TOWARD THE "SAMSON OPTION"

In the late 1970s, Israel agreed to give up the Sinai Peninsula to Egypt in exchange for a peace treaty. Many military and intelligence experts agree that further land concessions would leave Israel with indefensible borders and no effective conventional deterrent against attack.

Notice the emphasis on the word *conventional*. This is because Israel still has its non-conventional form of deterrence—nuclear weapons. And as we saw in Moshe Dayan's statement to Golda Meir, with these they have already formed a last-resort-battle-plan known as the "Samson Option." With the totally indefensible borders into which they are now being pushed, Israel would be quickly forced into launching the Samson Option. Is this really what Western leaders want?

There is within our State Department an appalling ignorance of the true situation in this volatile area. The current American president, Barack Obama, whom I believe is at heart a Muslim, seems to believe that the only way to resolve the Israeli-Palestinian problem is to force Israel to give into all of the Palestinian demands without even face-to-face negotiations. This thinking willfully ignores that Palestinian leaders are among the most vicious terrorists the world has ever seen. They refuse to renounce their charters, which call for the annihilation of Israel, much less recognize Israel as a state that has a right to exist. They will recognize Israel only as "the Jewish entity."

Israel's Hard Choice

Israelis live in the toughest neighborhood in the world. They have no other option but to stay tough and hold on to defensible borders. The citizens of Israel are weary of war, weary of seeing their sons and daughters killed in the prime of their youth. Understandably, there has developed an almost "peace at any price" mentality in many. But Israelis have basically one option, stay tough and fight or pack up and get out of the Middle East. This may sound harsh, but the facts are harsh and clear. Any sign of weakness or lack of resolve only encourages the Muslims to move toward destroying them. This is their irreversible goal. It is a fact that is not going to change, not even by "Obama charm offensives."

Islam Will Never Accept Israel

The present territorial concessions Israel is being pressured into making have absolutely no chance of appeasing the Muslims. History shows clearly that Israel will never be small enough to satisfy the Muslims. Their real quarrel with Israel has never been about its *size*, but about its *existence* on what they believe is sacred Muslim land.

In fact, the Muslim nations really don't care about the so-called "legitimate rights of the Palestinians." If that were so, Jordan and Egypt would have created a Palestinian state when they controlled the very territory they are now seeking to force Israel to give away for a state. They would have long ago helped the Palestinians out of the horrible refugee camps. No, it's the destruction of the Jewish state Muslims are seeking, and Palestinians have simply been used as pawns for achieving that goal.

As I have repeatedly pointed out, this is a blood feud that dates back to the tents of Abraham. That blood feud became an integral part of Islam. The ancient hatred against Israel is now sanctified and nourished by the Koran and the Muslim religion.

Allah's Honor

The devout Muslim believes that annihilating Israel and removing its occupation of Jerusalem has become nothing less than an issue of "removing an insult to Allah's honor."

"The rebirth of the Jewish state right in the midst of the Arab countries is a direct contradiction of Islamic teaching," explains author Elishua Davidson. "Has not Allah finished with the Jewish people?" And if Allah has predetermined all things, how is it possible that a Jewish state should have come into existence once again?"[235]

Before his death, the Ayatollah Ruhollah Khomeini set Iran on a course of Islamic Fundamentalism from which the government has not deviated. Muslim fundamentalists are determined to do Allah's will and destroy Israel—thus and proving to the world that the creation of the Jewish state was merely a historical anomaly. Iran is primarily responsible for the worldwide revival of Islamic Fundamentalism. And the so-called "moderate" leaders that have followed the ayatollah haven't changed the original direction of Khomeini's revolution one iota.

TREATY FROM HELL

Despite the continuing "friendship" between Russian leaders Vladimir Putin and Dmitri Medvedev with Presidents Bush and Obama, binding agreements between Iran and Russia continue to grow.

The "Treaty from Hell" was formed and put into action in February 1991 under the code name "the Grand Design." Russia was rightly terrified of Iran spreading the Islamic fundamentalist revolution into the five former Soviet Union republics that are all Muslim. The small state of Chechnya has demonstrated to the Russians how enormous a threat the five larger Muslim republics could pose if controlled by hostile Islamic fundamentalists.

So an exchange was worked out. Iran promised neither to encourage fundamentalism or hostility toward Russia in these states, nor to interfere with Russian "internal attempts" to put down Islamic terrorism whenever it appeared (including Chechnya). In exchange, Russia agreed to the following:

- Provide plants, equipment, and expert personnel for the development of nuclear power suitable for conversion to warheads

- Support Iranian development of long-range missile delivery systems
- Fight alongside Iran against the West in the event of an attack by Western forces

In keeping with this agreement, in late February 1991, 278 of Russia's best nuclear and missile scientists and technicians moved to Isfahan, Iran, and began helping Iran become a nuclear power.

As of the writing of this book in November 2010, it appears that the Russians achieved their mission. According to many intelligence sources, Iran could be only months from producing one or two nuclear bombs. We know that they have successfully tested a missile capable of accurately delivering a warhead on target more than sixteen hundred miles away. And they are pushing to build ICBMs that can reach the United States. As a result, Russia and Iran (Persia) have moved into the precise roles that Ezekiel chapters 38–39 predicted they would in the "Last Days" power alignments.

Israel in the Crosshairs

All of Israel is now in Iranian missile range—and parts of Europe are in range as well. As I said, Iran is determined to develop missiles that can hit the continental United States. When that happens, we are really in trouble. A fundamental part of the Iranian conceived "Grand Design strategy" is to checkmate the U.S. from coming to Israel's aid while the combined Muslim nations destroy it.

In April 1991, an intelligence source shared information with me concerning the Iranian "Grand Design" plan. I could not reveal these things until they became public knowledge.

For the next two years after this, I observed the amazingly accurate British-based *Intelligence Digest* warning about these secret alliances between Russia and Iran. The *Digest* revealed that because Russia recognized it couldn't compete with the economic power of the West, it linked itself with the Third World, where it can be the leader. This meant that Moscow had to make alliances with radical Muslim powers on the basis of Russian economic assistance in return for world-class military weapons and co-belligerence toward the West. The *Digest* confirmed the information about Russia's fear of Iran spreading Islamic Fundamentalism being the reason for these alliances. The *Digest* said outright that this meant the "Russians would be compelled to fight alongside the Muslims in the next major Arab-Israeli war."

The *Digest* continued, "Since the break up of the Soviet Union this service has consistently argued that Russia[236] will eventually return to its traditional role of heading up an anti-Western, predominantly Islamic, Third-World alliance.

"The motivating forces are various and complex, but of primary importance is its need to appease Iran. Only by making a strategic alliance with Iran, in which Moscow backs Tehran's southerly ambitions (i.e., the conquest against Saudi Arabia and Israel), can Russia ensure its own interests in Central Asia. . . . We now have further information on the Russian-Iranian relationship—this time from sources in Riyadh. Saudi Arabia is, of course, one of the countries most threatened by a Russian-Iranian strategic alliance. This information was confirmed on 26 July (1993) by a report in the Saudi daily *Asharq al-Awsat*. According to this report, Russia and Iran are in the final stages of putting together a 'nuclear cooperation treaty' under the terms of which Moscow will build two nuclear power plants, train nuclear technicians, and set up a nuclear research facility in Isfahan."[237]

Today, that work has been basically completed. Iran will soon have a nuclear arsenal. It's only a matter of time, unless Israel takes matters into its own hands and attacks Iran's nuclear facilities. Israel cannot count upon the "do nothing but talk" Western powers headed by President Barack Hussein Obama.

THE AHMADINEJAD FACTOR

A factor that most Western leaders are failing to take seriously is the Shi'ite prophesy believed by Supreme Leader Ayatollah Ali Khamenei and President Mahmoud Ahmadinejad. Their beliefs enormously increases, the danger of allowing Iran to get nuclear weapons. It puts all that I have previously said into an entirely new dimension.

President Ahmadinejad has publicly telegraphed his intentions many times recently. He has boasted on many occasions that "Israel will soon be wiped off the map." Like Western leaders' attitude toward Hitler before World War II, no one believes Ahmadinejad really means this threat. But I believe him. This is why he has defied the UN and all Western attempts to stop his headlong race to get nuclear weapons. He believes Allah has chosen him to play the key role in starting a global war that will cause the Muslim messiah called the Mahdi to return.

HELP FROM AN IRANIAN REPUBLICAN GUARD

One of the most effective CIA agents the United States ever tasked to spy on Iran is Reza Kahlili, a former member of the Republican Guards. He is no longer active with the CIA since he left Iran, but he risked his life to warn the United States about the danger posed by the prophetic beliefs of the Iranian leadership. What he says is so important that I am going to quote him extensively.

Ken Timmerman, writing for *Newsmax*, filed the following report:

Kahlili warned that the consequences of misunderstanding the ideology of Iran's clerical rulers could be disastrous.

"The ruling clerics, the fanatics right now in power, truly believe in the return of the last Messiah, the Shiites' 12th imam, the imam Mahdi," he said.

"This is not a joke. This is not a story. This is not something in comic books. They are counting the days for the reappearance."

"Iranian president Mahmoud Ahmadinejad and Supreme Leader Ayatollah Ali Khamenei both believe that their actions can hasten the return of the 12th imam.

"They believe that if they detonate nuclear bombs over Israel and the Persian Gulf, bringing horror and a breakdown in the global economy, this will result in the Imam Mahdi coming out of a whale riding a white horse, killing the rest of us," Kahlili said.

"Our problem is that we are trying to evaluate Iran and its leaders for the past thirty years through a rational mind, because we are used to rationality here.

"Western leaders think they can find economic pressure points and incentives that will compel the Iranian regime to change its behavior, even though this approach has failed time and time again," he said.

"Our problem is that we cannot think outside the box."

"If Iran's Islamic leaders are allowed to acquire nuclear weapons, "they will take the whole world hostage," Kahlili warned.[238]

To all of us who know Bible prophecy, these events have a familiar ring to them. Ezekiel predicts that a power from "the extreme north" of Israel in the "last days" will arm and lead a confederacy of nations against Israel and Western forces. The nations that Ezekiel names as allies of Russia are all Muslim today—and the first on the list is Persia, or Iran.[239]

WAKE UP TO THE "QURAYSH STRATEGY"

As noted before, Mohammad made a ten-year peace treaty with the forces of Mecca. Within a year, he had gathered enough strength to attack, which he did, ignoring the "peace treaty," annihilating the Quraysh tribe that was the custodian of Mecca, and taking over the city. This deception became known in Muslim history as the "Quraysh model" strategy. Yasser Arafat explained in a South African mosque that his signing of the 1993 Oslo Peace Accord was according to the "Quraysh model:"

> The late Faisal Husseini, Arafat's Jerusalem representative, confirmed that "Quraysh Model" was indeed the strategy behind the Oslo Accords. Husseini was a very cultured and sophisticated man. He was considered the "most moderate" of all the Palestinians. Yet shortly before his death on May 31, 2001, he expressed his true feelings in an interview with the popular Egyptian newspaper *el Arav*. Husseini said: "We must distinguish the strategies and long-term goals from the political-phased goals which we are compelled to accept due to international pressures." But the *"ultimate goal is the liberation of all of historical Palestine."* Explicitly he said: *"Oslo has to be viewed as a Trojan Horse."* He even added and clarified that it is the obligation of all the Palestinian forces and factions to see the Oslo Accords as "temporary" steps, as "gradual" goals, because in this way, *"We are setting an ambush for the Israelis and cheating them."*[240]

The United Nations, the European Union, and the current U.S. government are pushing Israel to grant the Palestinians a state. This despite the fact that the multiple terrorist organizations within the Palestinian territories will not even halt terrorist attacks long enough for the Palestinian state to be negotiated and granted.

For many years I have predicted that the United States will be neutralized as a major power. That appears to be taking place now via the unprecedented economic problems hitting the U.S. President Barack Obama's socialist ideas are accelerating the catastrophe. After America's fall, a great leader will suddenly rise out of the old Roman culture and people, and he will be miraculously healed from a fatal wound. He will quickly take over the ten strongest nations of the EU and make Rome his seat of power. He will then negotiate the final "peace treaty" between the Muslims and Israel. It is the signing of this treaty that begins a seven-year count down that will climax with the greatest war of all times, ending with the Second Coming of Christ.

IT IS ALL PREDICTED

As incredible as it may sound to some readers, the precise scenario of how this will all finally end was predicted over two thousand years ago. And events happening today are fitting into the forecasted pattern. But the timing for all of these things to happen is not quiet ready.

THE "WORM" THAT SLOWED A HOLOCAUST

While writing this section, there was one thing that kept bothering me. The time is not yet right for the Russian-Iranian confederacy to launch the predicted war I just outlined. And then came the announcement that a cyber attack was secretly launched against Iran's nuclear facilities a few months ago.

The Iranian government announced that they had arrested dozens of "cyberspies" in the wake of the discovery of what has been called the "Stuxnet," computer worm-virus. "Stuxnet" differs from the typical computer infections that normally target computers or servers. The Stuxnet worm breaks into the types of computers that control industrial machinery—things like pumps and motors and valves and alarms.

Stuxnet could, in theory, shut off safety systems at a nuclear plant and allow materials to overheat. It could contaminate water treatment plants. Or open pipeline valves. Or even cause explosions. According to the internet security giant Symantec, "Stuxnet can potentially control or alter how the system operates. A previous historic example includes a reported case of stolen code that impacted a pipeline. Code was secretly 'Trojanized' to function properly and only some time after installation instruct the host system to increase the pipeline's pressure beyond its capacity. This resulted in a three kiloton explosion, about 1/5 the size of the Hiroshima bomb."

Stuxnet has been found lurking in systems manufactured by the German electronics conglomerate Siemans Systems in India, Indonesia, and Pakistan.

Stuxnet is able to recognize a specific facility's command and control network. Once it does, it copies the data and transfers it to an outside system before destroying the local network. But it's apparently not designed primarily for espionage. Stuxnet was designed specifically for sabotage. The Stuxnet attack proves that Iran's entire industrial infrastructure is vulnerable to attack. Indeed, "whoever" did this has demonstrated that it's capable of melting down Iran's entire cyber-command infrastructure. So the war that most thought would never happen may have already been won—at least for the moment.

IRAN'S OTHER BIG PROBLEM

Another development in the aftermath of the discovery of "Stuxnet" may be even more damaging to Iran's nuclear weapons program than the "worm."

The Iranian Security Service announced that the infection could not have come from the outside via the Internet. The infected computers were never connected to the Internet. They were closely guarded and only connected to local infrastructure command circuits. No one outside of trusted Iranian workers was allowed near the computers—with the exception of the resident Russian nuclear scientists and specialists. The Iranian security agents say that the only way the "worm" could have been introduced is by someone using a small flash drive to manually download the virus-worm into each of the separate systems.

So when the Iranian agents began detaining Russian scientists and specialists for interrogation, and then arresting some, the Russians began packing up their families and leaving the country. This is a catastrophe for the Iranians at this stage of their pursuit of nuclear weapons. They need the expertise of the Russians more now than ever.

Furthermore, this could potentially cause a serious rift between Iran and Russia.

However all of this was orchestrated, I see the hand of the God of Abraham, Isaac, and Jacob sovereignly protecting His people in an impossible situation.

How all this ends is the subject of the next chapter.

FIFTEEN

ARMAGEDDON:
RESULT OF ANCIENT ENMITY

"They say, *'Come, and Let us wipe them out as a nation; let the name of Israel be remembered no more.'* They conspire with one accord; against YOU they make a covenant—the tents of Edom and the Ishmaelites, Moab and the Hagrites, Gebal and Ammon and Amalek [various Arab tribes], Philistia with the inhabitants of Tyre [Gaza and Lebanon]; Assyria [Syria] also has joined them . . ."

—PSALM 83:48 [241]

"The word of the LORD came to Jeremiah: 'Have you not noticed that these people [Israel's Arab neighbors] are saying, "The LORD has rejected the two families he chose"?' So they despise my people and no longer regard them as a nation. This is what the LORD says: 'If I have not established my covenant with day and night and the fixed laws of heaven and earth, then I will reject the descendants of Jacob and David my servant and will not choose one of his sons to rule over the descendants of Abraham, Isaac and Jacob. For I will bring them back from captivity and have compassion on them.'"

—JEREMIAH 33:23–26

"'I will lay waste your cities, And you will become a desolation. Then you will know that I am the Lord. *Because you* [the Arab people] *have had everlasting enmity* and have delivered the sons of Israel to the power of the sword at the time of their calamity, at the time of the punishment of *the end*, therefore, as I live,' declares the LORD God, 'I will give you over to bloodshed, and bloodshed will pursue you; since you have not hated bloodshed, therefore bloodshed will pursue you.'"

—EZEKIEL 35:46 [242]

OVERVIEW OF PROPHETIC SCENARIO

Beginning thirty-four hundred years ago and continuing for the next fourteen hundred years, the Hebrew prophets predicted a precise pattern of events that would all fit together during the same time frame. All the elements of this predicted pattern will lead to the apocalyptic war of Armageddon, which will draw all nations into it.

Even though different Bible prophets predicted the facets of this pattern at different times and from different locations, they can easily be identified and properly fit together because they all pertain to the great final conflict that begins in the Middle East and draws all nations into it. The prophetic scenario deals with all the events and peoples that lead to this final war, the war itself, and events that immediately follow the war. This great final conflict is a major theme of all end-time Bible prophecy. It is therefore like the "Grand Central Station" of end-time prophecy. Every facet of prophecy in the Bible that is to be interpreted as occurring in the end times somehow relates to the time of this great final war.

Concerning this global catastrophe, which is usually known as the war of Armageddon, Jesus Christ predicted, "For then there will be great distress, unequaled from the beginning of the world until now—and never to be equaled again. If those days had not been cut short, no one would survive, but for the sake of the elect those days will be shortened."[243]

The prophet Daniel foresaw this same war and also notes it

will be without parallel. He writes, "There will be a time of distress such as has not happened from the beginning of nations until then. But at that time your people—everyone whose name is found written in the book—will be delivered."[244]

The prophet Isaiah wrote about this war: "The earth will be completely laid waste and completely despoiled, for the Lord has spoken this word. . . . The earth is also polluted by its inhabitants, for they transgressed laws, violated statutes, broke the everlasting covenant. Therefore, a curse devours the earth, and those who live in it are held guilty. Therefore, the inhabitants of the earth are burned, and few men are left."[245] Note that Isaiah also predicts that very few people will survive this great final war.

THE KEY TO KNOWING THE GENERAL TIME

Israel Reborn

The key sign that would signal that the predicted pattern of events had begun would be the miraculous return—and national rebirth—of the scattered people of Israel to their ancient homeland. This prophecy was formally fulfilled May 15, 1948. Precisely as predicted, the ancient enmity of the neighboring nations, which are all Muslim today, immediately began to seek Israel's annihilation.

Jerusalem Recaptured

Jesus Christ predicted how Jerusalem would be central to this prophetic pattern, saying "They [Jews in A.D. 70] will fall by the edge of the sword, and will be led captive into all the nations; and Jerusalem will be trampled under foot by the Gentiles *until* the times of the Gentiles be fulfilled."[246] (emphasis added) Jesus made this prophecy just before his death. He predicted the destruction and dispersion of the nation would fall upon the generation that was rejecting Him. That literally happened thirty-seven years later.

But the second half of this same prophecy *puts a time limit* on the period of Jerusalem's desolations and captivity. Jesus predicted that it would be only *"until* the times of the Gentiles are fulfilled." The "times of the Gentiles"—the era of Gentile world domination"—began a gradual phasing out in June 1967 with Israel's recapture of old Jerusalem. This process will be completed with the coming of the Messiah to set up God's promised kingdom.

Islam's Jihad for Jerusalem

At around 520 B.C. Zechariah predicted:

> Behold, I am going to make Jerusalem a cup that causes intoxication to all the surrounding peoples; and when the siege is against Jerusalem, it will also be against Judah [the Jews]. And it will come about in that day that I will make Jerusalem a burdensome stone for all the peoples; all who attempt to lift it will be severely injured. And all the nations of the earth will be gathered [for war] because of it.[247]

As prophesied, Israel has regained control of its ancient capital city—Jerusalem—amid tremendous opposition from the surrounding nations. As the prophet Zechariah foresaw some 2,450 years ago, Jerusalem will cause all of the neighboring nations (which are all Muslim today) to become intoxicated with religious passion to repossess it.

The metaphor "a cup that causes intoxication" is used in the Bible to illustrate religious passions out of control. Just as a drunken person acts emotionally without reason, so it was predicted that the neighboring people would be intoxicated with religiously driven passion and hate.

Al Quds?

It is important to note that the name Jerusalem never appears in the Koran or the Hadith. The claim for Jerusalem arose years after Mohammad's death. The justification for this Muslim claim comes from a verse that says Mohammad traveled to the "uttermost mosque" (which is the meaning of *Al Quds* in Arabic) shortly before his death.

In the days of Khaliph Omar, who was the first Muslim to conquer Jerusalem, there is the first record of the legend that Mohammad, escorted by the angel Michael, flew on a winged horse named "Barak" to the Temple Mount in Jerusalem. According to legend, Mohammad ascended to the seventh heaven from the great rock that is on top of the Temple Mount. He then returned to the rock and flew back to Mecca.

In many parts of the Muslim world, the name *Jerusalem* isn't even known; instead the city is called "Al Quds." Omar was the first to erect a mosque over the sacred rock of the Temple Mount, and later, a magnificent mosque known as the Dome of the Rock was built there. There is no historical evidence that Mohammad ever was in Jerusalem. But in the Middle East, it doesn't matter whether something is actually true. It is what is believed to be true that matters. There, many have died for the sake of myths.

Jerusalem, the Burdensome Stone

As predicted by Zechariah, Jerusalem has become a heavy burden for all peoples. It is at the heart of the Muslim passion to destroy Israel and has been named Islam's third holiest place—on par with Mecca and Medina. True Muslims believe it is their sacred duty to Allah to retake Jerusalem and all of Palestine.

Because the Muslims currently control most of the world's oil reserves, whatever troubles them can be made to trouble the world. Zechariah's prophecy indicates that Islam's religiously driven obsession to retake Jerusalem and drive the Jews out of the Middle East will ignite a global war, for it is written, "All the nations of the earth will be gathered [for war] because of it."

THE FOUR SPHERES OF GENTILE POWER

The Last Days prophetic scenario features four dominant spheres of political power. It was predicted that these four power blocs would become identifiable during the general time of Israel's restoration and rebirth. The dispute over the land and Jerusalem draws all of these powers into it, much like a whirlpool irresistibly draws in all around it.

The four power centers would be:

- The Muslim sphere of power that Daniel calls "the king of the South"
- The Asian sphere of power called "the kings of the East"
- The power prophetically known as the revived Roman Empire heading the West
- The power known as "the king of the North," who comes from the extreme north of Israel

THE MUSLIM SPHERE OF POWER

Many Biblical prophets declare God's Last Days warning to the nations surrounding Israel. Great judgment is predicted for these nations because, God says, "They appropriated MY land and mistreated MY people Israel."[248]

When I wrote *The Late Great Planet Earth* in 1969, the Muslim nations did not represent anything like the threat to the West that they are now. Because of Bible prophecy, I recognized that with Russian help, they had to be one of the power blocs of the last days. Gamal Abdel Nasser of Egypt led the Islamic nations then, and he sought to unite the Muslim world under a kind of secular Arab socialism. The Soviet Union was, at the time, seeking to promote Islam's war against Israel in order to bring the Muslims under communist control. But this was an unnatural relationship, for neither socialism nor communism agrees with the Koran.

Iran's Importance

Ezekiel's prophesy names Persia, not Egypt, as the leader of the Muslim sphere of power that joins with the "king of the North" (also known as "Gog") for the final conflict. But at the time, the Shah of Iran was, next to Israel, the United States' best friend in the Middle East.

When the Shah of Iran was driven out and replaced by the Ayatollah Khomeini in 1979, a dramatic change in the Muslim world began to take place. As previously mentioned, the United States inexplicably withdrew help and support for the Shah at a critical time. America has paid and will continue to pay a terrible price for that, for it is Iran that has now become the leader of the whole fundamentalist Muslim world. Not through some secular political system, but through a return to the "pure fundamentals of the Koran." This is an almost irresistible pull upon the heart of virtually all Muslims.

The Islamic fundamentalist revolution began and continues through Iran. This movement's ability to appeal to young Muslim men to sacrifice their lives for a heavenly reward of fleshly pleasures they can only dream of on earth has produced the most formidable terrorists in history. This movement has the potential of wreaking havoc upon Western civilization—especially America.

Islam Warned by Jehovah God

When Ezekiel predicted the miraculous Last Days restoration of the land of Israel, he also warned the neighboring nations for confiscating His land. Just read how accurately the details of Ezekiel's prophecy fit the current situation in "Israel-Palestine":

> And you, son of man, prophesy to the mountains of Israel and say, "O mountains of Israel, hear the word of the LORD. Thus says the Lord GOD, 'Because the enemy has spoken against you, "Aha!" and, "The everlasting heights have become our possession."' . . . "Therefore, O mountains of Israel, hear the word of the Lord GOD. Thus says the Lord GOD to the mountains and to the hills, to the ravines and to the valleys, to the desolate wastes and to the forsaken cities, which have become a prey and a derision to the rest of the *nations which are round about.* . . . 'Surely in the fire of My jealousy I have spoken against the rest of the nations, and *against all Edom* [collective name for Arab peoples], who appropriated My land for themselves as a possession with wholehearted joy and with scorn of soul, to drive it out for a prey.' . . . "Therefore, thus says the Lord GOD, 'I have sworn that surely the *nations which are around you* will themselves endure their insults. But you, O mountains of Israel, you will put forth your branches and bear your fruit for My people Israel; for they will soon come [home].'"[249]

WHO OWNS THE HOLY LAND?

Who owns the land that the Romans out of spite renamed Philistia or Philistina after the ancient enemies of Israel—the Philistines? The Arabs couldn't pronounce "Philistina," so it came to be called by the Arab pronunciation—"Palestine." In the prophecy above, God makes it clear that the Arabs don't own the land—and neither do the Jews. He says it is "My land." The Lord declares that He will only give it to those He has promised it to—the believing remnant of Israelites.

The Lord expresses His fury at the Muslim nations for appropriating His land and desecrating it—reducing it to a state of utter desolation.

God then declares that He will bring His people back to the land and that it will flourish to their touch. In an earlier chapter, I noted that God would give back the land to the Israelites on the basis of His unconditional covenant with them, in spite of the fact they do not deserve it.

As the Lord explains:

Therefore, say to the house of Israel, "Thus says the Lord GOD, 'It is not for your sake, O house of Israel, that I am about to act, but for My holy name, which you have profaned among the nations where you went. . . . For I will take you from the nations, gather you from all the lands, and bring you into your own land.'"[250]

When God makes a promise, His name is at stake. He will not break a promise, no matter how unworthy the recipients may be. So He sovereignly announces that He will cause a remnant to believe and become the recipients of His ancient covenants with their forefathers, Abraham, Isaac and Jacob.

THE POWER FROM THE EXTREME NORTH

In the same general time of these events, Ezekiel predicts the rise of another key piece to the prophetic pattern. There are three major Biblical predictions about this northern power. They are found in Ezekiel 38 and 39, Daniel 11:40–45, and Joel 2:20. Ezekiel gives three clues by which to identify this power.

First, the Geographic Clue: In Bible prophecy, all compass directions assume Israel as their base point, unless specifically noted otherwise. The attacking nation in view in Ezekiel will come against Israel from its "uttermost or extreme north." This clue is repeated three times. Ezekiel predicts that the invader will come "from the remote parts of the north with all its troops—many peoples with you"[251]; that the attacker "will come from your place out of the remote parts of the north, you and many peoples"[252]; and that the Lord "shall turn you around, drive you on, take you from the remotest parts of the north, and bring you against the mountains of Israel."[253]

The Hebrew word translated "remote parts of the north" literally means "extreme north."

There is only one colossus that covers the entire great expanse to the north of the Middle East and Asia. Take a globe and go to the extreme north from Israel. There is only one nation there—Russia.

Second, the Time Clue: Ezekiel clearly identifies the time in history this nation would rise to power. He writes, "After many days you will be summoned; in the latter years you will come into the land that is restored from the sword, whose inhabitants have been gathered from many nations to the mountains of Israel which had been a continual waste; but its people were brought out from the nations, and they are living securely, all of them."[254]

Ezekiel predicts that this hostile nation will rise against Israel *after* it has been brought back from its worldwide dispersion and reborn as a nation in "the latter years." That can only be now—since the rebirth of the nation of Israel in 1948.

Third, the Ethnic Clue: Ezekiel writes that this northern power will be descended from the ancient tribes of Magog, Meshech, and Tubal. All these people spread north of the Caucasus Mountains at the dawn of recorded history.

The fifth century B.C. Greek historian Herodotus is quoted as mentioning Meshech and Tubal. He identified them with a people known as the Samaritans and Muscovites, who lived at that time in the extreme north of Asia Minor.[255]

Josephus, a Jewish historian of the first century, says that the people of his day known as the Moschevi and Thobelites were founded by Meshech and Tubal respectively. He also says, "Magog is called the Scythians by the Greeks." He reported that these people lived in the northern regions above the Caucasus Mountains.[256]

These fierce tribes later became collectively known as the Scythians. The Scythians are easily traced in history as the principle forefathers of the modern ethnic Russians.

Russia is not predicted as a world conqueror, but rather as a dangerous regional power with a vast arsenal of deadly weapons. Ezekiel predicts that this people will lead a confederacy of nations, which are all Muslim today, and will equip them with deadly weapons.[257]

Persia, or Iran, is the first confederate named.[258] It is no coincidence that Iran has signed a treaty with Russia that binds Moscow to fight along side the Iranians if the West attacks. Iran now troubles the world with its headlong plunge toward nuclear weapons. Iran's president, Mahmoud Ahmadinejad, has defied the sanctions of the world with his relentless pursuit of what he believes is his mission for Allah—to obliterate Israel and to start the last war that will cause the Muslim messiah, "the Mahdi," to return.

As mentioned in the last chapter, I have sought for years to warn about the Muslim prophecies that are passionately believed by Iran's ayatollahs and Mahmoud Ahmadinejad. And how the Russians are now in a treaty that requires them to side with Iran in future conflicts—just as predicted. As predicted in Ezekiel chapter 38, Russia continues to supply all manner of weapons to Iran and the Muslim world.

THE ASIAN CONFEDERATION

Also during this same era, predicts the Book of Revelation, the world will see the rise of an enormous power in Asia. The Apostle John writes of "the kings of the East"[259] who advance into the Middle East from east of the Euphrates River. In the Apostle

John's era, the Euphrates River was the dividing line between the Near East and the Far East. According to Revelation Chapter 9, this Asian confederacy will cross the Euphrates River with two hundred million soldiers. This advance is apparently to challenge the Russian-Persian invasion of the aforementioned strategic land bridge that connects Africa, Asia, and Europe—along with its vital oil reserves.

I believe China is destined to lead this Asian confederation and become a major world power. At the time of this writing, China is one of the top three economic powers in the world, and its military might is growing in tandem with its economic expansion.

It is important to note that *when* John made this cryptic prophecy of a vast two-hundred-million-man Asian army, there were not that many people in the world.[260] This sphere of power is destined to kill one-third of mankind. The Apostle John's first-century prophecy that describes the phenomena that kills this unprecedented number of people is a very good portrayal of the effects of a modern thermonuclear war. Just imagine this prophecy being fulfilled in terms of today's population. A third of the world's present population translates into 2.3 billion people killed in a matter of days. No wonder both Jesus and Daniel said about this time, "For then there will be great distress, unequaled from the beginning of the world until now—and never to be equaled again."

Growing Power of Asia

Asian nations like China, India, North Korea, and Pakistan already have nuclear weapons and missile delivery systems. They are rapidly improving their technology and enlarging their arsenals. Watch for China to move toward establishing hegemony over the Asian nations such as the Koreas, Japan, India and the Southeast Asian nations. On the basis of these prophecies, I believe these nations are destined to join together as both an economic and military power bloc.

In the light of recent shifts in the world's economic power, it is easy to see why any attempt by the other spheres of power to launch a hostile takeover of the Middle East's strategic land bridge and oil reserves would be immediately countered by a Chinese-led Asian attack.

THE WESTERN SPHERE OF POWER

Ultimately, this sphere of power will take over all other spheres of power for a short period. This Western power is predicted more often and in greater detail than all of the others. It will be a revived form of the old Roman Empire, and its capital will again be Rome.

We can have great confidence in this prophecy's fulfillment. The first four-fifths of it have already been dramatically fulfilled in history. The prophet Daniel predicted four successive gentile empires that would gain authority over the whole world.

In chapters 2, 7, and 8, Daniel predicted the details of these empires. The first was the Babylonian Empire, the second was the Media-Persian, and the third was the Greek. Even the career of Alexander the Great and the rule of his four successors were graphically predicted two hundred years before their rise to power occurred.[261] Now when you consider that Daniel wrote chapter 8 around 539 B.C., his prediction is awesome. It is important to note that the center of each succeeding empire moved further westward. The center of world power after the Roman Empire has remained in the west. The miraculous revival of the old Roman culture and people will be centered in the West, not in Mecca under Islam as some are seeking to teach today.

In 68 B.C., the fourth empire, Rome, conquered the remains of the Greek Empire. As predicted, the Roman Empire became the mightiest and longest lasting of all the others. The prophets did not forecast that the fourth empire would be conquered or utterly destroyed, but rather that it would disintegrate from within and go into a dormant form. Then it would rise to power again shortly before the coming of the Messiah to set up God's kingdom. Daniel specifically predicts, "*Out of* this kingdom ten kings will arise; and another will arise after them, and he will be different from the previous ones and will subdue three kings."[262]

Daniel predicts that it is "*out of*" the culture and people of the old Roman Empire that the ten nations will arise and come to power. It *does not* say the revived empire will be geographically coextensive with the old. There is only one specific part of the old that must remain the same—Rome must be the capital. The Book of Revelation predicts this with the symbol of a "woman": "And the woman whom you saw is the great city, which reigns over the kings of the earth."[263] When the Apostle John predicted this, there was only one city that was reigning over the kings of the earth—Rome. Muslims would never set up a world government centered in Rome; their authority would be centered in Mecca.

Rome's Coming Leader

Both Daniel, and then John in the Book of Revelation, predict that the revival of the Roman Empire will happen through the genius and supernatural power of a great leader. He will come out of Rome, because Daniel says he will be out of the people who destroyed Jerusalem and Israel in A.D. 70.[264]

John predicts that the ten nations will not receive power until this leader (which the Bible calls "the beast") comes and pulls them together, "And the ten horns which you saw are ten kings, who have not yet received a kingdom, but they receive authority as kings with the beast for one hour. These have one purpose and they give their power and authority to the beast."[265]

In 1969, I said that the European Common Market would become the United States of Europe.[266] Most critics said this would never happen. In fact, one cardinal in Rome branded me a "false prophet" because of it. But today, we have what Charlemagne, Napoleon, Hitler, and many others could not accomplish—the European Union. As I said earlier, this is not the final form of power predicted here, but it certainly is setting the stage for it.

I believe that this Roman leader is alive somewhere in Europe right now, just waiting for his appointed time to be unveiled. He is the one who will take ten of the strongest nations in the EU and form them into his power base, from which he will gain control of the whole world. John predicts that he will use a religious system to help bring the world under his authority. This man is called by many titles in Bible prophecy, but he is best known as "The Antichrist."

He will declare war on all those who believe in Jesus Christ. But as Revelation makes clear, he will be worshipped and followed by the entire world: "And it was given to him to make war with the saints and to overcome them; and authority over every tribe and people and tongue and nation was given to him. And all who dwell on the earth will worship him, everyone whose name has not been written from the foundation of the world in the book of life of the Lamb who has been slain."[267]

Apparently two events will be used to thrust this man into world prominence. First, he will receive a mortal wound from which he will be miraculously healed.[268] Second, he will settle the Arab-Israeli conflict by making a covenant with Israel that guarantees their security.[269] This will bring what appears to be a whole new era of peace and freedom from fear of war. Israel will even be allowed to rebuild their temple side-by-side with the Dome of the Rock mosque. The joy of freedom from fear of war is evident in the praise people give him: "And they worshiped the dragon [Satan], because he gave his authority to the beast [Antichrist]; and they worshiped the beast, saying, *'Who is like the beast, and who is able to wage war with him.'*"[270]

EVENTS THAT TRIGGER ARMAGEDDON

There will be a worldwide euphoria in the pseudo-peace the Antichrist brings. This will continue for three and a half years. Then the Antichrist will enter the Holy of Holies of Israel's rebuilt temple, take his seat there, and proclaim himself god.[271] This is the predicted ultimate desecration of the temple known as "the abomination that causes desolation" spoken of by Daniel and Jesus Christ.

It is at this point that the "great tribulation" breaks loose. Jesus warns that this is the sign that the great war of Armageddon is starting.[272]

DANIEL'S PREVIEW OF ARMAGEDDON

Daniel traces the movement of the military forces in this last great conflict:

> At the time of the end the king of the South [Muslim forces] will engage him [the Antichrist] in battle, and the king of the North [Russia] will storm out against him with chariots and cavalry and a great fleet of ships. He will invade many countries and sweep through them like a flood. He will also invade the Beautiful Land [Israel]. Many countries will fall, but Edom, Moab and the leaders of Ammon [Jordan] will be delivered from his hand. He will extend his power over many countries; Egypt will not escape. He will gain control of the treasures of gold and silver and all the riches of Egypt, with the Libyans [North Africans] and Nubians [Black Africans] in submission. But reports from the east [China-led Asian invasion] and the north [Antichrist-led Western forces] will alarm him, and he will set out in a great rage to destroy and annihilate many. He will pitch his royal tents between the seas at the beautiful holy mountain [Jerusalem]. Yet he will come to his end, and no one will help him.[273]

As mentioned in the last chapter, the initial attack is launched against Israel by an Iranian-led Muslim confederacy. "Him" refers to the Roman Antichrist and his partner, known as the False Prophet[274] from Israel (see description of "him" in Daniel 11:36–39).

The Muslims are immediately joined by the Russians in an all-out attack on Israel. But then the Russian leader takes over and also invades Egypt and Africa. While the Russian leader is in Egypt, reports from the east, which would be the oncoming Asian army, and from the north, which from Egypt would be the European-led Western army, trouble him.

So the Russian leader retraces his steps to make a stand in Jerusalem. It is there that the Roman-led Western armies of the Antichrist annihilate both the Russian and Muslim armies.

Then the two hundred million-man army of Asia will square off against the Western forces along the length and breadth of the Middle East, with its vortex in the valley of Megiddo. It is at this point that John foresaw a horrible vision of "blood standing to the horses' bridle for a distance of 200 miles." He indicates that the blood primarily flows from around Jerusalem. The Jordan River Rift Valley extends under the Jordan River's beginning at foot of Mt. Hermon, southward through the Sea of Galilee, the Dead Sea, and the dried up river bed (called a Wadi) that ends at the Red Sea at Aqaba-Eilat.[275] It covers a distance of about 200 miles. There are no other valleys in Israel that join with valleys from Megiddo (source of the name Armageddon) and Jerusalem. So this is the only valley that fits the prophecy from Revelation 14:20. It is here that blood will stand to the horses' bridle. It traverses the entire Eastern border of Israel.

Ezekiel predicts that this war will escalate to include the whole world: "I will send fire on Magog [Russia] and on those who live in safety in the coastlands [Continents], and they will know that I am the LORD."[276] The Hebrew word translated "coastlands" means continents today. So apparently the fire of thermonuclear weapons will reach most of the world.

It is at this point, when man is about to destroy all life on the planet, Jesus the Messiah will return to put down all armies. He will then judge the world. He will cast off all unbelievers into judgment. The surviving believers will go into a completely renewed earth and repopulate it. They will live in peace and prosperity for a thousand years.

WHAT ABOUT THE UNITED STATES?

This question has troubled me for the fifty odd years I have studied prophecy. I have not found one reference, either explicit or inferred, that applies to the United States in the final alignment of world powers. Now since the U.S. has been the leader of the West and the World since World War II, this has an ominous meaning.

I have said for over fifty years that the United States must fall from its position as the world's superpower. And now with its current economic problems that have been geometrically accelerated by the Obama Administration's reckless spending in the face of a disastrous national debt, it is easy to see this prophecy being fulfilled before our eyes. Mr. Obama seems to be bent upon destroying America's preeminence among the world powers and reducing us to a form that will have to submit to the one-world government movement that has gained enormous power in the Western political sphere.

The power center that will lead the West is clearly predicted. It will be a Roman-led union of ten nations out of the culture and people of the old Roman Empire. So this means the United States has to decline in power. I hate to even think of this because I love my country. But I see the United States being destroyed economically before my eyes by those who are determined to destroy our Constitution and capitalist system and turn it into a form of Marxist one-worldism.

However it happens, power must shift to Europe. Prophecy demands it.

NOW SOME GOOD NEWS

The really good news is that those who accept the free gift of pardon that Jesus gave His life to purchase will not be here in the fateful final seven years of catastrophe.

I was a young non-religious tugboat captain in New Orleans. I was satisfied with life and thought I had it all. I had a bachelor's pad in the French Quarter and the money to party non-stop. Then, after frantically experiencing all that I thought was fun, I found myself asking, "Is this all there is?" "What do you do for an encore?" I started searching and finally opened a Gideon's New Testament someone had given me years before. I had never read it, but I thought it was good luck to keep it with me—kind of like a rabbit's foot.

I read through the Gospels and came to the third chapter of the Gospel of John. Suddenly it became clear to me in this chapter that I had been born wrong the first time and I needed to be born again spiritually. I saw that the only requirement was to admit I could never measure up to God's standards. Then I simply asked God to forgive me on the basis that Jesus died for my sins and purchased a pardon for me. I received that pardon.

I didn't suddenly hear organ music or church bells ringing, but I sensed a peace come over me. I new God had touched me. That was the turning point in my whole life. Though I have had my struggles and failures, God has never let go of me. He has motivated me to learn His Word and fellowship with other believers. I wouldn't trade the life I have had since that day for all the world has to offer.

The wonderful thing is, God promises that all who believe in Him now are not appointed to the wrath that is about to come upon the world. I can't offer a global solution for the world, but I do offer you a personal solution. Right now, wherever you are, just bow your head and receive the gift of pardon Jesus purchased for you by dying in your place. Pray and ask Him to come into your life and make you what He wants you to be. If you just prayed that prayer, Jesus, who can't lie, has come into you and forgiven you. Continue with Him and seek out other true Christians for fellowship.

May you find peace as I found it. I hope to see you at the great reunion.

APPENDIX A

Transcription of the original handwritten note:

If the Arabs are established as I have asked in my manifesto of Jan. 4, to the British Secretary of State Foreign Affairs, I will carry out what is within this agreement.

If changes are made I can not be answerable for failing to carry out this agreement.

—Feisal ibn-Hussein

APPENDIX B:
THE FAISAL-WEIZMANN AGREEMENT

His Royal Highness the Emir FEISAL. representing and acting on behalf of the Arab Kingdom of Hejaz. and Dr. CHAIM WEIZMANN. representing and acting on behalf of the Zionist Organisation,

mindful of the racial kinship and ancient bonds existing between the Arabs and the Jewish people, and realizing that the surest means of working out the consummation of their national aspirations. is through the closest possible collaboration in the development of the Arabs State and Palestine, and being desirous further of confirming the good understanding which exists between them,

have agreed upon the following Articles; -

Article 1.
The Arab State and Palestine in all their relations and undertakings shall be controlled by the most cordial goodwill and understanding and to this end Arab and Jewish duly accredited agents shall be established and maintained in the respective territories.

Article 2.
Immediately following the completion of the deliberations of the Peace Conference, the definite boundaries between the Arab State and Palestine shall be determined by a Commission to be agreed upon by the parties hereto.

Article 3.

In the establishment of the Constitution and Administration of Palestine all such measures shall be adopted as will afford the fullest guarantees for carrying into effect the British Government's Declaration of the 2nd of November, 1917.

Article 4.

All necessary measures shall be taken to encourage and stimulate immigration of Jews into Palestine on a large scale, and as quickly as possible to settle Jewish immigrants upon the land through closer settlement and intensive cultivation of the soil. In taking such measures the Arab peasant and tenant farmers shall be protected in their rights, and shall be assisted in forwarding their economic development.

Article 5.

No regulation nor law shall be made prohibiting or interfering in any way with the free exercise and enjoyment of religious profession and worship without discrimination or preference shall forever be allowed. No religious test shall ever be required for the exercise of civil or political rights.

Article 6.

The Mohammedan Holy Places shall be under Mohammedan control.

Article 7.

The Zionist Organisation proposes to send to Palestine a Commission of experts to make a survey of the economic possibilities of the country, and to report upon the best means for its development. The Zionist Organisation will place the aforementioned Commission at the disposal of the Arab State for the purpose of a survey of the economic possibilities of the Arab State and to report upon the best means for its development. The Zionist

Oganization will use its best efforts to assist the Arab State in providing the means for developing the natural resources and economic possibilities thereof.

Article 8.
The parties hereto agree to act in complete accord and harmony on all matters embraced herein before the Peace Congress.

Article 9.
Any matters of dispute which may arise between the contracting parties shall be referred to the British Government for arbitration.

Given under our hand at LONDON,
ENGLAND, the THIRD day of
JANUARY, ONE THOUSAND NINE
HUNDRED AND NINETEEN

APPENDIX C:
THE SAN REMO CONFERENCE, 1922

The San Remo Conference, 1922
(Extract)

"The San Remo Conference decided on April 24, 1920 to assign the Mandate [for Palestine] under the League of Nations to Britain. The terms of the Mandate were also discussed with the United States, which was not a member of the League. An agreed text was confirmed by the Council of the League of Nations on July 24, 1922, and it came into operation in September 1923."[1]

The Council of the League of Nations
Whereas the Principal Allied Powers have agreed, for the purpose of giving effect to the provisions of Article 22 of the Covenant of the League of Nations, to entrust to a Mandatory selected by the said Powers the administration of the territory of Palestine, which formerly belonged to the Turkish Empire, within such boundaries as may be fixed by them; and

Whereas the Principal Allied Powers have also agreed that the Mandatory should be responsible for putting into effect the declaration originally made on November 2nd, 1917, by the Government

---

1 From *The Israel-Arab Reader*, edited, Walter Laqueur, New York, Bantam Books, 1976, pp 34-42. [NB: This is an edited version of the complete San Remo Agreement, and the ellipses found within form part of Dr. Laqueur's editorial process.]

of His Britannic Majesty, and adopted by the said Powers, in favour of the establishment in Palestine of a national home for the Jewish people, it being clearly understood that nothing should be done which might prejudice the civil and religious rights of existing non-Jewish communities in Palestine, or the rights and political status enjoyed by Jews in any other country; and

Whereas recognition has thereby been given to the historical connection of the Jewish people with Palestine and to the grounds for reconstituting their national home in that country; and

Whereas the Principal Allied Powers have selected His Britannic Majesty as the Mandatory for Palestine; and

Whereas the mandate in respect of Palestine has been formulated in the following terms and submitted to the Council of the League for approval; and

Whereas His Britannic Majesty has accepted the mandate in respect of Palestine and undertaken to exercise it on behalf of the League of Nations in conformity with the following provisions; and

Whereas by the afore-mentioned Article 22 (paragraph 8), it is provided that the degree of authority, control or administration to be exercised by the Mandatory, not having been previously agreed upon by the Members of the League, shall be explicitly defined by the Council of the League of Nations;

Confirming the said mandate, defines its terms as follows:

Article 1.
The Mandatory shall have full powers of legislation and of administration, save as they may be limited by the terms of this mandate.

Article 2.

The Mandatory shall be responsible for placing the country under such political, administrative and economic conditions as will secure the establishment of the Jewish national home, as laid down in the preamble, and the development of self -governing institutions, and also for safeguarding the civil and religious rights of all the inhabitants of Palestine, irrespective of race and religion.

Article 3.

The Mandatory shall, so far as circumstances permit, encourage local autonomy.

Article 4.

An appropriate Jewish agency shall be recognised as a public body for the purpose of advising and co-operating with the Administration of Palestine in such economic, social and other matters as may affect the establishment of the Jewish national home and the interests of the Jewish population in Palestine, and, subject always to the control of the Administration, to assist and take part in the development of the country.

The Zionist organisation, so long as its organisation and constitution are in the opinion of the Mandatory appropriate, shall be recognised as such agency. It shall take steps in consultation with His Britannic Majesty's Government to secure the cooperation of all Jews who are willing to assist in the establishment of the Jewish national home.

Article 5.

The Mandatory shall be responsible for seeing that no Palestine territory shall be ceded or leased to, or in any way placed under the control of, the Government of any foreign Power.

Article 6.

The Administration of Palestine, while ensuring that the rights and position of other sections of the population are not prejudiced, shall facilitate Jewish immigration under suitable conditions and shall encourage, in co-operation with the Jewish agency, referred to in Article 4, close settlement by Jews, on the land, including State lands and waste lands not required for public purposes.

Article 7.

The Administration of Palestine shall be responsible for enacting a nationality law. There shall be included in this law provisions framed so as to facilitate the acquisition of Palestinian citizenship by Jews who take up their permanent residence in Palestine.

Article 8.

The privileges and immunities of foreigners, including the benefits of consular jurisdiction and protection as formerly enjoyed by Capitulation or usage in the Ottoman Empire, shall not be applicable in Palestine.

Unless the Powers whose nationals enjoyed the afore-mentioned privileges and immunities on August 1st, 1914, shall have previously renounced the right to their re-establishment, or shall have agreed to their non-application for a specified period, these privileges and immunities shall, at the expiration of the mandate, be immediately re-established in their entirety or with such modifications as may have been agreed upon between the Powers concerned.

Article 9.

The Mandatory shall be responsible for seeing that the judicial system established in Palestine shall assure to foreigners, as well as to natives, a complete guarantee of their rights.

Respect for the personal status of the various peoples and communities and for their religious interests shall be fully guaranteed.

In particular, the control and administration of Waqfs shall be exercised in accordance with religious law and the dispositions of the founders.

Article 10.

Pending the making of special extradition agreements relating to Palestine, the extradition treaties in force between the Mandatory and other foreign Powers shall apply to Palestine.

Article 11.

The Administration of Palestine shall take all necessary measures to safeguard the interests of the community in connection with the development of the country, and, subject to any international obligations accepted by the Mandatory, shall have full power to provide for public ownership or control of any of the natural resources of the country or of the public works, services and utilities established or to be established therein. It shall introduce a land system appropriate to the needs of the country, having regard, among other things, to the desirability of promoting the close settlement and intensive cultivation of the land.

The Administration may arrange with the Jewish agency mentioned in Article 4 to construct or operate, upon fair and equitable terms, any public works, services and utilities, and to develop any of the natural resources of the country, in so far as these matters are not directly undertaken by the Administration. Any such arrangements shall provide that no profits distributed by such agency, directly or indirectly, shall exceed a reasonable rate of interest on the capital, and any further profits shall be utilised by it for the benefit of the country in a manner approved by the Administration.

Article 12.

The Mandatory shall be entrusted with the control of the foreign relations of Palestine and the right to issue exequaturs to consuls appointed by foreign Powers. He shall also be entitled to afford diplomatic and consular protection to citizens of Palestine when outside its territorial limits.

Article 13.

All responsibility in connection with the Holy Places and religious buildings or sites in Palestine, including that of preserving existing rights and of securing free access to the Holy Places, religious buildings and sites and the free exercise of worship, while ensuring the requirements of public order and decorum, is assumed by the Mandatory, who shall be responsible solely to the League of Nations, in all matters connected herewith, provided that nothing in this article shall prevent the Mandatory from entering into such arrangements as he may deem reasonable with the Administration for the purpose of carrying the provisions of this article into effect; and provided also that nothing in this mandate shall be construed as conferring upon the Mandatory authority to interfere with the fabric or the management of purely Moslem sacred shrines, the immunities of which are guaranteed.

Article 14.

A special Commission shall be appointed by the Mandatory to study, define and determine the rights and claims in connection with the Holy Places and the rights and claims relating to the different religious communities in Palestine. The method of nomination, the composition and the functions of this Commission shall be submitted to the Council of the League for its approval, and the Commission shall not be appointed or enter upon its functions without the approval of the Council.

Article 15.

The Mandatory shall see that complete freedom of conscience and the free exercise of all forms of worship, subject only to the maintenance of public order and morals, are ensured to all. No discrimination of any kind shall be made between the inhabitants of Palestine on the ground of race, religion or language. No person shall be excluded from Palestine on the sole ground of his religious belief.

The right of each community to maintain its own schools for the education of its own members in its own language, while conforming to such educational requirements of a general nature as the Administration may impose, shall not be denied or impaired.

Article 16.

The Mandatory shall be responsible for exercising such supervision over religious or eleemosynary bodies of all faiths in Palestine as may be required for the maintenance of public order and good government. Subject to such supervision, no measures shall be taken in Palestine to obstruct or interfere with the enterprise of such bodies or to discriminate against any representative or member of them on the ground of his religion or nationality.

Article 17.

The Administration of Palestine may organise on a voluntary basis the forces necessary for the preservation of peace and order, and also for the defence of the country, subject, however, to the supervision of the Mandatory, but shall not use them for purposes other than those above specified save with the consent of the Mandatory, Except for such purposes, no military, naval or air forces shall be raised or maintained by the Administration of Palestine.

Nothing in this article shall preclude the Administration of Palestine from contributing to the cost of the maintenance of the forces of the Mandatory in Palestine.

The Mandatory shall be entitled at all times to use the roads, railways and ports of Palestine for the movement of armed f forces and the carriage of fuel and supplies.

Article 18.

The Mandatory shall see that there is no discrimination in Palestine against the nationals of any State Member of the League of Nations (including companies incorporated under its laws) as compared with those of the Mandatory or of any foreign State in matters concerning taxation, commerce or navigation, the exercise of industries or professions, or in the treatment of merchant vessels or civil aircraft. Similarly, there shall be no discrimination in Palestine against goods originating in or destined for any of the said States, and there shall be freedom of transit under equitable conditions across the mandated area.

Subject as aforesaid and to the other provisions of this mandate, the Administration of Palestine may, on the advice of the Mandatory, impose such taxes and customs duties as it may consider necessary, and take such steps as it may think best to promote the development of the natural resources of the country and to safeguard the interests of the population. It may also, on the advice of the Mandatory, conclude a special customs agreement with any State the territory of which in 1914 was wholly included in Asiatic Turkey or Arabia.

Article 19.

The Mandatory shall adhere on behalf of the Administration of Palestine to any general international conventions already existing, or which may be concluded hereafter with the approval of the League of Nations, respecting the slave traffic, the traffic in arms and ammunition, or the traffic in drugs, or relating to commercial equality, freedom of transit and navigation, aerial navigation and postal, telegraphic and wireless communication or literary, artistic or industrial property.

Article 20.

The Mandatory shall co-operate on behalf of the Administration of Palestine, so far as religious, social and other conditions may permit, in the execution of any common policy adopted by the

League of Nations for preventing and combating disease, including diseases of plants and animals.

Article 21.

The Mandatory shall secure the enactment within twelve months from this date, and shall ensure the execution of a Law of Antiquities based on the following rules. This law shall ensure equality of treatment in the matter of excavations and archaeological research to the nations of all States Members of the League of Nations.

(1) 'Antiquity' means any construction or any product of human activity earlier than the year A.D. 1700.

(2) The law for the protection of antiquities shall proceed by encouragement rather than by threat.

Any person who, having discovered an antiquity without being furnished with the authorisation referred to in paragraph 5, reports the same to an official of the competent Department, shall be rewarded according to the value of the discovery.

(3) No antiquity may be disposed of except to the competent Department, unless this Department renounces the acquisition of any such antiquity.

No antiquity may leave the country without an export licence from the said Department.

(4) Any person who maliciously or negligently destroys or damages an antiquity shall be liable to a penalty to be fixed.

(5) No clearing of ground or digging with the object of finding antiquities shall be permitted, under penalty of fine, except to persons authorised by the competent Department.

(6) Equitable terms shall be fixed for expropriation, temporary or permanent, of lands which might be of historical or archaeological interest.

(7) Authorisation to excavate shall only be granted to persons who show sufficient guarantees of archaeological experience. The Administration of Palestine shall not, in

granting these authorisations, act in such a way as to exclude scholars of any nation without good grounds.

(8) The proceeds of excavations may be divided between the excavator and the competent Department in a proportion fixed by that Department. If division seems impossible for scientific reasons, the excavator shall receive a fair indemnity in lieu of a part of the find.

Article 22.

English, Arabic and Hebrew shall be the official languages of Palestine. Any statement or inscription in Arabic on stamps or money in Palestine shall be repeated in Hebrew, and any statement or inscription in Hebrew shall be repeated in Arabic.

Article 23.

The Administration of Palestine shall recognise the holy days of the respective communities in Palestine as legal days of rest for the members of such communities.

Article 24.

The Mandatory shall make to the Council of the League of Nations an annual report to the satisfaction of the Council as to the measures taken during the year to carry out the provisions of the mandate. Copies of all laws and regulations promulgated or issued during the year shall be communicated with the report.

Article 25.

In the territories lying between the Jordan and the eastern boundary of Palestine as ultimately determined, the Mandatory shall be entitled, with the consent of the Council of the League of Nations, to postpone or withhold application of such provisions of this mandate as he may consider inapplicable to the existing local conditions, and to make such provision for the administration of the territories as he may consider suitable to those conditions, provided that no action shall be taken which is inconsistent with the provisions of Articles 15, 16 and 18.

Article 26.

The Mandatory agrees that, if any dispute whatever should arise between the Mandatory and another Member of the League of Nations relating to the interpretation or the application of the provisions of the mandate, such dispute, if it cannot be settled by negotiation, shall be submitted to the Permanent Court of International Justice provided for by Article 14 of the Covenant of the League of Nations.

Article 27.

The consent of the Council of the League of Nations is required for any modification of the terms of this mandate.

Article 28.

In the event of the termination of the mandate hereby conferred upon the Mandatory, the Council of the League of Nations shall make such arrangements as may be deemed necessary for safeguarding in perpetuity, under guarantee of the League, the rights secured by Articles 13 and 14, and shall use its influence for securing, under the guarantee of the League, that the Government of Palestine will fully honour the financial obligations legitimately incurred by the Administration of Palestine during the period of the mandate, including the rights of public servants ,to pensions or gratuities.

The present instrument shall be deposited in original in the archives of the League of Nations and certified copies shall be forwarded by the Secretary-General of the League of Nations to all Members of the League.

Done at London the twenty-fourth day of July, one thousand nine hundred and twenty-two.

NOTES

CHAPTER 1

1   *Intelligence Digest*, January 24, 1992.
2   Robert Morey, *The Islamic Invasion*, (Eugene, OR: Harvest Publishers, 1992), 55–56.
3   *Newsweek*, June 3, 2002, 22.
4   Ibid., 22–23.
5   Ibid., 23.

CHAPTER 2

6   Zechariah 2:8–12.
7   Romans 3:2.
8   An example of how the Spirit of God uses historical accounts of how God responded to Israel's faith and lack of faith is in Hebrews 3:7 through 4:13. He quotes from Israel's history as a basis to teach Christians about believing God's promises today.
9   Isaiah 49:6.
10 An example of how the Spirit of God uses historical accounts of how God responded to Israel's faith and lack of faith is in Hebrews 3:7 through 4:13. He quotes from Israel's history as a basis to teach Christians about believing God's promises today.
11 Genesis 12:7 and 13:15–17.
12 Genesis 15:8.

13   Genesis 15:9–19 (NIV).

14   C. F. Keil and F. Delitzsch, *Commentary of the Old Testament*, 10 Vols (Grand Rapids, MI: Wm. B. Eerdmans Publishing Co., reprinted 1983), Vol. 1, 214.

15   Genesis 24:7–8 (emphasis added).

16   Romans 11:25–29 (verses 26 and 27 quote Isaiah 59:20–21 and Jeremiah 31:33–34) (emphasis added).

17   Romans 9:27–28 (quotes Isaiah 10:22–23). (emphasis added)

18   Deuteronomy 28:45–46.

19   Deuteronomy 28:49–50

20   Deuteronomy 28:64–68.

21   Deuteronomy 30:1–6.

22   Ezekiel 16:59–63 (emphasis added).

23   David Levi, quoted by Nathaniel West, *The Thousand Years in Both Testaments* (New York: Fleming Revel, 1880), 462.

24   Ezekiel 36:22–28. (emphasis added)

CHAPTER 3

25   The Hebrew for LORD sounds like and may be derived from the Hebrew for I AM ['Yahweh'], which was just revealed as God's special name to Moses in the previous verse. In most English Bibles, the translation of the name, Yahweh or Jehovah, is "LORD" in all capitol letters.

26   Exodus 3:15 NIV.

27   Isaiah 40:31 NKJ (emphasis added).

28   Genesis, chapter 17.

29   Genesis 18:12–15 NIV.

30   This is theologically a very important chapter. The three men are called God. The sovereign actions of God are attributed to the three equally. So here we have the first clear revelation that God is three persons within the one Godhead. They exist as co-equal and co-eternal beings in

the one Godhead. The mystery is how the one God exists in three persons.

31   Genesis 17:15–19 NIV (emphasis added).

32   Genesis 24:5–8 NIV (emphasis added).

33   Genesis 25:5 NIV.

34   Genesis 25:19–26 NIV.

35   Genesis 25:31–34 NIV.

36   Malachi 1:2–3 NKJV.

37   Genesis 27:27–29 NKJV.

38   Genesis 28:1–5 NKJV.

39   Genesis 31:3 NASB.

40   Genesis 32:24–30 NASB; read the full account in this passage.

41   Genesis 35:9–12.

42   Deuteronomy 10:9 NKJ.

43   Genesis 45:4–11 NASB.

44   Genesis 46:2–4 NASB.

45   Genesis 15:13–16 NIV.

46   Romans 8:28 NASB.

47   Genesis 50:19–20 NKJV.

48   Zechariah 12:10 NIV.

49   Muslims teach that the Israelites were entrusted with God's written revelation, but that they so changed and distorted its original message that Allah sent Mohammad to recover "the Truth," which he received in the Koran.

50   Exodus 3:15 NIV.

51   Matthew 22:31–32 NIV.

CHAPTER 4

52   Genesis 16:12 NIV. God made this prediction about Ishmael, Abraham's first-born son through his Egyptian maid, Hagar.

53   Genesis 16:1–4 NIV,

54   Proverbs 30:21–23 NIV, (emphasis added).

55   Genesis 16:5 NIV.

56   Orthodox Theologians agree that the Angel of the LORD, who appeared all through the Old Testament and ceased after the birth of Jesus, was the pre-incarnate Messiah Jesus, the Second Person of the Godhead. No doubt this is the phenomenon to which Jesus was referring when He said, "Your father Abraham rejoiced to see My day, and he saw it and was glad." Then the Jews said to Him, "You are not yet fifty years old, and have You seen Abraham?" Jesus said to them, "Most assuredly, I say to you, before Abraham was, I AM" (John 8:56–58).

57   Genesis 16:7–12 NIV. Note: all bracketed material in Bible quotes is alternative meanings from the original Hebrew.

58   Keil, C. F., and Delitzsch, F. "Genesis," in vol. 1: *The Pentateuch*. Translated by James Martin, *Commentary on the Old Testament*, 10 Vols. N.p.; reprint ed. (Grand Rapids, MI: Wm. B. Eerdmans Publishing Co., 1983), 220.

59   Job 39:5–8 (from Hebrew text).

60   Philip K. Hitti, *The Arabs: A Short History*, Washington, DC: Regnery Publishing, Inc., 1996.

61   Genesis 16:12 NASB.

62   Ibid.

63   Ibid (emphasis added).

64   Genesis 16:12, alternative translation from original Hebrew

65   Keil and Delitzsch, Ibid., 220–221. (emphasis added)

66   Genesis 21:9 NKJV.

67   Genesis 17:15–19 NKJV (emphasis added).

68   Keil and Delitzsch, Ibid., 244.

69   Genesis 17:20–21 NKJV.

70   Genesis 21:10 NIV.

71   1 Corinthians 12:11 NASB.

72   Genesis 21:17–19 NIV.

73 Genesis 21:20–21 NIV.

74 Genesis 25:18 NIV (emphasis added)

CHAPTER 5

75 Quoted from NASB (emphasis added).

76 Quoted from NKJV (emphasis added).

77 Genesis 12:1 NKJV.

78 See Genesis 11:27–32.

79 Genesis 12:4–7 NKJV.

80 Genesis 13:10–13 NKJV.

81 2 Peter 2:6–9 NKJV.

82 Genesis 25:1–4 NKJV.

83 Jeremiah 25:24 NKJ (emphasis added).

84 Genesis 25:6 NKJV.

85 The Hebrew word for *Jacob* is usually translated "he who supplants." But today it is best understood as "he who cheats by deception" or simply "Cheater."

86 Genesis 27:35–40 NKJV.

87 C. F. Keil and F. Delitzsch, *Commentary of the Old Testament*, 10 Vols) (Grand Rapids, MI: Wm. B. Eerdmans Publishing Co., reprinted 1983), Vol. 1, 278.

88 Genesis 27:40 KJV.

89 Genesis 28:8–9 NIV.

90 Numbers 20:21 NKJV.

91 Exodus 17:14–16 NKJV.

92 Ezekiel 36:5 NIV (emphasis added).

93 Amos 1:11–12 NIV (emphasis added).

94 Psalm 83:1–12 NKJV (emphasis added).

CHAPTER 6

95 Abdul Houssain Zarin Koub was the longtime head of the department of history religion and philosophy at the Univer-

sity of Tehran. He has also lectured at Columbia University and elsewhere. His book, *History of Religion* has been translated into over 60 languages. Zarin Koub's grandfather was one of the founders of Baghdad University.

96 Genesis 25:12–18.

97 Ezekiel 27:21 NIV (emphasis added).

98 Ezekiel 27:20, 22 NIV (emphasis added).

99 Genesis 25:3 NIV.

100 Isaiah 60:7 NIV.

101 Matthew 22:31–32 NASB (emphasis added).

102 Psalm 120:5–7 NIV.

103 Isaiah 21:13–18 NIV (emphasis added).

104 Genesis 21:20 NIV.

105 C. F. Keil and F. Delitzsch, *Commentary of the Old Testament*, (10 Vols) (Grand Rapids, MI: Wm. B. Eerdmans Publishing Co., reprinted 1983), Vol. 1, 264.

106 William Smith, *Smith's Bible Dictionary* (New York: Family Library).

107 Josephus, *Antiquities*, i, 12, 4.

108 Philip K. Hitti, *The Arabs: A Short History* (Washington, DC: Regnery Publishing, Inc., 1996), (emphasis added).

109 Genesis 27:39–40 NIV.

CHAPTER 7

110 Galatians 1:8–9 NASB.

111 Emphasis added.

112 Microsoft Encarta World Dictionary.

113 Robert Morey, *Islamic Invasion* (Eugene, OR: Harvest House Publishers, 1992), 71.

114 Dr. Anis A. Shorrosh, *Islam Revealed* (Nashville, TN: Thomas Nelson Publishers, 1988), 48

115 Robert Payne, *The Holy Sword* (Collier Books, 1962), 84.

116   Sir Norman Anderson, *The World's Religions* (Grand Rapids, MI: Wm. B. Eerdmans Publishers, 1976), 52.

117   Payne, Ibid., 84 (emphasis added).

118   Morey, Ibid., 72.

119   See 2 Thessalonians 2:9. All the Greek words that describe the miracles of Christ are also attributed to Satan's deceptive powers in this verse. Satan demonstrated enormous powers in the temptations of Christ (Luke 4:3–13), and in the first three chapters of Job. Satan is also called "the god of this world" (2 Cor. 4:3–4); "the ruler of this world" (John 14:30); "the prince of the power of the air [world's atmosphere]" (Eph. 2:2). Innate powers are attributed to Satan that are not attributed to any other created being. Believers are only able to resist him by depending on the power of the indwelling Spirit of God.

120   Deuteronomy 18:19–22 NASB.

121   See 2 Timothy 3:16–17.

122   2 Peter 1:20–21 NIV.

123   1 Corinthians 2:12–13 NASB.

124   See John 3:1–18

125   1 Corinthians 2:14 NASB.

126   Morey, ibid., 78–79.

127   It is important to note that Jesus is called "Isa, the son of Mary" in the Koran. He is never called the Son of God.

CHAPTER 8

128   Koran, translated by Abuallah Yusef Ali.

129   Palestina is a name given Israel by the Romans after they destroyed Israel in A.D. 70.

130   It is often confusing that we speak of the 12 tribes of Israel when there are actually 13 tribes. Levi was guilty of such a great sin that God removed him from having a tribal land

within Israel. But God later graciously made the Levites to be the priests of Israel. Though the Levites have no land, God told them that He was their portion and reward. The two sons of Joseph, Manasseh and Ephraim, were put in place of Levi (see Genesis 48:1–6).

131 Alfred Guillaume, *Islam* (Baltimore: Penguin Books, 1954), 10–11.

132 2 Chronicles 36:15–21 NIV.

133 Isaiah 39:5–7 NIV.

134 Joan Peters, *From Time Immemorial* (New York, Cambridge, Philadelphia, San Francisco, London, Mexico City, Sao Paulo, Singapore, Sidney: J. KAP Publishing, reprint 2000), 142.

135 Bernard Lewis, *The Arabs in History*, rev. ed. (New York, Evanston, San Francisco, London: Harper-Colophon Books, 1966), 31–32.

136 Peters, Ibid., 141.

137 Guillaume, Ibid., 11–12.

138 Ibid.

139 Robert Morey, *The Islamic Invasion* (Eugene, OR: Harvest House Publishers, 1992), 82.

140 John B. Noss, *Man's Religions* (MacMillian Publishing Co. Inc. 1974), 517.

141 Guillaume, ibid., 43.

142 Norman Stillman, *The Jews of Arab Lands* (Philadelphia, 1979), 17.

143 Peters, Ibid., 144.

144 Guillaume, Ibid., 47–48.

145 Ibid.

146 Ibid.

147 Philip Hitti, *The Arabs: A Short History* (Washington, DC: Regnery Publishing, Inc., 1996) (emphasis added).

148 Guillaume, Ibid., 49–50.

149 Ali Dashti, *23 Years: A Study of the Prophetic Career of Muhammad* (London: George Allen & Unwin, 1985), 86.

150 Peters, Ibid., 145.

CHAPTER 9

151 *Wall Street Journal*, December 18, 1992. (Hamas leader apparently quoted this as representative of the Hamas charter.)

152 Joan Peters, *From Time Immemorial* (New York, Cambridge, Philadelphia, San Francisco, London, Mexico City, Sao Paulo, Singapore, Sidney: J. KAP Publishing, reprint 2000), 33.

153 Tom Fontanes, *Islam, A History* (Special Report for *Countdown Magazine*: October 1991). To my knowledge, the full report was never published, but I express my gratitude for many valuable insights obtained from this work.

154 George Grant, *Blood of the Moon* (Wolgemuth & Hyatt Publishers: 1991), 64.

155 Chuck Missler and Don Stewart, *The Coming Temple* (Dart Press: 1991), 65.

156 Grant, Ibid., 59.

157 Peters, Ibid.

158 Deuteronomy 28:64–66 NASB.

159 Peters, Ibid., 34.

160 Ibid., 38.

161 Peters, Ibid., 36.

162 Ibid., 37.

163 Ibid.

164 Ibid., 39.

165 *New York Times*, July 27, 1992.

166 Adam Parfrey, *Extreme Islam: Anti-American Propaganda of Muslim Fundamentalism* (Los Angeles, Feral House: 2001), 291–292 (emphasis added).

CHAPTER 10

167 Historian/Author in 1985.

168 Grand Mufti of Jerusalem in Germany, 1937.

169 There is much factual material and numbers in this chapter. For some, it may be laborious to read. But I believe it will be worth the effort to have a balanced understanding of the true Middle East Problem.

170 Joan Peters, *From Time Immemorial*, (New York, Harper & Row: 1984), 25.

171 *Facts and Logic About the Middle East Report* (San Francisco, 1992).

172 Peters, Ibid., 116.

173 Ibid., 71.

174 Ibid., 80.

175 Mitchel G. Bard & Joel Himmelfarb, *Myths and Facts: A Concise Record of the Arab-Israeli Conflict* (Near East Reports, Washington: 1992), 120.

176 Ibid., 133.

177 Ibid., 78.

178 Ibid., 79.

179 Bat Ye'or, *The Dhimmi* (New Jersey, Fairleigh Dickinson University Press: 1985), 146.

180 Ibid.

181 Peters, Ibid., 174–175 (emphasis added).

182 John Hayman & Joseph von Egmont, *Travels* (London, 1759), cited by Katz in *Battleground*.

CHAPTER 11

183 EretzYisroel.org; Abdel Razak Kader, who is an Arab and not a Jew, said this in a 1969 speech.

184 Sydney Nettleton Fisher, *The Middle East* (New York: Alfred A. Knoff, Ohio University, 1967), 94–95.

185 Robert Goldston, *The Sword of the Prophet* (New York: Dial Press, 1979), 101.

186 Ibid., 101–104.

187 Bat Ye'or, *The Dhimmi*, (Farleigh Dickinson University Press, 1985), 371–372.

188 Ibid., 107–108.

189 Ibid., 109 (emphasis added)

190 Joan Peters, *From Time Immemorial* (New York: Harper & Rowe, 1984), 152.

191 Mark Twain, *The Innocents Abroad* (New York: American Publishing Company, 1869). It is written of this book, "The Innocents Abroad, or The New Pilgrims' Progress was published by American author Mark Twain in 1869. . . . It was the best selling of Twain's works during his lifetime."

192 Ibid., 167.

193 Ibid., 201.

194 Ibid., 213.

195 Ibid., 173.

196 Samuel Katz, *Battleground: Fact & Fantasy in Palestine* (New York: Steimatzky & Shapolsky, 1985), 120.

197 Ibid., 121.

198 Ibid., 121–123.

199 Ibid., 46.

CHAPTER 12

200 From Benjamin Disraeli's speech to Parliament in favor of allowing Jews to be admitted to hold office in the Parliament without swearing an oath of allegiance to the true faith of Christianity. He was admitted into parliament and later became Prime Minister because he was a Jewish convert to Christianity.

201 Barbara W. Tuchman, *Bible and Sword* (New York: Ballantine Publishers, 1984), 121.

202 Ibid., 122.

203 Thomas B. Macauley, *History of England*, Vol. 1 (Philadelphia, 1861), 71.

204 Tuchman, Ibid., 132.

205 Ibid., 141.

206 Ibid., 146.

207 Ibid., 178.

208 Ibid.

209 Ibid., 213.

210 Joan Peters, *From Time Immemorial* (New York: Harper & Row, 1984), 91.

211 Ibid., 311.

212 Ibid., 316.

213 Ibid.

214 David Fromkin, *A Peace to End All Peace*, (New York: Avon), 298.

CHAPTER 13

215 December 2, 1918, Toynbee minute: Foreign Office Papers; 371/3398, Amold Toynbee agreed with the Mandate: "It might be equitable [to include in Palestine] that part which lies east of the Jordan stream, at present desolate, but capable of supporting a large population if irrigated and cultivated scientifically . . . The Zionists have as much right to this no-man's land as the Arabs, or more." Cited in Martin Gilbert, *Exile and Return*, 115.

216 Barbara W. Tuchman, *Bible And Sword*, (New York: Ballantine Publishers, 1984), 339.

217 See the full text of this agreement in Appendix A.

218 Joan Peters, *From Time Immemorial* (New York: Harper & Rowe, 1984), 421.

219 Ibid., 238–239.

220 Ibid., 239.

221 Ibid., 240.

222 Ibid., 247.

223 Ibid., 249.

224 Ibid., 251.

225 Ibid., 259.

226 Ibid., 275.

227 Ibid., 299.

228 Ibid., 333.

229 Ibid., 336.

230 *Jerusalem Post International Edition*, December 19, 1992, 11.

CHAPTER 14

231 Jeremiah 31:35–36 NIV.

232 Not his actual name.

233 Seymour M. Hersh, *The Samson Option* (New York: Random House, 1991), 222–223.

234 *Intelligence Digest*, July 29, 1992.

235 Elishua Davidson, *Islam, Israel and the Last Days* (Eugene, OR: Harvest House Publishers, 1991), 92.

236 *Intelligence Digest*, August 1993.

237 Ibid.

238 Ken Timmerman, *Newsmax*, July 8, 2010.

239 Ezekiel 38:3–16.

240 Sharon Nader Sloan and Beth Kennedy, "We Have Been Had," *commentary* in *Israel Insider*, May 27, 2002 (emphasis added).

241 NASB, (emphasis added).

242 NASB, (emphasis added).

243 Matthew 24:21–22 NIV.

244 Daniel 12:1 NIV.

245 Isaiah 24:3, 5–6 NASB.

246 Luke 21:24 NAS (emphasis added).

247 Zechariah 12:2–3 (literal translation from Hebrew).

248 Ezekiel 36:5, summary of God's warning.

249 Ezekiel 36:1–8 NAS, (emphasis added).

250 Ezekiel 36:22, 24 NAS.

251 Ezekiel 38:6.

252 Ibid., 38:15.

253 Ibid., 39:2.

254 Ibid., 38:8

255 Walter Chamberlain, *The National Resources and Conversion of Israel* (London, 1854).

256 Louis Bauman, *Russian Events in the Light of Bible Prophecy*, (Philadelphia: The Balkiston Co., 1952).

257 See Ezekiel 38:5–6. Persia is Iran; Put (Hebrew word erroneously translated Libya) is forefather of the Muslim North African people of Libya, Algeria, Tunisia, Morocco, Mauritania; Cush is the Hebrew name for the forefather of all the black African people; Gomer is thought to be a forefather of various Balkan and European peoples; Togarmah, a son of Gomer, is the forefather of the Turkic peoples such as Turkey, Turkmenistan, Uzbekistan, Kyrgyzstan, Kazakhstan, Tajikistan and Afghanistan. The important thing is that all of these people are Muslims today.

258 Ibid., 38:5.

259 Revelation 16:12–16.

260 Revelation 9:14–16. This awesome army all come from east of the Euphrates River, which was the ancient boundary-line of the Near East and the Far East or Asia.

261 See Daniel 8:20–22. The first King of Greece was Alexander the Great. The "four horns" that took over his Empire at his death were Lysimicus, Seleucus, Cassander, and Ptolemy.

262 Daniel 7:27 NASB, (emphasis added).

263 Revelation 17:18. The Greek verb is present tense, which literally means, "*is reigning* over the kings of the earth" (emphasis added).

264 See Daniel 9:26 where it predicts "the Prince that shall come" will be from the people who destroy the city (Jerusalem) and the sanctuary (the Temple), which happened in A.D. 70 with Titus of Rome and the Roman Tenth Legion.

265 Revelation 17:12–13 NASB.

266 Hal Lindsey, *The Late Great Planet Earth* (Grand Rapids, MI: Zondervan Publishing, 1970), 94–97.

267 Revelation 13:7–8 NASB.

268 Revelation 13:3–4.

269 Daniel 9:27.

270 Revelation 13:4 NASB (emphasis added).

271 2 Thessalonians 2:3–4.

272 Matthew 24:15–22.

273 Daniel 11:40–45 NASB (explanations and emphasis added).

274 He is the second beast of Revelation 13:11–18.

275 Revelation 14:20.

276 Ezekiel 39:6 NIV.

INDEX